Stalin's Secret Services

Stalin's Secret Services

Henchmen and Poisoned Tipped Umbrellas

Andrew Sangster

First published in Great Britain in 2026 by
Pen & Sword History
An imprint of Pen & Sword Books Limited
Yorkshire – Philadelphia

ISBN 978 1 03614 741 9

Typeset by Mac Style
Printed in the UK by CPI Group (UK) Ltd, Croydon, CR0 4YY.

The Publisher's authorised representative in the EU for product
safety is Authorised Rep Compliance Ltd., Ground Floor,
71 Lower Baggot Street, Dublin D02 P593, Ireland.
www.arccompliance.com

For a complete list of Pen & Sword titles please contact:

PEN & SWORD BOOKS LIMITED
47 Church Street, Barnsley, South Yorkshire, S70 2AS, England
E-mail: enquiries@pen-and-sword.co.uk
Website: www.pen-and-sword.co.uk
or
PEN AND SWORD BOOKS
1950 Lawrence Road, Havertown, PA 19083, USA
E-mail: uspen-and-sword@casematepublishers.com
Website: www.penandswordbooks.com

I would like to dedicate this book especially to my patient wife Carol, and my two sons and their families with putting up with me living and seemingly dedicated to another world. Also, to my grandson Joshua for having shown an interest in Russian history, and to remind him he still has one of my library biographies on Stalin to return.

Contents

Acknowledgements   ix

Preface   x

Foreword   xi

Introduction   xiii

The introduction explores the nature of Intelligence work and secret police, from Tsarist Russia to Stalin's version of communism. It moves onto the way these agencies helped Stalin develop State terror, by selecting his henchmen to dominate as an autocrat, and concludes with an overview of Stalin the man, a criminal who ran a criminal State.

Chapter One: Lavrenty Beria   1

The life of Beria, Stalin's leading henchman in his secret world is outlined. Impoverished but intelligent he found himself working for the Cheka when he was 20. As a young man his ambition made him a cruel killer, he enjoyed participating in torture sessions, a manipulator, and a sex-addict. He rose in power, ensuring that Stalin was aware of his potential and he was made head of the NKVD in 1938 and by 1941 Deputy Chairman of the Council of People's Commissars. He was the organiser if not the promoter of the Katyń Massacres. During the Second World War Beria, mainly from behind his desk enhanced his power-status, becoming the most powerful security chief in Soviet history and the sense of State Terror increased. During the Cold War Beria's life was marked by the growing internal rivalries within the Soviet structure, with Stalin playing his usual policy of divide and rule. After Stalin's death the tussle for power was unabated. Beria fell to the intrigues of Khrushchev, was tried, executed and the chapter concludes with an oversight of Beria.

Chapter Two: Sudoplatov The Agent   97
This chapter is a brief summary of one of Beria's major secret agents who produced his own memoirs, written postwar but with a sense of honest revelation. He was the major agent who helped organise Trotsky's death, gained the top secrets about atomic bombs. It includes his work during the Second World War, his relationship with Beria and Stalin. His last conversation with the latter was the projected assassination of Tito. He played a role during the Cold War, participated in the dispute with Ukrainian nationalists, and like Beria stood trial, was imprisoned but survived to offer his reflections. He offers many insights into the criminal type of State which at first, he had admired.

Chapter Three: Criminal States   142
Explores the similarities of Stalin and Hitler's regimes and the inherent dangers arising from tyrannical autocracy.

Chapter Four: Evil Behaviour   146
Explores how autocratic political authority creates war and oppression by denying its own citizens intellectual and moral freedom and examines the reasons for human conduct and the nature and necessity of Free Will.

Appendix: Solzhenitsyn And The Gulag   174
Abbreviations   178
Notes   179
Bibliography   190
Index   193

Acknowledgements

I am grateful for the support of the publishers Pen & Sword for their support, for whoever manages the wonderful covers, and to Matt (only known through email) who finalises and organises the final manuscript with such care.

I am grateful to many colleagues not just for their support but for their friendship accepting the fact I seem to live on another planet, especially my closest friends, Simon Wright, Peter Doll, and Chris Ellis.

Preface

Soviet Russia was an important ally to the Western Powers during the Second World War, but promptly became a political opponent to the West as soon as Nazi Germany was defeated. The Cold War became a time of spies and Intelligence services for which Russia had already developed a much-feared system of Secret Police and Intelligence agencies, both at the national and international level. These structures had their origins in Tsarist times, but the new communist system developed them rapidly and widely because of its perceived importance for both internal and external security. Under Stalin's rule it became as oppressive as Nazi Germany, creating among its own citizens oppression, the Gulag Camps, the liquidation of suspected enemies both within Russia and beyond their borders, with many perceived opponents seeming to disappear, or having died in accidents, or committed suicide or from supposed medical reasons. It reached barbaric levels of action mainly because of Stalin's paranoid suspicious nature of any person who may challenge his authority.

In this study of the Soviet Russian State, the well-known Stalin is touched upon from time to time, and it explores these issues by focusing on the man Beria who was probably the most feared and formidable head of their various Secret Police and Intelligence agencies, and information gleaned from the memoirs of a major agent called Sudoplatov who admired Stalin. Sudoplatov later survived torture and imprisonment and looked back with a realistic appraisal at the way events unfolded. The book raises many incidents when the behaviour of the Soviet State can only be described as criminal and so immoral that the word 'evil' rises to the surface, as it often did in other autocratic countries such as Nazi Germany. This feature of human behaviour is the reasoning behind the concluding chapter, which explores why humans choose to behave in such an inhumane and evil way.

Foreword

Some historians are wary of introducing moral factors into their assessments. However, human beings are capable of actions of great evil as well as great good, and the choices they make have undeniable historical consequences. Political discourse at the moment is much preoccupied with being 'on the right side of history', and yet history does not have right and wrong sides. What has happened is what has happened. And yet if we are concerned for human flourishing and well-being in the present and the future, historians must make assessments of which political choices, which policies and actions have led to peace or war, prosperity or poverty, communal cohesion or chaos. Andrew Sangster has performed a notable service to the historical community by confronting the persistent challenge of the inhumane and evil choices made by the Soviet regime and seeking to understand what lay behind them.

Of course, whether those actions were evil or not depends on one's perspective; they are evil from the point of view of Western democracies which value personal freedom and human rights, but justifiable from the point of view of a totalitarian state which relies on its own absolute power and the implicit obedience of its citizens. The fall of the Soviet empire gave rise to hopes that the end of the millennium was witnessing the inevitable triumph of Western democratic capitalism, but it has transpired that in fact this was neither the 'end of history' nor the triumph of the West. If Western democracies hope that their values will prevail in a yet more uncertain world, they will need to pay more attention to their moral foundations.

Democratic ideals in the West emerged from Judaism and Christianity and their insistence on the ultimate value of the human person as created in the image and likeness of God, who endowed human beings with the capacity to make choices between good and evil thoughts and actions. That free choice enshrined in universal suffrage is at the heart of Western democratic traditions. It's not accidental that the Soviet regime and Nazi Germany both explicitly rejected Christian morality in favour of absolute subordination to the will of the leader. For those dictatorships, free will could only obstruct and confuse the one will of the people.

The values of the British state, which stand at the foundation of most English-speaking democracies around the world, are to be found in its coronation rite, an explicitly Christian ceremony more than 1,000 years old, in which the monarch, of his free will and on behalf of his people and government, acknowledges the moral purpose of the state. As the monarch is equipped with the orb and sceptre and the various other symbols of rule and power, he is reminded that government is to be exercised with 'gentleness and grace', 'equity and mercy', 'peace and justice', 'that by your service and ministry to all your people, justice and mercy may be seen in all the earth'. British monarchs and governments will all, in various ways, times, and places, have failed to live up to these commitments, yet these promises still stand as an ideal of humane and communal values.

If the 'right side of history' is to be understood as anything more than the triumph of market capitalism, then Western democracies will not achieve that without a renewed understanding of and commitment to those moral traditions of human dignity and free will which are the beating heart of our national identities. Historians will, like Andrew Sangster, need to be equipped to assess those moral choices and their consequences.

The Revd. Canon Dr Peter Doll.

Introduction

The introduction explores the nature of Intelligence work and secret police, from Tsarist Russia to Stalin's version of communism. It moves on to the way these agencies helped Stalin develop State terror, by selecting his henchmen to dominate as an autocrat, and concludes with an overview of Stalin the man, a criminal who ran a criminal State.

Nature of Intelligence Work

Before recorded history started there were what today we call Intelligence sources and agents. In tribal terms they would have been known as guards, trackers, or scouts. The guards keeping an eye on the tribe's area to ensure there was no hostile intrusion into their given area. The trackers to watch and monitor the movement of strangers or even some of their own tribe for whom there may be reason for suspicion. The scouts would watch an alien tribe or even infiltrate their area and life. This is of course speculation, but it makes sense as the early colonists found with the Australian Aboriginal people, who deemed these security measures as necessary for the safety of their home community. In one form or another this has become a feature of humankind's history. As the diplomatic service started with people like Sir Thomas More acting as an envoy in the early sixteenth century to the Holy Roman Empire, he also conveyed knowledge and insights of what was happening overseas to the English court. During the modern era, especially in the twentieth century, Intelligence and spies became a clandestine form of national necessity, and even today there are constant rumblings about cyber infiltration.

The very nature of these secret national organisations means that even over 100 or more years their work is often kept secret, and in some of the more nefarious events any evidence is destroyed, and in some countries even those involved 'disappear'. Any British journalist or historian looking for evidence in the archives finds that some files remain closed even fifty plus years after the event. It can be even longer in some countries. The reason is simply national security and sometimes embarrassment. When travelling as a guest of the Soviet Union in 1979, well into the post-Stalin era, this writer raised the question of the Katyń massacres only to be met with a total ignorance on the subject as if it were just a fairy tale.

The reasons for secrecy are diverse, ranging from the safety of the involved agents, the methods they deployed, covering up embarrassments, deceit, killings, useful and clever deceptions which may still be used. This is especially true of the Second World War followed by the Cold War, to this day. The French historian Henri Michel wrote of the years 1939–1945 that 'Europe became a prison, until such time as it would be a graveyard', and this led directly to the ramifications of the Cold War.[1] The 1939–1945 war was a time of total all-round barbarity which postwar was epitomised by the new legal terms of Genocide and Crimes against Humanity. The words Holocaust, carpet bombing, and Katyń summarise this era. When the famous convoy PQ17 was virtually destroyed because the Admiral of the Fleet, Sir Dudley Pound ordered it to scatter, it appeared that he failed to heed his own Intelligence sources, which indicated that the silence on the airwaves and lack of general traffic seemed to imply the battleship *Tirpitz* was not at sea, but there is no doubt that Ultra saved millions of tons of shipping and numberless lives. Secret Intelligence work is often instigated by governments, which can have long term embarrassing ramifications, which are often best put aside out of political interest, not least when some actions are obviously a blunder, immoral, or illegal.

There is another reason the work of the secret Intelligence agencies is ignored because they reflect badly on the involved government. The French service, known as the Deuxième Bureau in 1939 'seemed to have given fair warning to the French General Staff [of German intentions]… emphasised that hostilities might begin with a sudden attack…articles by General Guderian, the German expert on tank warfare, had been translated into French', which were ignored and the consequences were disastrous.[2] The senior Abwehr officer Hans Oster informed his Dutch counterpart, the Dutch military attaché in Berlin Colonel Sas, of the precise time of the intended invasion, yet the attack still came as a surprise. Such revelations are embarrassing in national histories.

This raises the question of the work of Intelligence agencies and their parameters of action. Their primary task is to issue warnings about the threats of a potential enemy so their own country can react appropriately. This is conveying essential information, but it can also lead to direct involvement on dubious grounds. When President Trump just after Christmas 2019 ordered that a drone should kill a leading Iranian military commander, he was utilising Intelligence sources in tracking the man's exact whereabouts, before the precise spot was selected to annihilate him, and all those who happened to be nearby in the attack. Over 100 years ago hot-air balloons were used to spot the general placement of guns and was regarded as a major advance in garnering information. As times have changed so the Intelligence services have kept pace. 'During 1913, about 100 people in the world worked fulltime in code-breaking or radio interception; by 1918 these numbers approached 10,000'.[3] Today, because of cyberspace, millions all round the world are watching and reading the plans and intentions of others, politically, militarily, and even economically.

The first signs of developing modern Intelligence gathering in the early twentieth century often involved operational deception, the use of agents (Humint), data processing systems, traffic analysis (Sigint), listening into the private conversations of prisoners, especially senior officers, and communications interception (Comint). During the Second World War the SIS department known as 'Y' eavesdropped on PoWs, and SIS MI19 recorded no 'fewer than 64,427 conversations between captured German generals'.[4] Intelligence services operate in peace time just as a check, but when another country becomes an enemy the situation changes, and a new alertness is always created. The nature and 'the quality of the Intelligence services changed as they switched from competitions of power-politics to those of war', which is understandable.[5]

Intelligence can be at the forefront of essential victories. It was the deployment of military Intelligence information which enabled the Allies to make amphibious landings, often by surprise. The British managed to convince Hitler that they were landing elsewhere than Sicily in their

Operation *Husky*, only Field Marshal Kesselring was not fooled.* Even at the Normandy landings the Germans were convinced that Calais and not Normandy was the focus of D-Day of 1944.

As such Intelligence has grown from tribal times of looking after one's valley to a global scale, and with humankind's aptitude for war never ceasing it has risen in importance and sophistication.

Secret Police

There are also the Secret Police who often work alongside the Intelligence Corps, sometimes away from their own country, but more often at home checking for what they deem to be traitors, spies or anyone who raises suspicion. In Britain, for example, the body known as MI5 keep an eye on home affairs, but often with support of the Special Branch, (created in 1883) technically police, but with a special remit in these matters.

British newspapers have often written about policemen who have gone undercover to investigate what some annoying organisation is planning. They have a counter-terrorism guide including groups such as Extinction Rebellion (regarding climatic change) and Greenpeace. The media reported that a twenty-four police guide was distributed to teachers and medical staff as part of anti-extremism.[6] In a democratic society there is nothing extremist about people taking peaceful action to stop any issue they feel strongly about, so the nature of a secret police force will always be a contentious problem. Nevertheless, for reasons few would quarrel with, in 2006 they merged to form the Counter Terrorism Command (SO15) which, as always, maintains contact with the MI5 domestic Security Service. They can carry the designation of detective, but they are not part of normal criminal police work, but most of the British public want people dedicated to stop music halls being blown up and general attacks by extremists.

---

* A well-known ruse by the British who used a dead body carefully swept ashore on the Iberian Peninsula to fool the Germans as to their plans. Two good books on this are: Montagu, Ewen, *The Man Who Never Was* (London: Naval Institute Press, 2001) and Macintyre, Ben, *Operation Mincemeat* (London: Bloomsbury, 2010).

However, while the Special Branch is not greatly feared, secret police are, mainly because of the history of such forces overseas. The one which caused the most fear was in Nazi Germany with Himmler's SS who had their own SD Intelligence and security branch, and who soon absorbed the slightly older Gestapo and eventually the military Intelligence known as the Abwehr. Eighty to ninety years later, the word Gestapo can still stir fear and is often used in the pejorative sense even outside Germany. If a person or an organisation is compared to the Gestapo this is the ultimate insult. In Tsarist Russia there were secret police (Okhrana) to protect the Tsar on the understanding they were therefore protecting the State but mainly guarding against internal opposition. The Bolsheviks within six weeks of their revolution established their own secret police (Cheka and later the GPU) which over the next 100 years changed titles and grew many specialised departments. The well-known NKVD (later the widely known KGB) were uniformed but had their secret components at home and abroad. In both these two countries, one an ally the other the enemy, their secret police had a much-feared reputation. In Soviet Russia they had the Troika system, and in Nazi Germany 'Special Treatment', both of which meant torture nearly always followed by execution, and for anyone to fall into their hands created widespread fear at all social levels. It is worth noting that the British Special Branch is not feared, but there is good reason for this sense of foreboding in any autocratic society. The well-known writer Hannah Arendt clearly outlined this issue when she wrote that all totalitarian regimes rely on secret police to instil a fear, to discover crimes and arrest people as enemies of the State.[7]

In learning from history, the dangers of a secret police force need to be disclosed and remembered. They tend to be a danger to their own residents but in many cases their work can take them overseas. In recent years it was Russian undercover agents who had used poisoned tipped umbrellas to exterminate what they considered as escaped traitors, and in Salisbury (UK) a developed poison was deployed which also endangered some of the innocent public. Historically secret police and agents are somewhat remote subjects, but it has been well covered in terms of Nazi German history both in history books, memoirs, and in journalism.

Not so well known is the Russian version of the secret police, and as elsewhere coupled with their Intelligence services. Even with what is identified, it would take many volumes to write, but the whole picture will never be known. Therefore, this exploration looks to key figures simply to garner insights into Soviet Russian secret agents and to make a murky subject as clear as possible. The selected key figures must be Joseph Stalin as he 'ruled the roost', then Lavrenty Pavlovich Beria for a critical time his top man, and Pavel Anatolyevich Sudoplatov one of Beria and Stalin's major secret agents. Before opening this aspect of this study, it is first essential to write a brief background to the Soviet system of the Russian Intelligence service and their secret police.

From the Tsar to Stalin

In Imperialist days, the Tsar had his own secret police known as the Okhrana, meant to protect the royal family and therefore the state of Russia. The Romanovs had ruled the vast expanse of Russia since 1613, and it was believed by other nations that their foreign intelligence was more advanced than any other countries. The 'history of the Soviet Union has often been interpreted as a great tragedy; a cruel deviation of a country from the general trajectory of human history', and it has been used to demonstrate that state power can sometimes lead to slavery.[8] As one historian noted, 'It is clear that revolutions do not usually break out unless there is a situation so bad as to invite revolution'.[9] When the British diplomat Bruce Lockhart arrived in Russia before the Great War, in the opening pages of his memoirs he noted that he was struck by the wealth of the few, and given the poverty in the working classes in Britain and other European countries, it must have been a stark picture for this gulf to be noticed.[10]

Nicholas II, as with his predecessors, had a gigantic Empire to govern covering not less than a sixth of the planet's ground surface, and he was constantly nervous about his land borders. His main attention was subsequently often focused on his empire's boundaries, and thereby ignoring the growing problems of the masses within his realm. In 1904 he had declared war on Japan because he was concerned about that country's expansion, only to be humiliatingly defeated at sea and on land. It has been observed that in terms of this conflict with Japan, 'one of the main factors was the diversity of ideas and aims within the Russian government, which prevented the adoption of any definite policy'.[11] It was during 1905 that Vladimir Lenin proposed the possible overthrow of the Romanov dynasty to be followed by 'a provisional revolutionary democratic dictatorship of the proletariat and the peasantry'.[12] Lenin had paid close attention to the developing power of the urban workers as well as the so-called rural peasants. However, Russia was in a similar state to many other European countries in the surge of nationalism. Lockhart, a British diplomat, noting 'here was a Russia I had never known – a Russia inspired by a patriotism which seemed to have its roots deep down in the soil'.[13]

It has often been observed that 'at the turn of 1917 there was no one in Russia, or anywhere else for that matter, who could have credibly foreseen that within the year the Russian State would have disintegrated – the Romanov dynasty swept aside'. This happened because the Tsar had no grip on the reality of all that surrounded him.[14] Nicholas II was not shrewd enough to recognise what was happening, the Duma meant little to him, and although he used the brutal Okhrana to arrest Mensheviks, Bolsheviks and any form of opposition, he had failed to see how popular was the gathering revolutionary storm that was brewing up.

The Bolsheviks had moved at speed, and Alexander Kerensky who led the Russian Provincial Government was overthrown on 25 October 1917, the famous Tsarist Winter Palace fell to the insurgents, and all those who opposed were threatened with life-changing retaliation. The Bolsheviks pinpointed capitalism as the cause of the Great War, and they claimed that social utility was better than private profit. To the oppressed workers this must have sounded attractive, just as many Germans believed Hitler's promises of a better future, and even in democratic Britain, the would-be fascist Oswald Mosley worked on this theme in the 1930s. The Bolsheviks used force and violence as their natural weapons, and called their government The Council of People's Commissars, widely known by the Russian acronym of Sovnarkom.

It was not an overnight achievement, because in general terms of Russian history, the years of 1918–21 are often referred to as the Russian Civil War, but it reflected not one civil war but many in which the Red Army eventually gained the upper hand. Lenin and Leon Trotsky used the terms civil war and class struggle as interchangeable terms, sometimes because of their principles, depending on how they worked at enforcing their grip on unfolding events. As the fraught years passed, it often resulted in the tussle for top leadership between the leading personalities. As it transpired a mere few years after the various wars the huge landscape of Russia was virtually under the control of Stalin, who had gained control of the Party's apparatus, and by promoting his supporters and dismissing others. From this time onwards he ruled under the aegis of fear, and as a consequence, 'the years of Stalin's rule stand out as one of the most violent chapters of the twentieth century'.[15]

Intelligence Background

The Russians were noted for their skilled code breaking, but the Tsar was more interested in quelling any revolution or demand for changes within Russia, so to be a trade unionist or any shade of socialist was dangerous. The Tsar's secret police had a reputation for sheer brutality, they once arrested Stalin as a young man and sent him into exile. Stalin's real name was Joseph Dzhugashvili, and he was born in Gori in Georgia. The Russian policing constituted a form of repression, especially when the fear of communism appeared on their doorstep. It was a difficult task as Russia is a vast geographical area, but the Tsarist system was adopted and re-adapted to suit the incoming communist regime.

After the Revolution in 1917 the Bolsheviks promptly created their own secret service having become all too aware of how useful such a force could be. It was first known as the Cheka and the VeCheka (Extraordinary Commission for Combatting Revolution and Sabotage) came into being, as always, and elsewhere, there was a confusing merger of duties and tasks both at home and abroad. During the year 1922 the GPU (State Political Directorate, Secret Police) a revamped Cheka, came into existence based within the NKVD (People's Commissariat of Internal Affairs), first known as the OGPU which was the Unified State Political Administration. In 1934 GUGB (Main Directorate of State Security within NKVD [1934–1941]) and the NKVD (The Peoples' Commissariat for Internal Affairs) were the key components and later formed the well-known KGB, which was the People's Commissariat for State Security. The changes were constant and continued to be so. Today it is the FSB, the Federal Security Service of the

Russian Federation. This is a confusing picture of abbreviations with many others barely worth much space, but essentially it was a growing organisation of secret police and agents operating at home and soon abroad. (Information on these abbreviations can be found on page 178 of this book.)

The original Bolshevik Cheka was in the early days of communism only viewed by the idealists necessary for a short-term existence, but Lenin 'little dreamed that it would rapidly become both the biggest political police force and the largest foreign Intelligence service in the world'.[16]

It started life at Bolshaya Lubyanka 11, but soon moved to Number Two, later to be the HQ of the KGB, an abbreviation widely known in the Western world, and the modern FSB is still in the same building. The Cheka was a child of the revolution, and as one Russian historian wrote, 'for twenty years the child of the revolution grew, matured, and under the never-resting tutelage of the General Secretary, (a post activated by Stalin after the Eleventh Party Congress in April 1922) developed full blown into the hired assassin of its mother'.[17] As early as 1921 the Troika system was announced which was a three-man committee empowered to judge and execute on the spot. This troika system amounted to rapid movement from judge and jury to executioner reflecting a form of state anarchy and exhibiting the dangerous aspects of a police-controlled state.

The Cheka was a weapon against counter-revolutionaries, regarded as a menace by wanting to counter the Revolution. It soon evolved from its original form as it became even more brutal and oppressive. It had been noted that 'the original measures approved by Sovnarkom [The Council of People's Commissars of the Soviet Union] to combat counter-revolution were non-violent, seizure of property, resettlements, deprivation of ration cards, publications of lists of enemies of the people, etc. The Cheka's main weapon, however, rapidly became terror.'[18]

Stalin would later use this body of secret police as his own, to rid himself of all his perceived problems. Initially its main task was to seek out counter-revolutionaries, but Stalin, having become an autocrat, used it to crush any opposition to him as a person. This contrasted strongly with Lenin's ideals who only wanted communism to survive, and as such the work stretched beyond Russia's borders, and during 1919–27 it 'began systematic foreign Intelligence collection'.[19] It was not only seeking out the White Guard opposition, often meeting in Paris, but supporting the ideal that communism itself was an idealistic improvement and genuine form of idealism, which the world's proletariat desperately needed to share. The organisation for this worldwide plan was the well-known Comintern who carried the hope of communism as far as possible.* The first Founding Congress of Comintern was held in Moscow in March 1919, but it was more of a show: a mere five delegates arrived from abroad, but it was the beginning. This organisation caused the most fear in the western world who were, perhaps understandably, almost paranoid about this emergence of communism, not least in the post First World War era burdened with uncertainty and news of street battles in German cities which included communists. Comintern's main efforts were inside Germany because of its extreme vulnerability, where they had tried to launch a Communist revolution in 1921, and then again in 1923, but even this was to prove unsuccessful. Comintern may have conducted several clandestine operations, probably much more than Western Intelligence agencies knew, but at this stage they lacked expertise with minimum training. This would soon change.

The Russian communists remained concerned with internal opposition (the Whites), especially with those who had fled Russia and attempted to organise attacks, which tended to gather in the French capital Paris, and it took considerable time for this fear to moderate.** However, the opposing White Movement was often naïve and gullible, and communist agents were able to infiltrate their ranks. As with secret service and police they would pinpoint the main figures and targeted individuals. A Boris Savinkov of the White Guards was regarded as the most dangerous, and he was lured over the Soviet border in 1924 and killed a year later. Savinkov had been unmasked by the Cheka in 1919 and had fled to Paris where he met Churchill, whose greatest wish was to find any opportunity to overthrow the Bolsheviks, however remote that opportunity might be. Churchill included Savinkov as one of his chosen candidates in his book *Great Contemporaries*, and was

---

* Comintern short for Communist International, was often known as the Third International (1919–1943) and advocated world communism. Its intentions were to overthrow the international bourgeoise by creating an international Soviet world-order.

** Lloyd George had sent British troops to Murmansk in March 1918, and other countries followed, involving some 200,000 who were embroiled in the Civil War. It transpired to be a needless waste of life and resources.

a great admirer of Savinkov, not only as a source of information but as a person, writing that 'when all is said and done, and with all the stains and tarnishes there be, few men tried more, gave more, dared more and suffered more for the Russian people'.[20]

The first Chairman of the Cheka (later GPU) was Feliks Dzerzhinsky who died in 1926. He was a Polish aristocrat who had turned communist and a member of the Polish Marxist Organisation.* He was acutely aware of Stalin's bid for power, and concerned about any split within the Party, and so he raised this at the Fourteenth Party Congress demanding Party Unity, but then died from a heart attack, although the Russian historian Anton Antonov-Ovseyenko expressed serious doubts about 'natural causes', which given Stalin's behaviour is understandable.[21] Dzerzhinsky had made it clear that he disagreed with Stalin that his national policy should be spread to other countries. In 1918 Dzerzhinsky had issued regulations about arresting people, stating that 'each and every one must remember that they represent Soviet power, the workers' and peasants' government, and that any verbal abuse, rudeness, injustice, or impropriety is a blot upon the Soviet power'.[22] However, these were barbaric days, with Trotsky introducing the old Roman policy of decimating regiments which failed to carry out high command orders, warning that 'a soldier who advances *may* be shot, but one who retreats *will* be shot'.

Ironically, Dzerzhinsky with Stalin had been a pallbearer at Lenin's funeral, and there had been a rumour that he was a possible contestant for the leadership. Stalin would have been aware with his habitual paranoid suspicion of others, that Dzerzhinsky, an old comrade, was therefore a possible opponent for his personal ambitions. Killing was for Stalin the normal method of building his personal empire. Whether heart attack or murder, Dzerzhinsky's death was convenient for Stalin, who was ensuring his position in the struggle for the hold on succession power, and during these years Stalin could be seen growing his paranoia for his need to be in total control whatever the cost in human life.

Dzerzhinsky was replaced by Vyacheslav Rudolfovich Menzhinsky, and both these early men had wanted 'to expand the application of methods

---

* In many texts he is given his Polish name, Feliks Dzierżyński.

of state terror' even though men like Lev Kamenev and Nikolai Bukharin disagreed.[23] As far as Stalin was concerned state terror was part of his policy and a permanent item in his armoury. Neither Dzerzhinsky nor Menzhinsky had been selected by Stalin, which was always a risk for them, nevertheless, they had always tended to follow his commands.

Menzhinsky was regarded as more pliant than his predecessor, and prior to the notorious Shakhty Trial of 1928, he had called for proof as head of the GPU. Such a normal demand would not work with Stalin, and Menzhinsky suffered from failing health and his deputy Genrikh Grigoryevich Yagoda took his place. The men who headed these organisations were critical and will be explored in the next section about the Stalin era.

Stalin's Men

The period between the 1920s and 1953 was an era dominated by the paranoid Stalin who continually used secret services to search for plots and opposition. Most people by this stage were terrified of opposing Stalin, including the secret services who often uncovered plots and their planners, often where they never existed in the first place, in the hope that they too would not fall under Stalin's paranoid suspicious nature. A mere 'two years after the civil war Russian society already lived under Stalin's virtual rule, without being aware of the ruler's name…strangely he was voted in and moved into all his positions of power by his rivals', and when they realised what had happened 'they found him immovable'.[24] Stalin emerged as the main leader, and 'the key to Stalin's power was his control of the Party apparatus in the Provinces', and 'he could promote his friends and rid himself of opponents'.[25] If Stalin suspected a person or a plot, or any personal opposition or even criticism, and the GPU uncovered it even though it never existed, then Stalin rejoiced at his own insight, or if he knew it were unfounded, he knew he had the GPU and its leaders precisely where he needed them, namely at his disposal.

Stalin's quest for power of an autocratic nature put him at odds with the traditional comrades of the past especially Leon Trotsky and all those associated with him. In November 1927 Trotsky, Zinoviev and hundreds of others were expelled from the Party. It was the beginning of a series of purges to rid Stalin of any opposition to his role of leadership, it often reflected his own bigotries, his sense of personal self-importance on the world stage, and the inbuilt desire that Soviet Russia should become all-powerful during his time of rule. This passion would continue until Stalin's death in 1953. Even as late as the 1950s there was the infamous Doctors' Plot and his then henchmen, including Khrushchev and Beria, (to be explored later in this study) were concerned that Stalin was about to purge them as his next targets. There is little doubt that Stalin had deep psychological problems, but he remained cunning, clever, and calculating all his life. It was known that he often encouraged his closest associates to become drunk during his frequent evening meals, if only for them to inadvertently expose their inner thoughts, and a grim look by a guest could be fatal. He used at the earliest opportunity the GPU to conduct witch-hunts against any opposition, pretending his personal distrust was seeking out counter-revolutionaries, or crushing subversion or traitors to himself, but always claiming it was for 'the communist cause'. All this effort was an ideal which for the ordinary Russian offered less hope, and it was Stalin's means to autocratic power. When Stalin's daughter later went to university to study history and social sciences she wrote, 'we seriously studied Marxism, analysed Marx, Engels, Lenin, and of course, Stalin. The conclusion I carried away from these studies was that the theoretical Marxism and Communism we had studied had nothing whatsoever to do with actual conditions in the USSR'.[26] The reasoning in Stalin's mind amounted to his personal position of total power and control. The word 'subversion' was the key theme for Stalin because its implications could be discovered in every occupation, including economic, political, military areas, and even in the cowsheds and shop floors. This was mainly an internal problem, but the threat of foreign aggression increased the hunt and took this obsession across the borders, always looking for counter-revolutionary plots. Behind every shortage or industrial accident, a plot could be uncovered or invented. The secret police and Intelligence services, often suspected themselves by the paranoid Stalin, were nevertheless always his key weapons in maintaining his position of power and its associate policies.

To achieve this unlimited power, Stalin needed the most ambitious men for the head of his secret agencies. The GPU in 1934 had accumulated increased powers within the NKVD, and it operated at the will of Stalin, who had in 1934 also prepared the way with the 'Special Board', imposing prison sentences by simple administrative methods. Stalin always ensured that he was to be regarded as the major founding figure of the new era, and the NKVD was therefore elevated above other institutions, and incorporated into the Party structure as his own guard, as well as his crusading force. He therefore needed ambitious amoral men, and Yagoda, mentioned above, the third director (following Dzerzhinsky and Menzhinsky) fulfilled this demand. Yagoda was noted for his cruelty, personal habits, and he was feared by everyone. It was not long before even Stalin distrusted his ambition.

Bukharin described Yagoda 'as an opportunist whose support could not be relied upon'.[27] Genrikh Yagoda (1891–1938) had been a secret police official who served as director of the NKVD 1934–36. His real first name was Enoch and had joined the Party in 1907, and became a 'corrupt careerist but he was, it has been claimed never a Stalin's man, and it was Yagoda under Stalin's authority who started to increase the notorious Gulag prison system.*/[28] The historian Gellately calculated that in 1930 and 1931 some 1.8 million people were deported to special settlements in the remotest of places.[29] Yagoda was arrested in 1937, and finally executed, having first been demoted in favour of Nikolai Ivanovich Yezhov (1895–1940. However, Yagoda's reputation has remained infamous, and his reputation was not rehabilitated in the post-Stalin era as were many of Stalin's victims. Yezhov headed the NKVD from 1936 to 1938 during some of the most devastating purges. Using a play on his Russian name he was nicknamed the 'Iron Hedgehog'. Like others he was infamous for his personal habits and brutality. Yezhov personally supervised the tortures, and the 'Cheka had long had a cult of torture, and Leonid Zakovsky, one of Yagoda's men, had written a guide to torture' for him.[30] It was reported that Yezhov beat his victims so badly that their eyes popped out. It appeared that men like these were chosen by Stalin because of their psychopathic leanings. Yezhov fell from grace with Stalin and was condemned and executed in 1940. This gave the appearance that to be one of Stalin's key men often meant execution ordered by their master Stalin. It has often been noted that of the major figures working with Stalin 40 per cent

---

* The Gulag was an acronym for 'Main Administration of Camps'. Established as a Tsarist tradition and continued by Lenin, but they reached their peak under the barbarity of Stalin's times.

died in the purges, 20 per cent assisted him, 5 per cent were assassinated, 10 per cent suddenly died from illness and only 25 per cent died from old age: this was a risky and dangerous time and place in which to live.

The NKVD had rapidly become the rule of terror, and Yezhov's new Deputy Lavrenty Beria, who had arrived in Moscow in July 1938, soon took over control as he and Stalin had planned. Stalin in his usual slow but determined fashion decided that Yezhov's day for retirement was approaching. He decided a special commission would investigate the NKVD and appointed Vyacheslav Molotov, Georgy Malenkov, Andrey Vyshinsky and Beria to the task.* It was decided that 'honest men' were required, and 'an *honest* people's commissar was needed. On a motion by Kaganovich, Beria was appointed to the post of first deputy of the NKVD'.[31] Whatever the devious machinations in the summer of 1938 Stalin transferred Beria to Moscow as Yezhov's first deputy of the NKVD. This was undoubtedly in preparation for Yezhov's dismissal on 8 December, by which time effective power had passed to Beria. Stalin had watched Beria over the years and his servant had accomplished precisely what Stalin demanded, namely 'Beria had crushed not just the Georgian Mensheviks but also the Georgian Bolsheviks', all of whom Stalin had become suspicious.[32] Stalin chose men who were obedient to his will but they were dismissed and executed the moment they raised the slightest suspicion in Stalin's mind, not because of their cruelty.

Stalin the Man

There can be little doubt that Stalin was a tyrant as can be seen above in the way he treated many of those who served him. During the Second World War, when allied to America and Britain against the Nazi regime from the need for pure mutual survival, Stalin was often seen as popular in the West and was referred to as 'Uncle Jo' which he deeply resented. The Western leaders, especially Churchill, were aware of Stalin's danger as a leader, but came to terms with him to win the war.

---

* Andrey Vyshinsky (1883–1954) was a politician, jurist, and diplomat. In 1935 he was the Procurator General of the USSR and headed up Stalin's Moscow trials and attended the Nuremberg trial. From 1948 to 1953 he was Foreign Minister. He died in New York.

Stalin was frequently referred to as 'the boss', and it did not take long for people to become extremely cautious in his presence and to whom they talked. It had been pointed out that when his wife Nadezhda was rumoured to have argued with him following a social occasion in late 1932, she then went outside and allegedly shot herself. According to a British diplomat working in Russia at the time, the gossip was that Stalin's wife was against the oppression in the countryside, and Stalin had ordered her arrest. However, the truth of these events will probably never be known, and it may simply have been a mere domestic argument.[33] However, the Russian historian Anton Antonov-Ovseyenko related in detail how Avel Yenukidze had been the first to find Stalin's wife 'with the marks of the killer's fingers still on her throat'.[34] Yenukidze was himself later killed but his account sounds plausible with the benefit of hindsight.* Later Yezhov investigated Yenukidze and a terrorist cell was uncovered, but it has been claimed that 'Stalin had surely not forgotten that Yenukidze had swayed Nadya politically, and had been the first to see the body'.[35] Stalin's daughter always denied that her father had killed her mother though she was only a child at the time, and the facts were often withheld from her, but she noted her mother's picture retained a prominent place in Stalin's rooms, which may well have been a ploy by Stalin, but the truth may never be known.[36] She wrote in her later account that 'Some say my mother was a saint, others that she was mentally unbalanced. Neither of these things is true, any more than the story that she was murdered'.[37] Whatever account or history is read about Stalin leaves little doubt he was a tyrant who used the communist cause to boost his own power as an autocrat.

It was clear to some outside observers that the Soviet Intelligence and policing agencies were merely a tool for Stalin's machinations at home and abroad and dedicated to looking after Stalin's self-perceived interests. Stalin's early supporters were men like Sergei Kirov (1886–1934), Lev Kamenev (1883–1936) and Grigory Zinoviev (1883–1939) and although close to Stalin all died under his directions. Lev Kamenev was a revolutionary and one of

---

* Avel Yenukidze (Enukidze) (1877–1937) published Lenin's revolutionary papers during Tsarist times and was accused of diminishing Stalin's literary contributions. In July 1935 he suggested to Stalin that he relinquish power. Stalin expelled him and two years later he was shot in the purges.

the first seven members of the Politburo (the others were Lenin, Zinoviev, Trotsky, Stalin, Soloiniknov and Bubnov). He was Trotsky's brother-in-law and acting Premier during Lenin's last year (1923–4), and he was executed in August 1936 during one of Stalin's ongoing purges. Grigory Zinoviev (1883–1936) a Bolshevik revolutionary travelled the same route. He had been one of the original members of the first Politburo in 1917 who helped manage the revolution. He became the head of Comintern and tried to make Germany communist in the 1920s. Stalin dismissed him in 1926, and he was executed following the first major Show Trial in August 1936. This happened to countless other one-time leaders and is cleverly reflected in one of Arthur Koestler's historical novels, *Darkness at Noon*, in which prominent one-time leaders find themselves imprisoned without hope even though they had supported the 'leader'.[38] Koestler who had opposed Nazi Germany and the Spanish dictator Franco had been an ardent communist until he saw the cruel repression under Stalin.

There are many questions about the arrest of Sergei Kirov, a prominent Bolshevik leader and part of the 1905 revolt. He was a supporter of industrialisation and collectivism, and at the 17th Congress supported Stalin. It is occasionally suggested that Stalin had him killed. He was laid to rest in the Kremlin Wall and Stalin helped carry his coffin. However, the sheer intrigue surrounding Kirov's death provides an illustrative picture of life in the Soviet Union under Stalin, adding to the confusing picture of unravelling the truth. Kirov had been viewed as an alternative to Stalin during the February Congress and was allegedly shot in his office, and Stalin used this incident (which some claim he possibly manipulated from his usual distance) to grant more authority to the NKVD to arrest and execute at will. Some reliable historians are convinced, with a possibility of truth, that Kirov's death was organised by the NKVD or at least originated from Stalin. Anton Antonov-Ovseyenko's history gives carefully noted evidence to this effect.[39] In her biography of Beria, Amy Knight also provides some insights into Beria's possible involvement, including Beria's sudden visit to Moscow to meet Yagoda, the then NKVD chief. Kirov's closest friend Ordzhonikidze who was taken mysteriously ill after visiting Beria had been ordered to stay in Georgia by Stalin as he recovered, it was then Kirov was killed.[40] Notably, the well-known historian of secret Intelligence, Christopher Andrew boldly states that it is wrong to assume that Stalin was behind Kirov's death.[41] As in all secret services the truth is rarely available and can lead to sensible speculation or silly conspiracy theories. The various possibilities relating to Kirov's death are placed here to demonstrate the impossibility of ascertaining the truth in the studies of Soviet history. For this writer, the fact that Kirov had been seen as an alternative to Stalin during a Party Congress seems persuasive that Stalin was involved, as the Purge Trials demonstrated.

The Soviet security system, which was inextricably combined with the penal system, and with the increased powers granted by Stalin to the NKVD, clearly indicated that Stalin was the spider at the centre of the complex web. The purge of Party Members had started in 1933, if not earlier, technically to root out so-called corruption, but by 1935 it was clearly a political move because it was personal to Stalin who was paranoid about critics, and this upsurge of trials became known as 'The Great Terror'. These public trials and confessions became the centre of considerable worldwide attention. For the individual victims it was a question of facing torture in the Lubyanka with threats of being sent to the Gulags with their families, and nearly always under false charges as to why they were on trial in the first place.

Stalin, who is now well-known for not believing the threat from Nazi Germany lost some of his best military commanders through his purges just as the Second World War was looming, 'with the like of [generals] Tukhachevsky, Blucher and Yegorov, the tragedy of 22 June 1941 could have been avoided'.[42] The purges meant the state of the Russian air force was in a weak position as the war years approached, not least because Stalin had liquidated three of his five Soviet Marshals and three of his four Fleet Commanders. 'Stalin had [also] shattered his own remarkable spy network: of the 450 secret police officials stationed abroad, at least 275 had been arrested by his regime'.[43] In 1957 it was noted that 'it was thought the Beria clique [operating under Stalin's orders] had picked up a giant crystal vase containing 82,000 of the best, most experienced, and qualified commanders and political workers in the army and navy and smashed it on the rocks. On the eve of the war, we found ourselves decapitated'.[44] These activities later included whole swathes of the population with Poles deposited in Kazakhstan, Kurds driven out from their homelands, and Koreans ousted from eastern Siberia. There was no compassion shown as they forcibly moved whole populations to new and often disastrous areas, which was nothing short of tyrannical evil. This amoral behaviour was the work of the Soviet secret police using the Intelligence agencies and always under the command of 'their boss' Stalin.

Stalin's initial reaction to Nazi Germany clearly indicated that he was easily misled in his pursuit of power and too sure that he was always right in his judgments. He allied Soviet Russia with Nazi Germany in dividing Poland by mutual conquest as a result of the Ribbentrop-Molotov agreement, then ignored all Hitler's warnings about *Lebensraum* in the east of which many had some knowledge. The West appeared relieved that *Lebensraum* was intended only in the east of Europe. Stalin simply could not believe that Russia was the next Nazi target despite the fact that many of his best secret agents had warned him.

One of his best spies was Richard Sorge who had been able to find his way to what could be best described as normally inaccessible levels and dispatched considerable Intelligence acquired by access to high authority within Japan. Sorge had considerable information from Hotsumi Ozaki, a member of the entourage of the leading Japanese statesman Prince Konoye. Despite Sorge's warnings about Hitler's intentions, Stalin ignored him and failed to 'join the dots' from Sorge and many other warnings, even those from the western powers. Moscow should have been the best-informed centre in the world having built up a network of secret agents for both internal and external use. It was Stalin's dangerous paranoid personality that was the cause of the problem, as even those closest to him were terrified of causing him offence by doubting his judgements. It is now known that some invaluable information was not passed on to him because of the traditional fear that the messenger of bad news often paid the price. Stalin always believed in his own analysis and was suspicious of anyone who challenged his views or perceptions, because like all emerging autocrats his self-belief in his genius of always being right was a dominant feature of his personality.

The NKVD and GRU had considerable information about the build-up of German forces on the western borders, and Dekanozov, who was the Soviet Ambassador in Germany, knew from reliable sources and his own perceptions about Hitler's intentions, but was ignored. Even Vyacheslav Molotov was aware of the danger because Dekanozov had spoken to him about the issue, but when he informed Stalin, it was rebuffed on the grounds of being disinformation emerging from the capitalistic west.* Beria, who will be explored in the next chapter, and who was the up-and-coming leading man in the secret world, was aware of the threat, but was cautious with his ability to read Stalin's mind and knew the ramifications of offering unwelcome news which contradicted his master's thinking. Immediately before Operation *Barbarossa* started 'Stalin told his military Intelligence Chief Filipp Golikov, that any reports about a German attack on the USSR were false, that it was the product of officers trapped by British deception'.[45] Sorge continued to send warnings, and later historians and many others would ponder over Stalin's refusal to listen to Intelligence reports about Germany's Operation *Barbarossa*. When the Germans started to invade Stalin was for once concerned that his position was in jeopardy, but his well-trained henchmen turned to him for help. The enormity of Stalin's misjudgement in refusing to listen to the advice from overseas and his own secret agents soon impacted when Russia was overrun to the outskirts of Moscow.

There is no question that Stalin was in his own way clever and cunning when it was required. Stalin knew that Comintern was regarded as essential for the communist cause, but he ordered it to stop functioning in May 1943 to impress the West that the Soviet Union was improving, because he needed material resources against the Nazi invasion. Also, against the communist grain 'there were indications of a new religious tolerance when in September 1943 Stalin permitted the Russian Orthodox Church to appoint a new Patriarch'.[46] It was well understood that Stalin had no time for religion, was anti-Semitic, despised the West, but he was desperate to keep the West on side and needed Christians and Jews to assist in the war. It would have taken a gifted genius to work out what Stalin's current thinking and suspicions were at any given moment.

Churchill may have had this in mind when he famously said that 'Russia is a riddle wrapped in a mystery inside an enigma' … 'but Stalin remains the central mystery within the Soviet enigma'.[47] The way Stalin remains a mystery

---

* Vyacheslav Molotov (1890–1986) was an old Bolshevik and a leading figure during the 1920s as a protégé of Stalin. He was Chairman of the People's Commissars 1939–41 and Minister of the Foreign Office 1939–1949 and again in 1953–1956. He was First Deputy Premier between 1942–1957 but was dismissed from the Presidium by Khrushchev. He was aware of the Katyń massacre and may have opposed Khrushchev's de-Stalinisation.

is the way an autocratic tyrant managed to destroy the ideals of the original communist state. He may have surrounded himself with congresses and the paraphernalia of the projected communist ideal, but he eliminated any who opposed his individual rise to be the overall leader. He was as much feared as Hitler, Franco and other dictators, making Mussolini look even mild. He was more powerful than the Tsars and like them used secret agents to dig up and dispose of any opposition, but with more cruelty and deaths. It was essential for him that he had at his disposal the secret Intelligence, Police and Agents to act according to his orders, and only those who never asked questions survived his regime.

The background to these services, as seen from above was complex and would take volumes of intricate and confusing detail. To illustrate the power of Stalin and the way he used his 'support team' this study has turned to the microscope to explore two such prominent members of his secret squad. The first is Lavrenty Pavlovich Beria, Stalin's lead man in the secret services, a man who understood Stalin and therefore survived until Khrushchev came to power.* The second study is Pavel Anatolyevich Sudoplatov, one of Stalin's and Beria's most successful agents used in many different scenarios. For the reader they will appear as they were, dangerous, dedicated to what they always called The Cause, but in reality, they were mere obedient servants to Stalin, and both these men should provide some insights into the life and nature of the Soviet Intelligence agencies and their obedience to Stalin.

---

* Lavrenty comes in many forms of spelling, the y sometimes an i, or iy, and many others, and is the Georgian version of Laurence.

Chapter One

Lavrenty Beria

The life of Beria, Stalin's leading henchman in his secret world is outlined. Impoverished but intelligent he found himself working for the Cheka when he was 20. As a young man his ambition made him a cruel killer, he enjoyed participating in torture sessions, a manipulator, and a sex-addict. He rose in power, ensuring that Stalin was aware of his potential and he was made head of the NKVD in 1938 and by 1941 Deputy Chairman of the Council of People's Commissars. He was the organiser if not the promoter of the Katyń Massacres. During the Second World War Beria, mainly from behind his desk, enhanced his power-status, becoming the most powerful security chief in Soviet history and the sense of State Terror increased. During the Cold War Beria's life was marked by the growing internal rivalries within the Soviet structure, with Stalin playing his usual policy of divide and rule. After Stalin's death the tussle for power was unabated. Beria fell to the intrigues of Khrushchev, was tried and executed. The chapter concludes with an oversight of Beria.

His Early Youth

Beria was born on the 29 March 1899 in a small village in Georgia, with the full name of Lavrenty Pavlovich Beria. The village was on the northwest corner of the Black Sea and Beria belonged to the Mingrelian ethnic class, who were something of a minority clinging to their traditions. The Mingrelians tended to be agricultural workers, including wine production, and at times could be rebellious. Beria's mother was Marta Ivanovna (Jakeli), and she was deeply religious. She was widowed earlier, but she married a Pavel Khukhaevich Beria by whom she had one daughter and two sons, including Lavrenty. Her second husband died while Beria was at junior school, and as with Stalin, who was also born in Georgia, Beria was brought up by his mother. She later married a Georgian Jew called Levan

Loladze, but by sixteen Beria had left home. It had been rumoured that Beria's real father was an Abkhazian landowner which might account for the patronage he received during his education.[1] Georgians were regarded as people for whom loyalty and personal pride were the characteristics of their ideal. Geography was not all that Beria shared with Stalin, because they were both raised in a rural community, by their mothers, and lived the life of the Russian peasant. Their background had so much in common it is tempting to describe them as potential *alter egos*.

The experience of living as children in an impoverished landscape where the wealthy were living on another planet, would naturally have left resentment, and created a deep influence, which Beria and Stalin probably shared with others of this typical background. The tendency to project national characteristics is often wrong and limited, but stark poverty creates its own mark, though this does not account for a reliable picture of every person. The cultural background of any individual has a bearing, but it is not a mathematical formula, and human beings have their own individuality.

It has even been suggested but without any substantive evidence that Beria was descended from a Mingrelian prince, but as far as is known, his birth was humble and in a small village. However, it is believed that like Stalin, he probably had a rich patron, who was possibly his mother's one-time employer.[2] His birthplace was in that area of Caucasia in Georgia, which was a meeting place between the East and the West. From tribal times onwards Caucasia was a well-placed area for wider control and influence because it was a meeting point for east and west. Georgia has its own history, but by the mid-nineteenth century it was part of the Russian empire.

With such beginnings in a remote area, it is not surprising that little is known about the young Beria. The Polish writer Thaddeus Wittlin wrote in his biography of Beria that he was known as 'the man without history'.[3] However, Wittlin uses many pages on his early life, how he dressed and even his thought processes, how he behaved at school and from this the reader can only assume it is mere conjecture and speculation, although his work gives the impression that he almost knew him personally as a young boy, which he did not.

What is known is that when Beria was five years old there were serious developing political divisions. The opposition to the Tsarist regime was growing, mainly led by Marxist Social Democrats who were divided between the Bolsheviks and Mensheviks. Lenin led the Bolsheviks and demanded a central disciplined organisation under proletariat-class rule, whereas the Mensheviks insisted on the more flexible democratic elements. At first the Mensheviks prevailed, but as Beria developed during his teenage years Lenin was gaining control. It was an age of political divisions and violence, influencing Beria's youthful background. However, not too much should be read into this because there are many examples where people have not automatically developed according to where they were brought up.

According to a family friend called Danilov, Beria was not a bright student and was considered 'cunning and devious', but how far such teenage observations can be trusted is dubious.[4] Given his background he must have been intelligent because after school in Sukhumi he went in 1915 to the oil centre of Baku in Azerbaidzhan, where he joined the course in the Poly-Technical School for Mechanical Building Construction. There is a degree of uncertainty if not mystery about what he actually studied, one researcher claiming he was an architect, but such is the vagueness of his background it can only be assumed that his course was something to do with architectural design or building,[5] though it is interesting to note that later he designed his own dacha. His course was in Baku, which was nearly 500 miles from his home, which must have been an arduous distance for a young teenager. Like many in that generation he had to make his own way even though he was incredibly young.

Leaving home at sixteen to move to Baku was not necessarily unusual, but it indicated that Beria was brighter than Danilov had described, and like many youngsters he would have been trying to improve his status. By this age he would have been more than aware of the First World War, and undoubtedly alert to the opposition against the Tsarist control. He had been in Baku barely a year when he joined with fellow students (in October 1915) to organise an illegal Marxist group to study communism, helping to create connections with the new workers' groups. This was nothing unusual as students today frequently become politicised and often on the anti-establishment side, but Beria's political interest never evaporated as he grew older.

Following the Tsar's abdication Beria joined the Bolshevik wing of the Russian Social Democratic Labour Party, which was receiving less support than the Mensheviks, except in Baku itself. It was at this point in time that world events caught up with Beria and he was conscripted into the Russian army in June 1917 to serve on the Romanian front. This increased his political activity, and he was soon elected the chairman within his detachment for the Party, helping to provide propaganda. This did not last long, and after the conflict he returned to the school and concluded his studies in 1919 as an architect-builder technician. Given his poverty-stricken background this was an achievement, and his political activities clearly demonstrated not only his ability, but a determination to succeed, indicating a man driven by ambition.

The Secret Agent

It was at the stage when Russia had descended into a series of civil wars that in Baku the main fear was the Turkish army, with the Bolsheviks in this area being in danger. There was violence, and the lack of food was serious, which the student Beria survived. A new governing body in the area called the Musavat had shifted somewhat to the Right and opposed the Bolsheviks.* It is worth noting that despite his youth in 1919 Beria was asked to work in counter-intelligence against the Musavat government, as the Bolsheviks remained an underground organisation. However, Beria's involvement with the Musavat government would create problems for him to his final days, decades later. Some historians claim he worked for the Musavat, but whether they were right or not is impossible to know because his role demanded subterfuge.[6] It was later decided that the Bolsheviks had asked him to take on this role, but many times, Beria had to offer evidence to defend against such charges.

Beria was only twenty when he had found himself in a new world in which he would one day dominate through his personal ambitious route to power. In this chaotic setting of intrigue, it helped shape him as a person who later became well-known for his political power. From an impoverished

---

* The Musavat (Equality) government consisted of Azerbaijani nationalists seeking an independent republic which it started to establish itself through the offices of the Turks and British occupying forces. It was therefore regarded as foreign.

lifestyle, he took the opportunity for his ambition to become a person of status. He had been used as a spy, the nature of such an assignment makes any person deceitful because it is part of the role. Being a 'mole' or secret agent was a task which placed the subject in both camps, which, as he later discovered, left him open to accusations by all sides. A spy can be treated by some as a hero, others a threat, but to this day the task of a secret agent is often looked down on with denigration. To this day a spy is always open to denunciation, rejection, and suspicion. Beria was a typical example, as he had been instructed (according to him) to pose as a member of the Musavat, and this left him wide open to doubt, which persisted throughout his life and was used by all his enemies and detractors. It was generally ignored by Stalin who always protected his favoured henchman. However, when Frinovsky a police chief in Azerbaijan passed on this information to Nikolay Yezhov, it is highly likely, given Stalin's paranoid personality, that he kept the material to himself because of his habit of needing information in case Beria became a suspect in Stalin's personal world.[7] Nikita Khrushchev certainly found it useful in 1953 when rendering Beria powerless.

Back in March 1920, he left this activity to work, but he was soon asked to return to underground activities in Georgia in gathering Intelligence for the Bolshevik Eleventh Army. His power increased when he was ordered to establish his own network in Tbilisi. He was captured, but with intervention was released on the promise that he left Georgia at once. He did not keep that promise, but he adopted the new name of Lakerbaia and worked from the newly established Russian embassy, who were determined to overthrow the Menshevik hold on power in that region. He was arrested again despite protests from Kirov, but again Beria was released, this time being expelled from Georgia in a prison convoy.

On his return to Baku in the summer of 1920 as a student in his educational establishment, he continued to work for the Bolsheviks on a committee dedicated to seizing property for their movement. For a brief time, he worked at his studies, but the Party appointed him to work in the Azerbaidzhan political police, namely the Cheka. Baku was an area which Lenin had demanded should be brought under Bolshevik influence, probably because of its oil resources. It was at this time there was a remote possibility that Beria may have seen Stalin who arrived in the area to give a speech in November 1920. Beria had also established connections with Kirov and Sergo Ordzhonikidze.* It was Ordzhonikidze who helped him escape the Musavat spy charges.

As a young man Beria was being moulded to think not in terms of his natural homeland of Georgia, but the broader picture of Marxist belief of a world union based on communism. As with so many in these turbulent political times it is impossible to ascertain Beria's deeper motivations with some suggesting he was the idealist of Marxist theories, others that he was using this to further his own personal ambitions, and speculatively it may have been the human mix of both elements.

Beria in the Cheka

When Beria signed into the Cheka, (technically the AzCheka as all regions had their Cheka forces controlled by the Moscow VeCheka), he had found, by hindsight, his natural habitat. Their task was revealing counter-revolutionary plots, upon which they were granted powers of prompt justice, typically reflective of kangaroo courts. The Red Terror (1918–1920) was a time of brutality as the Bolsheviks imposed their will as they assumed power. It provided an opportunity for an ambitious man like Beria to seize the moment by belonging to the Cheka, where he and his comrades had the power of life and death over others. The work carried its own risks as it was a world of suspicion, often leading to distrust and suspicion. Beria was mistakenly arrested again but released, and he learned that a lack of human trust in another was a common feature in this style of life. Stalin would one day confide he trusted no one not even himself, an attitude which was rampant amongst those who worked in the political underworld. This was part of Beria's youth, forming his reputation as the feared man of later years.

The Bolsheviks gained the loyalty and support of young men like Beria because their youth made them exploitable, very much as later in Germany the most fanatical Nazis (the SS) frequently emerged from the Hitler Youth.

---

* Sergo Ordzhonikidze (1886–1937) was Georgian Bolshevik about whom there is a great deal of mystery and lack of verifiable knowledge. He was instrumental in incorporating the Caucasus into the early Soviet Union. He fell out with Stalin and was apparently killed, but it was publicised as death by illness.

The Jesuits once claimed that if you gave them a child until they were seven years of age, they would give you the man. The Bolsheviks were no different when they recruited young ambitious men like Beria. However, the question remains as to Beria's personal motivations. His energy and ambition 'seemed willing to do anything that was required of him by his Bolshevik superiors', but at this distance in time his personal incentives remain elusive.[8] The question as to whether he was an idealist or careerist at this age will always remain indefinable.

Beria's immediate boss was Mircafar Bagirov, the twenty-four-year-old head of the local Cheka who had been involved in some bloody reprisals against the local population, and like Beria, had adapted with ease to the brutal repression.* He recruited Beria, 'and, after a few weeks, named him deputy secret police chief, at the age of twenty-one'.[9] Beria and Bagirov formed their own alliance looking after one another to the bitter end in 1953. Bagirov had known Beria before he joined the Cheka, and he may have been the reason that Beria's future blossomed so rapidly. Beria was made chief of the Secret-Operative Department and deputy Chairman of the AzCheka, with Bagirov's personal support. Beria appointed as his secretary a young ex-medical student called Vladimir Dekanozov who remained close to Beria.** These were difficult and dangerous times, and it was essential to have friends with genuine trust, but difficult when Stalin threw the dice. Beria was now in a world of intrigue and secrecy, which he seemed to find natural adapting to, by seeking and crushing the enemy. It was also the start of his life-long habit of intrigue against his superiors in the hope he could undermine them for his own advantage. It has been noted by one historian that 'His next boss, Ivan Pavlunovsky, pleaded at staff meetings for his deputy Beria to cease intrigues against him'.[10] In such an office it was not just about seeking out subversives but being careful as to who had the desk next door.

---

* Mircafar Bagirov (1896–1956) was always close to Beria. He had taken part in the October Revolution and the Civil War. He was the Communist Leader of the Azerbaijan SSR from 1932 to 1953. He tried to survive the downfall of Beria but was tried in 1954 and executed in 1956, though some claim he died in Siberia.

** Vladimir Dekanozov (1898–1953) served in the Red Army in 1918, joined the Bolshevik Party on 1920. He was a secret agent in Transcaucasia and member of the Cheka in Azerbaijan where he befriended Beria. He joined the NKVD in 1938 as Beria rose in national status, then became Deputy Chief of NKID (Foreign Affairs) in 1939; in 1940 he was Soviet Ambassador in Berlin. He was executed in 1953.

The Cheka's main task was to crush counter-revolutionary groups which could be sought from spying or overhearing a joke. It was a time and place of distrust and mutual suspicion, a major feature of the Soviet regime. It was in 1921 the Troika system, mentioned above, was announced. This three-man committee was empowered to judge and execute on the spot, and Beria played a major role in these proceedings. From his youth he had become accustomed to killing people, not as a fighting soldier, but often dragging them from their beds and their families in the middle of the night, very much like the Gestapo's *Nacht und Nebel* (Night and Fog). The Cheka relied upon political orders, but it is known that they often selected and executed suspects with motivations not touching on any political necessity. The fact is that by the age of twenty-one Beria's character was forming into a killer, lacking any compassion, and showing signs of becoming a violent sex addict. In the concluding chapter of this book where immoral and illegal behaviour is explored, it might cross the reader's mind that Beria from a young age was showing signs of a psychopathic disorder.

It is perhaps no surprise that as a young person Beria developed into the most feared man after Stalin, and he was already becoming the person of future years, feared at all levels on the Soviet ladder of power. On one occasion Beria was criticised by Mikhail Kedrov for convicting the wrong people and allowing serious opponents to escape. Kedrov (1878–1941) had been a Soviet politician and secret policeman who was himself known to be cruel. He slaughtered people and threatened to annihilate whole communities. He and his son Igor often complained about Beria to Stalin, but Beria later had Kedrov executed under his own orders.

Throughout Soviet history there was always a delicate relationship between Party members and the political police, especially in the upper echelons. This was and is typical of a country which has secret police focused on political matters. Even the major leading figure of Göring in Nazi Germany was at one time concerned about Himmler's investigations, and he awarded his detested colleague flyers wings to placate him. When there is a Gestapo or a Cheka, suspicion and fear dominate daily life at all social levels. Later, in Russia it was initially agreed after a period of tension over such matters, that the Cheka should not arrest members of the Party. Many of the complaints had been against Beria who was soon to become a controversial and feared figure. At a young age he was already well known and seen extending his power by serving on various governmental bodies outside the Cheka within his given area.

Beria married Nina Teimurazovna Gegechkori in 1921, having proposed to her when she was sixteen in secret in case of family objections. Curiously, Stalin's daughter later claimed that when Nina was living in her home village and 'hearing that Lavrenty Beria, Head of the GPU of Georgia, had arrived, she went to plead with him for her brother's release – he had been arrested. Beria had arrived in a special train, and Nina entered his car, and never again saw her native village, her beauty having caught the police boss's fancy. He locked her up in a compartment. That was how she became his wife'.[11] The truth remains a mystery, but these rumours abounded, and it may simply be that because it was a secret marriage that such rumours took hold. However, this account which Stalin's daughter provided, more probably grew from his well-known sexual predatory nature, the marriage lasted and 'she remained in love with her "charmer" throughout her long life', it has been claimed.[12] Whatever the truth, Nina stayed with Beria, and she became a student of pioneering chemistry and was obviously a science-academic in her own rights.[13]

The Bolsheviks were facing continuing opposition in Georgia, and Beria was transferred to Tbilisi in November 1922 to the same position he had held in Baku, because Moscow knew that local people were necessary for success. Georgia was unsettled because of the Mensheviks who tended to be more popular, there was serious land shortage, the economic situation was poor, and Georgia had always demanded its independence. As this is being written in November 2025 there are still political disturbances in that country.

Despite these major problems, Stalin helped by Beria's friend Ordzhonikidze enforced a treaty on Georgia uniting it with Azerbaidzhan and Armenia into a form of federation of Transcaucasian republics in the March of 1922. Lenin who was ill at this stage protested at this manipulation, but Stalin was determined on a total centralising of power.* As such, the new federation was incorporated into the USSR within a month, despite

---

* The Trans-Caucasus is an important area, the Caucasus Mountain range is a natural barrier separating Eastern Europe from Western Asia. The Caucasus region was separated between North Causcasus (Cis-Caucasus) and Trans-Causcasus (South Causcasus).

Georgian efforts to keep their identity. Stalin always wanted his own way, and Georgian rights diminished as Stalin ordered his men like Beria not to waver in carrying through his plans.

Beria's Early Ascendancy to Power

Beria's transfer to the Georgian Cheka was the beginning of his rise to power. The Cheka was needed to ensure that Georgian politics rid itself of the wish to remain independent and not be totally subjected to Moscow. Beria was undoubtedly chosen because his ruthlessness and determination to please had been observed. Beria, aware of his own progress, always suppressed any opposition with noted ferocity which he knew would mark him as a necessary component for the movement. There is no question that Beria was a driven man in his pursuit for recognition and he was overly ambitious.

Beria rose through the local ranks of power, eventually transferring to the highest Party offices in 1931: it was what he was seeking but at times it was a balancing act for Beria. It was, as is well known, the time when the new Bolshevik order took over the best bourgeois homes and hotels. Most of the well-off had fled, kept a low profile, or had merged with the new political elements. Beria with his wife Nina took over a large apartment at 57 Kiacheli Street, Tbilisi, which was to remain his residence throughout his time with the Georgian police. In the same apartment building lived Beria's chief Nika Kvantaliani and his family, as well as Ordzhonikidze's brother. Other young serving men, the lesser mortals, lived in hotels now transformed into barrack-like dormitories. The photographs of Beria indicate he wore *pince-nez* glasses as he did throughout his life, and his physical features were somewhat diminutive, as noted by Stalin's daughter Svetlana who described his face as repulsive.

Beria's character was apparent to those who knew him, he was a man determined to rise and be successful. He once said, 'When we Bolsheviks want to get something done, we close our eyes to everything else'.[14] Nikolai Bukharin later noted that he was extremely intelligent and charming and 'he dominated his entourage with his intelligence'.[15] As noted Beria's chief moved into the same premises with Beria, probably because he was encouraged to do so, as it would benefit any ambitious man to have friendly access to his superior. Beria would frequently join in the social gatherings of his superiors, as well as the lower orders of the offices to ensure his personal success. He gathered around him keen young helpers who would do his bidding, and they were often referred to as 'Beria's gang'. Many of whom were poorly educated young soldiers, and like Beria were looking to their futures, doing so by carrying out barbaric orders. Beria often selected Mingrelians of his own ethnic background, and he never lost this habit of surrounding himself with loyal minions, who gravitated towards a person they knew was climbing the Party ladder. Beria rewarded them with apartments and security, and they in return also 'admired him as a professional in police work and a patron'.[16] One early important comrade was Vsevolod Merkulov who assisted Beria with his Russian language, which at this time was not polished in its grammar and idiom.* Merkulov stayed loyal to Beria to the end, and he only turned against him to save his own skin, which failed.

The Georgian Cheka had been established in early 1921 and was critical for the Bolshevik policy of centralising and bringing everything under Moscow's control. It was this particular demand which had led to Beria's new chief, Kvantaliani who had replacing his predecessor, who had been less enthusiastic about centralisation, and subsequently died from tuberculosis while in prison. By 1922 the GPU replaced the Cheka, but it conformed to the policy of centralising Soviet control by brutal control-force.

A major issue faced by the Bolsheviks was the opposition to their control in these Georgian borderlands. This led to brutal repression by the Cheka demanded by the government. It was not only an attack on the counter-revolutionary elements or vendettas against those bourgeois who had stayed, but on any individual who attracted the attention of the secret police. Mass executions and burials were the order of the day, with fear dominating the region. The Mensheviks at first were ignored but soon came under the same threat of annihilation. By the end of 1923 there was a move for independence in Georgia but the Cheka, with Beria as one of the leading components, brutally crushed the effort. It has been suggested that

---

* Vsevolod (Boris) Merkulov (1895–1953) started as a detective for the Cheka in Georgia, then from 1925–31 was the Deputy Head of the GPU in Ajaria. For a few months he was the Peoples' Commissar of State Security but following the reorganisation from 1941–43 he was Deputy Peoples' Commissar of the NKVD. He was deeply involved in the Klaus Fuchs atomic spying episode. In 1946 for a brief time, he was a minister of MGB but was executed in 1953.

Beria and his superior Kvantaliani all but encouraged this revolt claiming it would bring the insurgents to the surface with a view to crushing them more effectively.[17]

During these years Beria proved to be efficient in finding any opposition. Whole families and villages could be contaminated in his search simply because they were neighbours, and the Cheka murdered people with the same surname or with any family connection, there was no mercy shown. There are, expectedly, no records of those killed, but it is known that it amounted to thousands of victims. It has been argued that because they had direct orders from the Moscow government, Beria and his men were not entirely responsible. It was the blind obedience to immoral and illegal orders condemned at the Nuremberg Trials. Being the sort of government which was developing under Stalin's paranoid fear of the slightest opposition, it often meant that any dissent in the ranks could not avoid vicious purging.

Stalin was constantly searching for any critics within the Communist party, and many so-called subversives were sent to the camps, including Lavrenty Kartvelishvili 'who had not been able to get along with Stalin's protégé and favourite in Georgia at that time, Lavrenty Beria'.[18] Beria, to demonstrate his character, insisted this old rival be brought from Tbilisi where he made him dance to the blows of his club. Beria and many others at this time, generally young men mainly in their twenties, often indicated a willingness if not pleasure to kill people with any form of torture. For them killing people had simply become a task to be carried out upon the demands of their superiors. The sheer fear experienced by the victims rapidly brought submission, and Beria's effectiveness was noticed by his superiors and also by Moscow. Such was the brutality in subduing any national Georgian identity, and crushing the Mensheviks, that some observers raised questions, and Moscow was obliged to send Sergo Ordzhonikidze to investigate the situation. As already noted above Beria knew Ordzhonikidze well, his brother lived in the same apartment, and this may well have saved Beria from the pseudo-blame game which followed for a brief time. As in any society it was and is a matter of who knows who. When in 1924 Beria's wife gave birth to a son, Beria named him Sergo after Ordzhonikidze who was also a godfather which helped Beria's ambitions. The repression had worked, and the Mensheviks and any form of related opposition was subdued in this area by terror.

It is believed that Beria personally met Stalin in the mid-1920s, probably when Stalin decided to take his home holidays in the area. It was rumoured that Beria arranged to use prison labour to have a holiday home built for Stalin. In 1925, Mogilevksii, the chairman of the Transcaucasian Cheka was killed in a plane crash, and there was speculation that Beria hoped for immediate promotion. There was even speculation that Beria had organised this death, but there is no evidence to give substance to such a claim, though because of Beria's character even at this stage it was understandable why this suspicion arose. Beria wrote his ex-boss's eulogy, in which he promoted himself.[19] It was too early for Beria's ambition, but not long afterwards he was promoted to the post of Chairman of the Georgian GPU and his boss Kvantaliani was moved sideways. As he started to rise in authority Beria's pursuit for power, he was always looking for the next step up the ladder. It was well-known that he was always seeking for information which could undermine any rival's reputation, creating for him many personal enemies, as can happen in any office scenario.

On one occasion he was attacked on a military road leading to Tbilisi by Georgian terrorists or bandits, and apparently some of his colleagues were killed, but it is claimed he fought them off and won a medal for bravery. Other accounts claim it was his bodyguard Boris Sokolov and the driver who fought them off, and it was Sokolov who was wounded, but it is impossible to know how many of these stories were exaggerated.[20] On another occasion Beria was reputed to have covered Stalin's body with his own on a launch when some shots were fired from the shore.* It has even been suggested that Beria contrived the attack so he could undermine the hated Nestor Lakoba who was responsible for security in that area.[21] It certainly brought him closer to Stalin.**

---

* This incident happened in 1933 when a guard had supposedly challenged the launch which had not responded, and warning shots were fired. Stalin appeared to accept the explanation, but Beria pursued the matter relentlessly. See Kotkin, Stephen, *Stalin, Vol II: Waiting for Hitler, 1928–1941* (London: Allen Lane, 2017), pp.141–2.

** Nestor Lakoba (1893–1936) was the Communist leader in Abkhazia when incorporated into the Soviet Union, and Lakoba remained somewhat independent because of his close relationship with Stalin. Because of his status Beria clashed with him, he was then regarded as an enemy of the people and died in 1936 by Beria's machinations. In 1953 his reputation was rehabilitated.

His 1927 promotion at the Fifth Party Congress also saw the departure of his supporting acquaintance Sergo Ordzhonikidze to Moscow. This old friend was now closer to Stalin and carried political influence of which Beria was well aware. Beria stayed in touch with Ordzhonikidze, obsequiously informing him of all that was occurring, or grovelling, dependent on the circumstances. Beria was determined to rise in the ranks as far as possible. He was already becoming known as the arch-manipulator and Machiavellian in his devious manipulations. It only needed Beria's slightest suspicion for any individual to come under scrutiny, and although Party members were immune from outright arrest, this did not stop secret files being compiled on them, a habit fastened onto by the Nazi leader Himmler, with whom Beria was often compared. The developing Soviet system was becoming a police state of terrifying proportions, and as the Georgian opposition was crushed Beria turned more to what he considered the inside-enemies lurking within the Party system. Moscow was aware of the infighting in Georgia, but Stalin was more concerned that his Party objectives were implemented.

Complaints still emanated from that part of the communist controlled areas, and in September 1929 a delegation was dispatched from Moscow to investigate irregularities, and to inspect some abuse by major figures, and Azerbaidzhan was the first republic to come under scrutiny. This investigation may possibly have been prompted by Beria's letters of criticism about senior men, but he would have been aware that the investigation might give attention to his conduct, so he astutely warned Ordzhonikidze that everyone tended to blame him. It was a clever prophylactic move, pointing out that those under investigation would of course blame the GPU. In a letter to Ordzhonikidze, he suggested he should be transferred out of Georgia, no doubt seeking promotion, which his political mentor ignored, but on the other hand he shielded Beria from criticism.[22]

There were changes amongst senior men, but Beria kept his position, and his work of repression focused on his opportunities to serve Stalin's policies. Stalin had started to activate his policy of collectivisation, (part of the Five-Year Plan mainly affecting agriculture when individual holdings and labour were merged) and the anti-Kulak (the wealthier farmers) campaigns were started to ensure these polices were implemented throughout the old empire. The average peasant in Georgia was less well-off than his Russian counterpart, but Stalin had no time for the economic circumstances of its citizens and demanded prompt action. Beria turned his already well-known brutality on to the peasants, knowing that this would please Stalin.

During the years 1929 to 1930 the repression was severe, and vast numbers were being shot, which led to opposition from the peasants leading to more repression by the GPU assisted by army support. Those who were seen as protesting about their traditional way of life were simply analysed as anti-Soviet elements opposed to communism. The reactive barbarity against the ordinary workers eventually caused a reaction in Moscow when Stalin in March 1930 suddenly decided to remove the demanded emphasis on rapid collectivisation.

Stanislav Redens, Beria's local superior was reputedly feeble, and he tended to follow Beria's lead who was undoubtedly behind the belligerence of this repression.* This was a tenuous moment for Beria who inveigled Redens at the Transcaucasian HQ to send a message to the OGPU (see list of abbreviations on page 178 if necessary) leadership in Moscow.** This carefully composed message intimated that there were anti-government movements in Georgia amongst Party leaders, and the collectivisation policy was being used as an excuse for a counter-revolution. The paranoid Stalin read this note from Beria and Redens, and the officials were ordered to let the GPU continue their work. This letter to Stalin advanced Beria's ambitions and increased his standing with Stalin, leading to another shake-up of the Georgian leadership. Beria had proved able to discredit others while always elevating himself.

Beria continued to plot that his value was recognised, ensuring there was no potential leader who could block his elevation. This included his weak boss Redens who was transferred by Stalin, based on Beria's typical information that Reden when drunk had battered down the door of a female employee who had called for the local police, which Beria promptly

---

* Stanislav Redens (1892–1940) was born of Polish parents and a secret police official. He joined the Cheka in 1918, and the Crimean GPU in 1922–23 where he became widely known for his brutal repression of the Kulaks. In 1928 he was Chief of the Transcaucasian GPU but was side-lined by Beria. In 1933 he was recalled to Moscow and elected to the Supreme Soviet of the Soviet Union in 1937. He was accused of running a Polish underground group and was arrested and shot in 1940. In 1961 under Khrushchev his reputation was rehabilitated.

** Because of this Redens was sometimes referred to as 'Berens'. See Knight, Amy, *Beria: Stalin's First Lieutenant* (Princeton: Princeton University Press, 1993), p.43.

reported to Stalin.[23] Another account is that Beria made Redens so drunk he walked home stark-naked.[24] These accounts may or may not be true, but Beria ensured the way ahead was free from rivals.

On one occasion when Beria's wife Nina's uncle was caught with a prostitute, Beria stifled any investigation of the matter, but it is easy to speculate he did not act out of family compassion but for his own reputation, because the uncle was family which might raise questions about Beria.* Beria's reputation was important to him as he tried to climb the ladder of success, and in November 1930 he became a member of the Georgian Central Committee, involved in policy making. Much of this political elevation was due to Ordzhonikidze and Stalin's interest in this obedient servant. Whenever Stalin took his holiday breaks at Sochi, it was Beria who organised his residence security. Stalin was beginning to be more aware of how useful Beria would be and proposed he should be First Secretary in Georgia, and then as Second Secretary of the Transcaucasian Central Committee against which there were many protests. However, there were changes in the leadership, and by the age of 32, Beria was in the ascendancy.

The Ladder of Power

The Tbilisi Party committee members were strident in their protestations about Beria's rise through their ranks, based on his known habits of undermining anyone seemingly barring his progress. Many threatened to resign rather than work with a man who would have them denounced if they were in the least critical of him. However, few wished to cross swords with Stalin, who eventually met the opposition stating 'We'll settle this question the routine way…and angrily concluded the meeting by appointing Beria Georgian First Secretary and Second Secretary of Transcaucasia over their heads. Beria had arrived'.[25] Beria promptly asserted his authority, making sure the Georgian Party understood his areas of responsibility as First Secretary, which included not just the feared GPU, but agriculture, oil-refining, resorts, and later in 1936 he would publish a report on his success.

---

* Later this same uncle embezzled government funds but committed suicide rather than face the consequences.

In January 1932 Beria made his first public appearance as the local Party chief, and his report carried a full-sized photograph of himself, indulging in his characteristic policy of self-promotion. He sent out his usual warning against the Mensheviks and the Kulaks, claiming they were counter-revolutionaries against Bolshevism. Later he attacked deposed Party leaders constantly referring to Stalin, which was a cunning ploy he used. In his attack on the ex-Party leaders, he had support from Stalin who wanted to rid himself of the original Party members who knew too much about him, and he had probably noted their lack of veneration towards him. As far as Stalin was concerned Beria was an up-and-rising cohort prompting Stalin to write to Kaganovich that 'Beria makes a good impression' meaning he was a useful tool.[26]/*

Beria continued his habit by insinuating to Stalin that two senior men, Mamia Orakhelashvili and Lakoba were failing, but raising the issue inspired by his personal ambitions. Beria wanted to broaden his power beyond Georgia, and he had cast his ambitious eyes towards Mamia Orakhelashvili the Party leader of Transcaucasia, the area which included not only Georgia but Armenia and Azerbaidzhan.** This ambition meant that Beria spoke as if he were representing the whole of the Transcaucasian Federation.

To ensure Moscow knew of his dedication, he maintained his compliant correspondence with Ordzhonikidze, knowing that his old friend was close to Stalin. He corresponded on many matters ranging from the Kulaks and agricultural problems to the conditions in Tbilisi, and the need to allow the Mingrelian language to be used at an official level. However, this relationship with Ordzhonikidze showed signs of faltering, as Beria became aware that many of the people he had 'fingered' had gone to see Ordzhonikidze, not just about the complaints, but the critical way Beria had spoken about Ordzhonikidze. As soon as Beria realised this was happening, he wrote immediately denying their accusations as a sheer fabrication for his victims to have their revenge. Nevertheless, the relationship became somewhat tense

---

* Later Kaganovich's brother Mikhail was accused by Stalin of building airfields too close to the border; Beria and Malenkov interviewed him, and he allegedly shot himself in the toilets. He had become a scapegoat for the developing aircraft blunders at the start of the war. Despite this hideous attack on his brother Kaganovich stayed loyal, denying that he had any part.

** Mamia Orakhelashvili (1881–1937) was an active Bolshevik politician in Transcaucasia and later part of the *Pravda* board. He died during the Purges in 1937.

when Ordzhonikidze's brother Papulia was sacked from his post with the railways, and Ordzhonikidze realised that Beria had done nothing to help. Beria protested he had tried, but it started a degree of tension between the two men. Ordzhonikidze may also have been aware of Beria's machinations to dispose of Orakhelashvili, but Beria was eventually successful because Orakhelashvili was demoted, and by January 1934, Beria held both posts. One Russian historian noted that 'Beria was a confirmed criminal type who had pursued his calling by serving the secret police…and with meticulous cruelty he massacred the Party veterans in the other Transcaucasian republics as well as Azerbaidzhan and Armenia…later Beria was to tell his boss how he had gloated over Mamia Orakhelashvili, one of the true founders of the Bolshevik organisation in Transcaucasia'.[27] It would have been more than apparent how dangerous Beria could be even to those closest to him.

Beria's relationship with Ordzhonikidze continued but the mutual trust evaporated. Nevertheless, Ordzhonikidze visited Transcaucasia in 1934 and travelled the area with Beria, even recommending that Beria and his close friend Bagirov should receive the Order of Lenin for their work in oil-extraction. However, compared to the earlier days the relationship was strained. It was noted that Beria was developing a deep interest in economics, as he knew how important this was for Stalin. The state of economics in Russia was poor which was an ongoing problem of which Stalin was aware and sensitive about.

Beria always responded to Moscow's demands, producing long written reports or addresses to indicate how much he was achieving. The harvest had been poor, and the repressed Kulaks were blamed, but tea production increased, and he inspected the major oil resources in Baku and explored the tobacco and wine produce areas. All this activity gave him the opportunity in 1934 with a speech to the Seventeenth Party Congress, for Beria to boast of his progress, presenting his personal development on the national stage. It was no surprise that he was elected 'to full membership on the Central Committee of the All-Union Communist Party'.[28] Beria knew precisely what Stalin was seeking, and the total support and loyalty he demanded, needing men who would follow him and never challenge his position. Beria was intelligent and politically astute, understanding Stalin and he knew what was needed to stay close to his demanding leader.

At this Seventeenth Congress Stalin had not received the number of votes he had anticipated, but he and his henchmen 'were automatically elected but here was another blow to Stalin's paranoia and self-esteem, confirming that he rode alone among two-faced double dealers' and he needed a Beria to resolve these self-obsessive problems.[29] Beria was Stalin's man because he was pro-active in promoting the Stalin cult and managed to build his own platform to ensure his rise to the upper echelons. Nearly all dictators have an obsessive need to promote their own image which is why Göbbels was so important to Hitler, and Franco sought the support of the Falangists and had a few close henchmen to boost his image. Beria ensured Stalin's picture appeared everywhere he could arrange, even organising a monument over Stalin's birthplace in Gori.* He even went so far in this reverential behaviour to bring Stalin's mother to Tbilisi where he and his wife took care of her. When Stalin visited his mother in 1935 it was with her carer Beria.** He was making every possible effort to ingratiate himself in the leader's eyes with one historian writing that he behaved 'like a courtier looking after a dowager empress'.[30]

Stalin was aware that he was making history, and Beria even involved himself in either writing or influencing the way the records and histories of the time should be written, and in doing so tried to construct what may best describe as a Stalin cult. An official history called *On the History of Bolshevik Organisations in Transcaucasia* was produced, it carried Beria's name, but it has long been accepted that it was the work of others. Beria later admitted a man called Bediia along with other contributors had produced the history. It was common at that time for 'committee-writing' to be followed by a senior name as the author. However, according to one witness Merkulov, 'Beria didn't do a single bit of work on the book' because to achieve this 'he would have to know history'.[31] The book was presented as a lengthy lecture, published in the press, and sold thousands of copies with additional editions. The central apparatus instructed all Party organisations to organise study groups on Beria's book, which 'offered the richest material on the role of Stalin as a supreme leader and theorist of our Party', and Beria received all

---

* It is curious that Saddam Hussein was born not far away and studied Stalin. Beria's building was almost a temple.

** When Stalin's mother died, he did not attend the funeral, but Beria and his son took his place.

the credit.[32] The Politburo reprimanded Beria for not seeking permission to publish Stalin's work, to curb his ambition. The danger for many was that Stalin was being made into the superhero which had led to a web of lies, and as one of Beria's biographers wrote, 'in short, Beria's book, hailed as path-breaking work, transformed Soviet historiography into fiction'.[33] Those who knew that Beria had not done the work while claiming total authorship often suddenly died, and the historian Robert Service noted that Beria had 'commissioned and appropriated the text and then shot the writers'.[34] The book was essentially based on a Stalin cult and offered a justification for his repression of the Mensheviks. 'There were various Soviet hagiographers competing to portray Stalin as just such a humble man of the people and their instrument of destiny', and Beria watched this happening and later boosted it by depicting Stalin as the Lenin of the Causcasus.[35]

It has been suggested that Kirov's sudden death marked the beginning of the purges, as it was a matter of Stalin removing possible contenders who might challenge his reach for power. During the mid-1930s Beria would follow and imitate Stalin's malicious machinations, and one Russian historian wrote, 'In Georgia, Lavrenty Beria, the Little Pope, in imitation of the Big Pope, held show trials of the "Trotskyists" in those parts'.[36] It was a huge web of denunciation and conspiracy, and the old revolutionaries were the first to suffer. In 1934, the OGPU had become the NKVD and with increased authority, reacted to the will of Stalin, establishing the 'Special Board' which imposed prison sentences by simple speedy administration.

Beria's main concern was the drafting of a new constitution in 1936 which meant the dissolution of the Transcaucasian Federation, which indicated a reduction of Beria's powers, because he would only have Georgia within his grasp. 'Beria had ruled the three-republic South Caucasus Federation – Stalin's homeland – like a Persian Shah'.[37] Because of his friendship with Bagirov he had some influence in Azerbaidzhan, but Armenia was headed by Khandzhian who was known for often being critical of Beria.* Given the benefit of hindsight it was perhaps no surprise that Khandzhian had purportedly committed suicide, but it created considerable scepticism amongst

---

* Aghasi Khandzhian (1901–1936) was First Secretary of Communist Party in Armenia. He was a charismatic leader and popular in that area. He was denounced and although his death was a mystery it now seems Beria was involved. After Stalin's death his reputation was rehabilitated.

his friends. The surrounding circumstances were highly suspicious and the evidence years later, when it was safe to raise the issue, seemed to indicate that Beria had shot Khandzhian in his office, having the body dressed up as suicide. When Stalin heard from the concerned South Causcasus Party he replied that 'It was unnecessary to send its own representative to ascertain the circumstances…since in this matter everything is clear, and no investigation is required'.[38] Khandzhian was buried under a concrete block and forgotten. This singular brutal act allowed Beria to launch into the Armenian political government.

Nestor Lakoba, the chairman of the Central Executive Committee of Abkhazia (part of the Georgian Republic) also suffered a similar death, and Beria's involvement could almost be taken for granted, because for some time Beria had wanted Lakoba's downfall. On one occasion when he and Stalin were guests at Lakoba's house Beria had switched plates with Stalin insinuating that Stalin's portion may have been poisoned.[39] Lakoba was supposed to have died from a heart attack, but he was young with no history of illness, and Beria would not have acted without Stalin's validation. Stalin had dined with Lakoba, and all had seemed well on the surface. However, two months later Beria invited Lakoba to dine with him, and following this meal there was a trip to the theatre when Lakoba suddenly felt ill, and he returned to the hotel where he claimed, 'That snake Beria has killed me'.[40] He died that morning at 4.20 aged only forty-three from a supposed heart attack. Beria took his cruelty further by torturing Lakoba's family and drove his widow to medical madness by placing her in a cell with a snake, and by beating her teenage children to death.[41] Lakoba, unlike many was buried with full honours, and 'Lakoba's suspicious death, after Khandzhian's suicide, enhanced Beria's mystique and power', and the possible dangers of challenging or not supporting him must have been apparent to all who stood in his way. and for the modern reader demonstrate the personal unpleasant aspects of Beria the person, and why he had some appeal to the paranoid Stalin.[42]

The Purges

As the purges developed in Transcaucasia Beria authored an article in *Pravda* attacking the enemies of the Soviet state, demanding that anyone with the slightest official capacity should be aware of subversion within their ranks. The article had a demanding and puritanical tone, ensuring the purges were regarded as essential for the well-being of Russia, with one historian noting that 'Beria incarnated the terror-facilitated ascendency of the NKVD vis-à-vis the Party, but he had achieved that status years before', and he was feared and hated until his fall decades later.[43] Shortly after this the NKVD chief Yagoda was replaced by Yezhov to prepare for the major purges, and it started with the persecution of Nikolai Bukharin.* This was significant because Bukharin was from the old school, deemed close to Stalin, but far too popular for Stalin's taste. Even Beria's old friend and mentor Ordzhonikidze knew he was personally in danger as his family members and closer colleagues were under scrutiny. His brother Papulia had been arrested by the NKVD, his younger brother Valiko was in trouble, so Ordzhonikidze turned to Beria for help.** However, their friendship was now a matter of mere necessity.*** It was clear however that Stalin was moving against Ordzhonikidze who shot himself to avoid the inevitable torture which preceded the inevitable execution. Once again, his death was displayed as a heart attack.

Stalin announced that Party officials should not be members of small cabals looking after one another's interests. This was an anxious time for many and even Beria may have wondered whether he was in danger. When Stalin ordered new elections, they remained in the control of the local Party men, and Beria and his cohorts survived, but an article had appeared in *Pravda* which was critical of the Georgian procedures. Beria had powerful political instincts, responding with a detailed report to Stalin, thereby managing to survive a potential disaster. Stalin eliminated any opposition and Beria

---

*   Nikolai Bukharin was an early revolutionary and a Marxist theorist described by Lenin as valuable. Later he was the editor of *Izvestia* and a member of the Central Committee.

**   Papulia had been arrested under Stalin's orders by Beria, see Kotkin, Stephen, *Stalin, Vol II: Waiting for Hitler, 1928–1941* (London: Allen Lane, 2017), p.504.

***   Such was the growing tension between Ordzhonikidze and Beria that the latter built a special fence between their two dachas and refused to shake Beria's hand, See Montefiore, Simon Sebag, *Stalin: The Court of the Red Tsar* (London: Weidenfeld & Nicolson, 2003), p.180.

imitated him. Whereas Stalin was motivated by paranoia about opposition, Beria was driven by his thrusting ambition. For Stalin, the purges were to take total control, for Beria it was a passion to rise as close as he could to the political domination of Stalin's throne.

The Russian historian Anton Antonov-Ovseyenko once described Stalin as the 'Big Pope' and Beria as the 'Little Pope', which reflected a degree of reality, because Beria responded to Stalin's demand for the purges with enthusiasm.[44] Beria always followed Stalin's lead without hesitation because it was his personal pursuit for power. Beria returned from Moscow in the summer of 1937, calling a meeting of the NKVD and trusted leaders to demand the prompt search for traitors at once, even if they did not exist. They were ordered to employ torture as authorised by Stalin's instructions, which Stalin had pushed through his Central Committee. This indicated a warped personality, and it was well known that Beria participated in torture sessions; unlike Stalin and later Himmler in Germany, he did not just organise such brutality but became personally involved in these repulsive procedures. 'Many targets like Eihe were beaten not only in Beria's presence but by Beria himself', and it was noted that military commanders often referred 'to having tea with Beria' as a euphemism for a beating.[45] On the occasion that Maxim Litvinov was under suspicion, Yevgeny Gnedin his press officer of foreign affairs, recalled how 'Beria and Bogdan Kobulov put me on a chair and sat on either side and punched me in the head, playing "swings"… they beat me horribly, with the full force of their arms, demanding I give testimony against Litvinov'.[46] There are many available testimonies of the way Beria appeared to enjoy his personal involvement in the various means of torture. Stalin was a distant murderer and took no part in the rituals, he simply ordered the procedures. Beria, on the other hand appeared to revel in such grotesque situations. The torture was frequent, and most people feared such pain that it made death feel welcome. History has clearly revealed that very few men can withstand torture and will confess to anything demanded of them in the hope of a quick death, making confessions unreliable, not that this would have worried Beria. One serious problem is that the fear of torture often means some victims may implicate others hoping that such denunciations will stop their pain. This sometimes worked, and when Beria eventually took charge of security in Moscow some were released out of sheer necessity, which gave a false public impression about Beria. There were very few public trials in Georgia until the torture had ensured that the so-called culprit was not likely to say anything in public. Beria was well-aware that torture never led to the truth, and later admitted that it was possible to make anyone say anything, with one historian noting that 'a person that's beaten will give the kind of confession that the interrogating agents want, will admit that he is an English or American spy or whatever we want'.[47] Most of the early trials were held *in camera* and the Troika system, mentioned earlier, was widely employed. This was the three-man justice group which often acted as judge, jury, executioner and torturers, and cases could be started and finished within half an hour or even less.

A prominent Georgian Bolshevik called Mdivani had once opposed Stalin on the Transcaucasian Federation and had appealed to Lenin. Stalin had not forgotten this request, and Mdivani's destruction was inevitable. He was one of the very few who bravely failed to confess, and so his trial was held *in camera*. He was regarded as a ringleader and he and those of his suggested cohorts were taken out of the trial and shot, all of which was accomplished in one day. There were innumerable trials like this, including Beria's old colleague Kvantaliani mentioned earlier, and Beria used the occasion to eliminate his own opponents, including Bediia who was probably the real author of Beria's so-called book. He was just one of countless numbers who passed through the hands of the notorious NKVD Troika system and was shot on 27 December 1937. Beria also attacked the intelligentsia, especially writers. Initially he had encouraged their contributions only to demand a series of articles in praise of Stalin and himself. Beria had the habit of killing those who had responded to his demands, possibly because they knew too much and could later reveal the facts.[48] On one barbarous occasion, in the occupation of music, a young and talented orchestra conductor called Evgenii Mikeladze with his children were tortured through the Troika system with Beria personally involved. It transpired that the unfortunate Mikeladze was married to the daughter of Mamia Orakhelashvili, and for that reason alone the whole family suffered. Lakoba's wife and mother were rounded up, and all his associates, making no one safe, and perpetuating the growing sense of fear. Georgia's population was about 3.4 million and only about two per cent of the Soviet totality, and about nine per cent of these were victims.[49] It was just as appalling in the Ukraine where this brutality was also widespread.

Beria always ensured that Stalin knew he was obeying the letter of the law which meant obeying Stalin's demands. Bagirov survived but probably because of Beria's support. Another survivor was Khrushchev in the Ukraine who had also 'developed a reputation for bootlicking', and was as shrewd if not more so than Beria, to Beria's eventual misfortune.[50] In Beria's final days it would be Khrushchev who would bring him down, but in these earlier times Khrushchev admitted 'after the first encounter with Beria, I got closer to him...I liked Beria – a simple sharp-witted person'.[51] Khrushchev was right that Beria was sharp-witted, but he was never simple.

On reading the various individual accounts of sadistic torture it defies belief as to where such cruelty arose from, and elements of this will be explored in the concluding chapter. It could be argued that what Stalin demanded he achieved, and the same question can be asked of Nazi behaviour in Germany and in many other countries. The question does not go away with the answer that men like Beria always obeyed their masters, but more often than not it was in the pursuit of their own ambitions even though they became dehumanised and were bereft of any human sensitivity.

Stalin succeeded in what he demanded, namely the elimination of the old Bolsheviks, and any personal criticism he detected. He never allowed any popularity amongst his underlings, no men with memories of his younger past, and he ensured he was the one man at the top of the political pyramid which he was building from the ashes of Marx's ideals. The numbers killed will never be known in detail. During the great purges of the mid-1930s Beria himself 'reported that over 12,000 had been arrested and more than half of them convicted', which would have pleased Stalin.[52] Over the Soviet Union more than 1.7 million people were arrested in 1937–39, the population of the Gulag increased by 600,000 inmates, but under the leadership of the 'new people's commissar, Lavrenty Beria, conducted the same work in the same tenacious and systematic manner. True, its methods became more secretive, and hence more sinister'.[53]

Trusted by Stalin

Beria at this stage had gained Stalin's confidence. When, for example, Grigory Gofman, the Soviet Commissar for health, suddenly announced in the June 1937 Central Committee plenum in Moscow, that Beria had worked for the Musavat and was therefore a British spy, it must have been a stunning shock that anyone (apart from Stalin) could dare announce this powerful criticism. There was a telling silence, and why he made this suicidal claim remains a mystery. He must have known that even if there had been truth in this repetitious claim Beria had been officially exonerated. Stalin called for a break, allowed no discussion and Gofman was expelled from the Party and arrested the next day. Gofman received 'ten years without the right of correspondence, which meant he had been executed'.[54] Beria had powerful backing from Stalin and not until after Stalin's death was the Musavat spy charge mentioned again, this time by the then all-powerful Khrushchev.

In Beria's areas of responsibility in Georgia there were many different nationalities and as noted Beria was Mingrelian but amongst Abkhazians, Svans, Adzharians, Imeretians, and Lezghians, a country divided by ancient tribal and basic racial affiliations. Stalin was not interested in this but demanded that their Party cadres should cease, and he entrusted this work to Beria. Beria used Stalin's orders as an opportunity to eliminate his own enemies and build his own powerbase. Beria tightened his grip, and many leaders simply disappeared. Control of life even in faraway Republics such as Transcaucasia changed, and their governmental systems became, as Stalin intended, centralised in Moscow, and it was supported by a growing sense of fear. Beria continued his rise to power because he was in the all-powerful NKVD. It was not always straightforward for Beria, and in 1938 his name was not given the prominence he sought. He was criticised for not following some protocols, and his cohort Sumbatov-Topuridze head of the Azerbaidzhan NKVD was removed by Yezhov and replaced by his own man. For a moment the political life appeared to turn against Beria, as he was not the only bullyboy on the block seeking power. He heard from his faithful servant, Goglidze, the Georgian NKVD chief, that Yezhov was planning a move against him by trying to implicate him in an ongoing military-fascist plot. There was a rumour that Beria was on the move to safety, but it was only as far as Moscow to defend his cause personally with Stalin.

Stalin's daughter later described Beria as 'a magnificent modern specimen of the artful courtier, the embodiment of oriental perfidy, flattery and hypocrisy', and this appeared to work for Beria even with a man of Stalin's paranoid nature.[55] He explained the situation to Stalin, and having a sharp political mind he garnered the support of Lazar Kaganovich who fortunately, like Beria, had discovered that Yezhov was investigating him.* Stalin in his determined fashion changed direction and decided that Yezhov's day for retirement had arrived. He ordered a special commission to investigate the NKVD and appointed Molotov, Malenkov, Vyshinsky and Beria to the task.** They decided honest men were necessary, and on a motion by Kaganovich, Beria was appointed to the post of first deputy of the NKVD.[56] Stalin then informed Yezhov that he needed a deputy and asked his advice, and being cautious of all that had happened, enthusiastically agreed when Stalin suggested Beria. It was not that Yezhov wanted Beria alongside him, as the historian Robert Service noted that 'daily collaboration with Beria was like being tied in a sack with a wild beast'.[57] There is no doubt that in Stalin's mind Yezhov was finished, and Beria would replace him 'to cause the leader himself to shine more brightly', as Solzhenitsyn cynically noted, later writing that 'in any case, Stalin had to remain innocent, his sacred vestments angelically pure'.[58]

Vsevold Merkulov who was later given the task of writing about Beria's life following his arrest in 1953, claimed Beria was unhappy about his appointment to Moscow, and Khrushchev stated the same.[59] According to this account, Beria had reputedly said to Khrushchev 'What are you congratulating me for? You yourself did not want to be Molotov's deputy…I also did not want to transfer to Moscow, I'd be better off in Georgia'.[60] There was always the possibility that Stalin needed Beria closer to home because he was aware that Beria had been building up his own powerhouse in Georgia. The chief of the Union of Soviet Writers, Fadeyev had informed Stalin that a bust of Beria stood in the main public square, and he described

---

* Lazar Kaganovich (1893–1991) who, during this period, was the People's Commissar of Heavy Industry. He was a staunch and brutal stalwart of Stalin and was sometimes known as the 'Iron Lazar'.

** Andrey Vyshinsky (1883–1954) was a politician, jurist and diplomat. In 1935 he was the Procurator General of the USSR and headed up Stalin's Moscow trials and attended Nuremberg. From 1948 to 1953 he was Foreign Minister. He died in New York.

the habit of Congress members who stood up every time Beria entered their proceedings, whether this it true or not is questionable, on the grounds that Beria was all aware of Stalin's cast of mind in terms of his officials becoming popular.[61] In addition to this Stalin was knowledgeable of the number of letters of complaint Beria frequently wrote on economic matters regarding his home territory. Beria had demanded extra allocations of grain and flour, complained when hydroelectric equipment had not arrived from Leningrad, and demanded more industrial goods. On the other hand, Beria may well have missed the adulation he received, genuine or otherwise in his home country, and Stalin may therefore have wanted him relocated away from this possible adulation. It has also been suggested that Stalin wanted a Georgian close to him, a Party man of the same ethnic background. However, it seems more likely that Stalin recognised in Beria a tool for his devious machinations, and it is known that Beria was ambitious to be close to Stalin.

In the summer of 1938 Stalin transferred Beria to Moscow as Yezhov's first deputy of the NKVD, but it was certainly in preparation for Yezhov's dismissal on 8 December of the same year, when power was given to Beria. Stalin had been impressed by Beria because he always achieved what Stalin demanded, not least when 'Beria had crushed not just the Georgian Mensheviks but also the Georgian Bolsheviks' of whom Stalin had been suspicious.[62] Stalin had wished 'to purge the ranks of the secret police and wind down the Great Terror', as he was alert and therefore suspicious of the growing powers of his own policing officers.[63]

In Moscow it appeared that Beria and Yezhov worked well and socialised together, but it was the organised Commission's report which denounced the work of the NKVD during the purges. Yezhov was attacked and his reputation had not helped. According to their sources 'there were homosexual affairs, bisexual orgies, bouts of heavy drinking and fantastic stories that his wife was an English spy'.[64] There may have been some validity to these stories, but even if Yezhov had been clear of these taints, Stalin had decided his subordinate's role had finished.* In his biography of Stalin, Robert Service

---

* 'Yezhov characterised his homosexual liaisons as mutually active. How much of this Beria embellished cannot be known; history does not record the prudish Stalin's reaction'. Kotkin, Stephen, *Stalin, Vol II: Waiting for Hitler, 1928–1941* (London: Allen Lane, 2017), p.620.

suggested working with Beria had been the source of his sexual misconduct, but at the very least it seems that working with Beria was dangerous.[65] 'Yezhov's dismissal enabled Stalin to make him the scapegoat for such excesses of the *Yezhovshchina* [a term associated with the worse period of the purges] as could be publicly admitted'.[66] The same Commission 'also advised that the purges came to a halt. It was clear that Stalin had slowly realised that it had to stop soon, and Stalin was able through this Commission to shift the responsibility from himself'.* Yezhov was given no room for manoeuvre or protest and had no alternative but resign. Yezhov had been aware that he was in serious danger and was so 'distraught with fear and foreboding that he started shooting prisoners who might incriminate him'.[67] Beria was just as cruel, but he had more cunning and deep survival instincts.**

Stalin cultivated Beria on his arrival in Moscow making him feel welcome. He was granted better accommodation and a two-storey detached mansion. This had been 'the former residence of General Alexei Kuropatkin, war minister during the Russo-Japanese War fiasco, at Little Nikitskaya Street' and he replaced this dacha with an upmarket model.[68] In 1937 when the purges were at their height, Stalin explained to Beria that 'an enemy of the People is not the only one who does sabotage but one who doubts the rightness of the Party line. And there are a lot of them, and we must liquidate them'.[69] Beria was new to Moscow, and he was. as always, ready to obey Stalin's every command.

At a personal level, Stalin's daughter wrote that 'Beria's pince-nez was already gleaming in a corner somewhere, thought he was still humble and inconspicuous, everyone in the family loathed him and felt a premonition of fear'.[70] Stalin's daughter was accurate in her attitude, with the possible benefit of hindsight, adding that her family, by 'letting Beria into the family was like locking a fox in a chicken coop, but Stalin shared responsibility for their fates'.[71] It has been noted that Stalin's one time lover Zhenya Alliluyeva

---

* Because Yezhov was the driving force behind the major purges, (which Stalin needed to divert his own image from these appalling times), the term *Yezhovshchina* was thereafter used to describe the purges.

** Amongst the papers discovered in Yezhov's apartment were incriminating pieces of evidence against Malenkov and it has been suggested that Beria and Malenkov formed their alliance from this time. The discovered papers disappeared into Beria's rooms. See Montefiore, Simon Sebag, *Stalin: The Court of the Red Tsar* (London: Weidenfeld & Nicolson, 2003), p.263 and p.263fn.

in 1934, that her husband Pavel, an apparent innocent suffered a suspicious death at the same time as his associates were arrested. Medical murder was becoming popular amongst Beria's henchmen, because it gave a legitimate explanation, though this fooled no-one.* Stalin treated the wives of his victims in the same vein, assuming they had supported their husbands and so the children suffered as well. He always showed an interest in the wives of his henchmen and Beria understood this characteristic trait of Stalin, ensuring Stalin was suspicious of everyone except himself.

Beria insisted that everyone associated with Yezhov were purged, replacing them with his own men, although he remained alert to Stalin who had warned him that too many Georgians would not be good. Stalin never trusted any form of cabal, and to play safe it is alleged (by Merkulov) that Beria had to return some of his appointees.** Beria personally killed one of Yezhov's men, a man called Blokhin, following Stalin's order of thinking. Stalin had stated that the Party (meaning himself) needed a man prepared to do the dirty work. Beria was that type of man Stalin required, who from behind his desk could order a death or do it himself. Through this immoral political culture Stalin ensured 'he had many more senior willing executioners, who spoke and thought like thugs', and Beria had become a prime asset.[72] As far as is known Stalin ordered thousands upon thousands of deaths, but he always tried to keep his distance from public awareness.

Beria was in a stronger position than his predecessors of the NKVD because he was also a politician as well as a policeman. This enabled him to shape, with Stalin's permission, the NKVD organisation into a powerful body, because he needed security and supremacy. This gave Beria room to expand his personal power with occasional warnings from Stalin, so Beria's standing grew until after the Second World War. Stalin had warned Beria there would always be the question over his reliability when in 1919 it had been suggested he had been spying against the Bolsheviks. Merkulov was sent to Baku to find the papers relating to this time which appeased Stalin because he never raised the issue again, but others did later. He worked

---

* Zhenya Alliluyev was Stalin's lover in 1934.
** Merkulov had always been one of Beria's cohorts, but in the Khrushchev purge of 1953 he was obliged to co-operate.

hard in his post, making the NKVD offices efficient, and because Stalin had ordered an end to the purges this was sometimes known as the 'Beria thaw'.[73]

There was almost a sense of relief at Beria's appointment, with one observer writing 'we were overjoyed by the appearance of this pure and ideal figure, as Beria appeared to us, remembers Mark Laskin, who hoped like many people, that all the innocents would now be released, leaving only the real spies and enemies in jail'.[74] This sentiment was far from any reality, a few were released but the purges continued, but the victims were more carefully selected, and there were no major pronouncements in the newspapers. During the early months of 1939 Beria presided over the 'executions of 413 important prisoners, including Marshal Yegorov and ex-Politburo members Kosier, Postyshevm and Chubar', the last of these whose dacha plot was already inhabited by Beria.[75] Even the professional assassin Sudoplatov, to be explored next, wrote 'we hoped that the appointment of Beria as Yezhov's deputy in July 1938 might correct the evident mistakes. Naturally, [he later reflected] we were naïve, since we sincerely believed in the decency and honesty of our leaders'.[76]

Yezhov had instilled terror, but Beria, known as coldly efficient, made the system more effective, and the fear of the state security grew exponentially. The influence of the NKVD developed at a political level and Beria, along with Merkulov, achieved the status of being elected to the candidate membership in the Politburo.* Once again Stalin made sure that Beria was aware of his superiority by not giving him the top rank which he did not achieve until January 1941. Beria told his political colleagues he had removed the sense of frenzy from his predecessor's reign, but that was his way of creating his image. 'In general, Beria consolidated and institutionalised the system. From the *Yezhovshchina* [mentioned above] he developed, rather than an emergency operation against the people, a permanent method of rule'.[77] There may have been some hope for a few that times were changing, but it was only a change of personnel, although the 'frantic atmosphere of the Great Terror had been dissipated but Stalin's state remained a murderous madhouse – and most of the leading madmen were confirmed in power'.[78]

---

* Khrushchev also joined the Politburo at the same time on 10 March 1939.

The labour camps (GULAG) were expanding, and all classes of people were terrified by the appearance of the NKVD men. The Gulag population appeared to have peaked in 1938, and '837,000 detainees were released from camps and colonies following a re-examination of their cases under Beria's authority during a rectification campaign ordered by Stalin. In 1939, however, the repression resumed afresh, and on 1 January 1940 the number of inmates of camps and colonies reached 1,979,729, most of them best described as common-law prisoners'.[79] Regarding the 'Beria thaw' mentioned above, it was clear to the discerning that Beria was making the system more efficient, but not less cruel.

These camps were well-known but not a topic for conversation because of the bad publicity, and silence was demanded and the brutal interrogations were never publicised. To help this new policy, 'Beria wrote to Stalin and Molotov on 7 December 1939 to say that defence lawyers and witnesses should not be admitted during the preliminary investigations [instigated to review illegal proceedings], in order to prevent disclosure of the way in which these investigations are conducted'.[80] Unlike Yezhov, Beria's approach was more clandestine and thereby more sinister. All operatives of all grades were 'trained in the traditions of Stalinist obedience to the Party line, they were a docile group of functionaries, quick to bend their principles when they sensed a shift of power at the top'.[81] Whenever Beria or any other Party leader announced a change of direction, the hyper-sensitive politicians and all their functionaries knew it must have emanated from Stalin.

The camps were part of the NKVD's economic empire (this was a similar feature later in Nazi Germany when Himmler tried to turn the concentration camps to economic purposes) whereas originally, they were regarded as a better way of life than detention in prison cells. It has been argued that at times the conditions were less rigorous than detention 'with the exception of those that held political prisoners, notably on the Solovki Islands on the White Sea, which was the sole camp under the jurisdiction of the GPU'.[82] The NKVD under Beria became more interested in playing a role in the country's industrialisation and transformed the camps into a major work sector. This was the original meaning of Gulag or General Camp Directorate (Correctional labour Camps).

The first NKVD showpiece had been in constructing the White Sea Canal launched in 1931–32 dedicated to the workers and their overseers, namely the secret police.* The dedication was a travesty because 'the systematic exploitation of convict labour would also build the symbols of heroic modernity by which the regime would present itself'; the White Sea Canal had been the prime example, but ' all these came together to produce mass death on a previous unimaginable scale'.[83] There were other similar major tasks such as the construction of railways (in the Trans-Baikal region), a series of canals, one connecting Moscow and Volga, plus a myriad of factories and saw-mills. Stalin was obsessed with what he called the *Great Transformation of Nature*, which was taking natural resources for granted as they were free and not expendable. Russia's timber was cut down without thought (Russia accounted for more than a fifth of the planet's timber resources) and this policy was continued by Khrushchev and Leonid Brezhnev so that an area the size of France became a huge swamp, and the Aral Sea's sources were diverted for industrial purposes, and in time became a toxic salt desert.[84] Building the 200 mile Great Fergana Canal to move water to cotton fields was another propaganda feat which was based on slave labour, and was the last nail in the coffin for the Aral Sea.** In Beria's time the required labour was provided by the Gulag camps and their slave labour. In 1940 Beria, with an NKVD report to Stalin, stated the Gulag system was paying for itself. Beria as with Himmler in Germany was recognising and using the economic value of slave labour.[85]

Had it not been for the outbreak of war the system would have continued enlarging, but the work blossomed again post 1945. Beria wrote a report on the Gulags to Molotov in 1940 and according to this report 'the camp labour force, employed in constructing enormous factories, railways, port facilities and special sites [namely for defence needs], or logging and producing timber for export, was not used to the full because the inmates were fed too little and clothed too badly to face the difficult climatic conditions'.[86] The camps

---

* The White Sea Canal was economically worthless, built in record time it was not deep enough and cost thousands of lives. See Ings, Simon, *Stalin and the Scientists: A History of Triumph and Tragedy 1905–1953* (London; Faber & Faber, 2017), p.431.

** The Aral Seas was an endorheic lake (without an outlet) which shrank in the 1960s and dried up in 2010.

were remote, criminality amongst the inmates was rife because of the need for survival, but their sheer isolation meant the camp administration was often corrupt as each constituted its own little empire. Appendix One offers some of Aleksandr Solzhenitsyn's insights into these camps.

Stalin Allied with Hitler

After the purges it was realised that Stalin had deprived the Soviet Union of many critical military commanders and even some of his foreign agents, but he remained in 'a state of mind that made him, if anything, less equipped to analyse the dangerous international situation' which was developing on his very doorstep.[87] He had never been well-tuned into foreign countries because he had concentrated his energies on his personal power and ridding himself of critics. However, as Germany invaded Poland, Stalin moved in to take his agreed share (Ribbentrop-Molotov Pact) and Beria worked closely with Stalin on all these matters. There were huge numbers of prisoners to be held, and in the Baltic States and in Poland it was decided there had to be population adjustments, with the need to move any potential intelligentsia or political leaders to the east. As a consequence 'there were three deportations, in February, April, and June 1940. The operations were meticulously organised. In February, for example, 100 trains took away the equivalent of a large city's population in a matter of hours'.[88] Documents have clearly indicated this was Stalin's policy which was carried through by Beria. 'We learn from a secret letter Beria wrote to the TsK [central committee of the All-Union Communist Party] in September 1940 that, under a resolution of the SNK [Council of People's Commissars] dated 10 April of that year, members of twenty-five thousand Polish families – old people, women and children – were exiled from the new western oblasts [regions] of Ukraine and Belorussia. All they were guilty of was that their men had served in the Polish army or the state apparatus, or had been classified as bourgeois – landowning, counter-revolutionary elements'.[89] As Himmler would try in the west to move populations for political and racial reasons, Stalin and Beria proved even more adept at this appalling policy. It was the general theme in both the Nazi regime and Soviet Russia that ordinary people were of no consequence, and any intelligent persons or leaders were considered a potential danger.

The most notorious situation arose over Polish prisoners taken in the brief Polish occupation. Many were sent to the Gulag camps, but it was soon evident that some 15,000 were simply missing. Their deaths through an organised Russian massacre were uncovered in 1943 by Nazi forces in the Katyń area, where the bodies of Polish potential intelligentsia and officers were found buried, and still identifiable with the information in their clothes. The Germans were delighted to announce their discovery, but no one in the western world cared to believe the facts because the Soviet Union at this time was an indispensable ally. It took decades and the breakdown of the Soviet Union before it was revealed as one of Stalin's crimes, conducted by Beria's NKVD troops. There were many sites but together they are generally known as the Katyń massacres. The orders were carried out by the Kharkov NKVD under Beria's orders. It was Beria who had informed Stalin of the perceived danger, and it was Beria who signed the necessary orders along with Molotov and Mikoyan. Stalin avoided having Beria as a member of the troika and changed him for Kobulov, probably because Beria was working elsewhere.[90] It was Stalin's decision based on his paranoid fear that these Polish citizens might cause a revolt, but it was Beria and a few others who suggested and committed the deed. Stalin rightly carries the blame, but a known letter from Beria to Stalin proves that it was Beria's suggestion to eliminate what he perceived to be potential enemies.[91] In the words of the historian Bob Moore 'the failure to convert them and other members of the Polish intelligentsia to a pro-Soviet attitude led directly to an order by Lavrenty Beria on 5 March 1940, for their execution and the mass murder of up to 22,000 victims in the forest of Katyń and two other sites'.[92] As in most cases the movement of captured population areas and the mass of prisoners remain unknown in terms of precise figures. However, it has been estimated that the operations started in the spring of 1941 and about 140,000 Lithuanians, Latvians, and Estonians were taken into the Soviet Union, and about 400,000 Poles were sent to the labour camps.[93]

For Beria, the labour camps provided economic benefit, and it is known that the conditions were barbaric. As the war continued their conditions deteriorated, but there were prisoners who were potentially useful, such as scientists and engineers. One example was the aeroplane designer Tupolev, released the moment the Germans invaded. It was Beria who arranged the *Sharashka* (special prisons) probably prompted by the scientists who rather than be imprisoned pointed out they could use their talents for the state.[94] Beria's personal powers were widespread and, in the ascendancy, and in early 1941 he became deputy chairman of the USSR Council of People's Commissars, the most important state body.

Stalin's Blunder

As Hitler prepared to invade Russia, Stalin still appeared to trust the Nazi leader, ignoring Richard Sorge his most reliable spy, arguing that the capitalist states were deliberately trying to activate a war between Germany and Russia. Stalin instructed Beria to find those who thought otherwise, seeing them as subversives and who therefore were colluding with the capitalists.[95] The NKVD and many others had considerable information about the build-up of German forces on the western borders, and Dekanozov, the then Soviet Ambassador in Germany, communicated Hitler's intentions. Molotov was also aware of the situation because Dekanozov spoke to him directly, but when he told Stalin it was promptly dismissed as disinformation. Beria also knew the facts but was only concerned about a possible attack in the Caucasus oil fields. It reflected the central problem in the Soviet Union, that by this stage Stalin had become a totalitarian leader and Marx's ideals had been crushed. Such was the fear of Stalin no one wanted to disagree with him or even suggest he was wrong, with its inevitable consequences of annoying him with obvious consequences. It has been noted by the historian Hastings that Beria told Stalin that the Germans were at a high state of readiness on 2 June but was ignored.[96] Beria naturally would not disagree with the Master, and he even accused the head of military Intelligence, Golikov, of being a liar even though his own information backed Golikov's observations. It was all a gigantic blunder, but 'the war they had inadvertently helped to promote brought them new rewards, promotions, and prestige'.[97]

Stalin's incredible blunder in not reading the Nazi German mindset has remained something of an enigma. It had been the same in the West where appeasement had been the keynote, many of these issues may have been understood earlier had more attention been paid to Hitler's thinking processes, clearly laid out in *Mein Kampf* but rarely studied properly because it was so long, badly written, and tedious in the extreme. Stalin had ignored the obvious warning signs, and he refused to accept their validity. However, he had ordered that the borders should be defended by Beria and the NKVD, which organisation was growing in power and had the latest weapons, because for Stalin this body represented the power of the Party over the military.

Stalin had made an incredible error of judgment by leaving it so late for the western borders to be fortified, even having some of the traditional areas demolished to supply materials. Beria having no military insight of his own followed his master's command to the letter. Even when his own men had warned Beria of the gathering onslaught, he must have realised the enormity of the imminent danger, but he persisted in supporting Stalin's views even when they were so evidently mistaken. Sudoplatov, the secret agent to be explored later, blamed the Soviet Intelligence for not estimating the power of the German forces, and for being reliant on the belief that the Germans could not sustain a long war, claiming the NKVD and GRU were too 'preoccupied with political intentions'. He was probably right in both criticisms, but ignored Stalin's serious error of judgement.[98]

When the military complained they were again ignored. Three times communist inspired German soldiers had crossed the lines to warn the Russians, but Stalin simply viewed this as a German ruse, a matter of total self-delusion.* The preparations for the defence line, even simple anti-tanks ditches, were half-finished or non-existent when the onslaught started. Although Beria used camp-labour there was insufficient time for such a major task. They increased their mistakes by building new airfields too close to the border, placing their aircraft within easy reach of the Luftwaffe, neatly lined up for easy destruction. Perhaps the greatest blunder was allowing a German reconnaissance plane to fly deep into Soviet territory for fear of provoking a German reaction. According to Sudoplatov a German Junkers 52 landed in May 1941 unannounced and undetected, which led to several executions.[99]

---

* The third deserter was Alfred Liskov who swam the River Pruth, but Stalin's own response was to order his execution for sowing disinformation. 'Even on such a night, it was impossible to break the Stalinist routine of brutality' ... Montefiore, Simon Sebag, *Stalin: The Court of the Red Tsar* (London: Weidenfeld & Nicolson, 2003), p.317.

Kesselring, who led the initial air-attack, recorded his disbelief of 'Stalin's unbelievable trust in Hitler which greatly assisted Kesselring's Luftwaffe attack. Stalin had issued an order that restricted flying over German territory so that the Russian bomber force (which had largely escaped the first Luftwaffe strike, owing to its bases being farther from the front) took off obediently in accordance with an already outdated operational plan. Over 500 were shot down'.[100] In a biography of Kesselring it was noted that 'Kesselring had flown his FW-189 over the projected war-zone to familiarise himself with the territory, to see the gathering of German forces, and in his memoirs confesses that it was incredulous that Stalin would not believe all his informants'.[101] Beria had forbidden his troops or any military to fire on intruding German planes in Soviet air-space prior to the invasion, and although Beria was later denounced as a traitor in the Soviet history of the war, he was following Stalin's orders which he never questioned.[102]

Beria had in fact warned Stalin on 12 June writing that 'in a few instances they [the German aircraft] had penetrated 60 miles or more in the direction of military installations and large troop concentrations'.[103] Stalin still remained frozen in his own thinking, and he had decided not to move for fear of provoking the Germans. Stalin knew that Hitler's troops had taken Scandinavia, France, they were in the Balkans, and Britain had retreated. The Nazis had occupied many east-European countries and Italy was appearing sub-servient, but at least Stalin had a non-aggression pact, and the memory that Napoleon had failed in 1812. Stalin would not permit any combat preparation and Beria's men ensured there was no aggression on the Russian front to provide an excuse for German over-reaction. Hitler would be guilty of underestimating Russia, but Stalin, like many western politicians, had failed to grasp the machinations of Hitler's mind. Within hours of the attack the results were devastating, and in days huge tracts of Soviet territory and Russian military were in the hands of the Germans. Even as the initial attack started, and Timoshenko had ordered Zhukov to phone Stalin about the heavy shelling, 'like a schoolboy rejecting proof of simple arithmetic, Stalin disbelieved his ears. Breathing heavily, he grunted to Zhukov that no countermeasures should be taken'.[104]

Such was the shock for Stalin that for years it was believed that he had a nervous breakdown, disappeared into his dacha thinking he would be arrested.

Stalin's behaviour indicated that he had fallen into depression, believing his credibility as a leader had been destroyed because there was no one else he could blame. However, his cohorts came begging him to take the reins of government. He was pursued by Beria, Kaganovich, Molotov, and Kliment Voroshilov who convinced him he was needed. The four, along with Anastas Mikoyan and Nikolai Voznesensky, went to Stalin's dacha on the evening of 30 June.* When he saw them, as noted, 'he expected they were there for his arrest'.[105] It has also even been suggested that Stalin staged this scenario, as a 'pose successfully employed from Achilles and Alexander the Great to Ivan' to test possible opposition, causing Beria to note that 'Mikoyan had been right to hide' having stood outside the visiting group at the very back during their visit to Stalin's dacha.[106]

As news of the overwhelming German success came through Stalin had hurried to the Kremlin at 5.30 a.m. summoning Beria, Timoshenko, Zhukov and Mekhlis. He ordered Molotov to make the radio broadcast to the nation about the invasion, probably because Molotov had arranged the Soviet German Pact with Ribbentrop. The reality of these days remains evasive. There seems little doubt that he was in a deep state of depression as news percolated through of the continuous onslaught of the Germans. Probably more out of a sense of freeing himself from any blame he fastened on to finding out the traitors who had allowed this to happen, even though it was his miscalculations which were the main cause, and it had been Stalin who had opposed considerable sound advice which had left the Soviets unprepared. The visiting group had agreed that Molotov should take Stalin's place if they found him unable to be himself, but had Stalin found out 'it could have been the death of all of them'.[107]

In the early phase of Operation *Barbarossa* Stalin was still looking for peace, not out of humanitarian grounds but the situation was looking potentially disastrous for the Soviet Union. When General Georgy Zhukov was later summoned into Stalin's presence, he found Beria already there and

---

* Nikolai Voznesensky (1903–1950) was an economic planner overseeing Gosplan (State Planning Committee) and Deputy Premier in May 1940. He clashed with Stalin over economics but was hated by Beria as a possible contender for Stalin's favour. Later Beria would inform Stalin that Voznesensky was failing to produce enough guns and was given his job. Later Voznesensky found himself caught up in the Leningrad Affair and was tried and executed on the same day in 1950. His reputation was rehabilitated in 1954.

discovered that both men were thoroughly convinced of imminent defeat. Stalin's relationship with this soon to be well-known and efficient general was never going to be easy, as Zhukov on one occasion had said to Stalin 'Comrade Stalin, have we permission to get on with our work?'[108] Beria was shocked at this approach to Stalin rebuking Zhukov in Beria's fashion and Stalin, silent for a moment after this dressing down, warned Zhukov the Party opinion was important.

It was in Zhukov's presence that Stalin instructed Beria to seek a peace settlement with Hitler, even knowing that it would probably mean losing the Baltic States. Beria then asked his special agent Sudoplatov (his trusted henchman) to approach the Bulgarian ambassador in Moscow called Ivan Stamenov, to act as an intermediary. Contrary to some historical accounts he agreed 'but his overtures to the Germans were brushed aside'.[109] Others claimed the Bulgarian never made the effort, telling Sudoplatov that even if the 'Russians had to retreat to the Urals you will win in the end'.[110] This effort was made a second time on 7 October but again to no avail. It was apparent that Stalin 'felt less than confident about the Red Army's defensive capabilities'.[111]

Proper administration for the war became essential with the creation of *Stavka*, the General Headquarters of the Soviet High Command. Marshal Timoshenko headed this military command structure with some civilian advisers, notably Beria, but Stalin remained in charge. In addition to this a five-man State Defence Committee (GKO), a form of war cabinet appeared, and its members could sit in on *Stavka* meetings. It is generally believed that it was Beria who introduced the idea of a New State Committee of Defence (GKO) which would streamline the bureaucracy.

The war consolidated Beria's power, and in July 1941 the NKGB was reabsorbed into the NKVD making Beria the most powerful security chief in Soviet history. His powers during these years would grow exponentially. It transpired that some 140 Intelligence officers had been imprisoned during the purges, a list supplied by Sudoplatov and all but three (already executed) on Beria's orders were released to help in the crisis. Sudoplatov later noted that 'Beria did not question the guilt or innocence of the people I recommended; he only asked, are you sure we need them?'[112]

After his initial stalling and inactivity Stalin became obsessed with the war and the international scene, leaving Beria and Malenkov responsible for all domestic affairs. Beria's administration team organised the prompt removal of heavy industry east beyond the Urals, and was also made responsible for internal security. As his American biographer wrote, Beria 'like other members of the leadership threw himself into his tasks with the energy of desperation, motivated not so much by his patriotism as by self-interest and fear. He could ill-afford a Nazi victory over his country'.[113] As unpleasant as he was Beria was an excellent organiser, and this time people worked for him to resist the Nazis, he was also too venomous, like Stalin, to challenge.

One ruse Beria authorised in August 1941 was when NKVD agents disguised as German parachutists suddenly dropped into the Volga area to assess the loyalty of the citizens. Those who helped were killed, and eventually the whole population was transported to Siberia and Kazakhstan.[114] The method of moving populations meant many died during the journey, and it should be recalled that 'the Germans and the Soviets used exactly the same methods to deport huge numbers of people: a few minutes to pack some necessities before being shipped off in cattle wagons to an unknown fate'.[115] Beria was remorseless in his pursuit of making sure his given tasks were completed, and he ensured his efforts were noted by Stalin. It was pertinently noted by one historian that 'no industry was too complex or vast for Beria to master: he was in many ways not only the Himmler of Stalin's entourage, but also the Speer, another architect'.[116]

Stalin's habitual paranoid suspicion made him constantly mistrust his leading commanders, and therefore Beria had the similar attitude. It was almost bizarre that with the force of the German invasion that Beria continued a purge of the high command looking for so-called traitors, which was identified as being any commander who dared raise doubts about Stalin's battlefield orders. The war never stopped the terror, and Russian PoWs who returned or who escaped, were to suffer the fate of the postwar returnees and found themselves interrogated as potential spies and sent to labour camps. In the early months, General Meretskov had been arrested and was tortured by Merkulov under Beria's orders. It was noted 'that brutal continuous torture was applied to Meretskov by high-ranking officials…he was beaten by rubber rods until he was covered in blood'.[117]

As Stalin ordered the scorched earth policy, and Moscow was under threat, Beria reported that 638,000 men had been detained, and 505 deserters shot. A deserter was often defined as someone being in the wrong area which can easily happen in battle circumstances. Preparations were made to evacuate everyone to Kuibyshev (the old city of Samara on the Volga) and families and many others went, but Stalin was hesitant and eventually followed Zhukov's advice that the Germans could be halted. Before their anticipated departure Stalin had informed Beria and Shcherbakov that they would have to stay to organise the underground resistance. How effective Beria would have been is questionable, he was a man of violence, but he had never been involved in any serious military battle experience.

During the nights of 15 and 16 October the NKVD had moved its essential systems to Kuybyshev along with their prisoners. It was a major exercise for which there was not enough transport, so 300 were disposed of, by being shot. As hundreds of high-ranking officers sat in prison their junior officers were at the front trying to hold the line.[118]

Stalin's mind was impenetrable, and he suddenly decided to hold the annual military parade while Moscow was under attack, and he refused to be dissuaded. The fraught public were gathered, with the Politburo nervously grouped closely together on the top of the Mausoleum. Beria's agent Sudoplatov was placed as a lookout from where he could warn of a German air attack, but this was unlikely because the snowing wintery weather conditions were appalling.[119] Tanks and soldiers passed by in what to many must have seemed unbelievably bizarre. The German attacking forces were a mere fifty miles away, but the November parade had to happen because Stalin needed to be seen by the people as in control. As it happened Zhukov fought the Germans to a standstill on 5 December having lost some 150,000 men in three weeks. As Sudoplatov observed it might have encouraged people to believe everything was under control, noting that 'the parade strengthened our belief in the defence of Moscow and our inevitable victory'.[120]

Stalin took on the appearance of the top military commander, but during the war his constant attempt at controlling military affairs often, as with Hitler, created disaster. For example, it later led to his refusal to evacuate Kiev, despite the advice of his commanders, with the loss of over half a million prisoners in September 1941, and 'after Order 227 in August 1942 he decreed "not a step back," and General Vasily Chuikov, defending Stalingrad, shot an estimated 13,500 of his own men to stiffen morale'.[121] Four out of every five German fatalities occurred on the Eastern Front, Germany had 80 million people and the Soviet Empire 171 million, but Germany had 208 divisions in 1941, 167 at full strength and 146 deployed to attack Russia. The statistics were astonishing.[122]

Some Germans lived in the border regions of Soviet territory, and it was rumoured that they had welcomed the German army, and 'Stalin lashed out and told Beria to get rid of the lot'.[123] War can be barbaric and men like Stalin and Beria only increased the suffering of their population and soldiers. Stalin instructed Beria to instil the strictest discipline and enforce it with punitive action. As early as 16 July the system of political commissars was given the right to share the command with the military. A few days later he had ordered that military units should be purged of unreliable elements, looking for political reliability rather than military strength.

Those men who had escaped and returned to their lines were to be investigated by the NKVD and its special OO units (*Osobye Otdely*) who checked for political security and military counterintelligence. On 25 July these OO units rounded up over 1,000 so-called deserters and shot the majority. These were men who had bravely escaped and could have fought again. Some senior officers were shot including the mentioned General Pavlov who had been the commander of the Western Front when *Barbarossa* started. Beria, on Stalin's orders, eliminated men who had fought and escaped against appalling odds, because Stalin needed scapegoats for his own failure in allowing Germany to attack while the Soviet Union remained unprepared.

Stalin gave the orders, Beria carried them out through his Chief of this Special Department Viktor Abakumov, who was notorious for his brutality.* Abakumov and Beria were distrusted and feared by the military as was Abakumov's deputy Ryumin. Abakumov's rise to power was noted by

---

* Viktor Abakumov (1908–1954) was later Head of SMERSH, 1943–1946, then Minister of State Security, 1946–1951; he fell out of Stalin's favour over the Doctors' Plot, survived Stalin but was executed in 1954. 'Abakumov remains the most shadowy of Stalin's secret-police bosses…many atrocities were Abakumov's doing, not Beria's, even though most histories blame the latter'. Montefiore, Simon Sebag, *Stalin: The Court of the Red Tsar* (London: Weidenfeld & Nicolson, 2003), p.477.

Sudoplatov when he wrote that Abakumov 'went from being a subordinate of Beria's to be a rival', even in a war-crisis Beria was watching his own career.[124]

Beria had considerable experience at interrogation and political machinations, but no war experience. Repeatedly Beria used threats to gain control over the military, prompting them to appeal to Stalin to stop this interference, and they developed a deep but silent animosity towards Beria. Beria was always seeking to arm his troops who were only rear-guard and security men, but at the expense of frontline troops. Beria managed to clash with the top men, including military commanders such as Voronov and even Zhukov. When Voronov had brought Beria's allocation of rifles to Stalin's attention Beria was beside himself with rage, and as they left the presence of Stalin, Beria whispered to Voronov 'just you wait, he hissed, we'll fix your guts. Voronov hoped this was an Oriental joke. It was not'.[125] Beria and Stalin both distrusted General Zhukov when he became popular with his military successes. On one occasion Beria fed false information about German incursions but to contradict Beria was dangerous. As to why Beria should do this can only be answered by the possibility that he was intent on appearing essential, by having access to important Intelligence. He did the same to impress Stalin over his knowledge of Rudolf Hess's well-known flight to Britain, suggesting a Western connivance which was unfounded. It simply served his own ambitions to make him the master of even foreign Intelligence.

As it transpired, the sheer necessity brought about by the German threat of winning lessened the NKVD's influence. Stalin appeared to recognise that if Russia were to survive, the military had to be trusted more than hitherto. Beria concentrated his efforts on gleaning Intelligence about the enemy, and when Moscow appeared under direct threat the NKVD was evacuated to Kuibyshev, although the GKO remained in Moscow after assurances by Zhukov, mentioned above, that the line could be held.

The parts played by Beria from behind his desk in Intelligence work in organising activity behind the enemy lines were deemed important. He used his man Sudoplatov and others like him for sabotage and information, and he formed an Administration for Special Tasks in July 1941 to carry out these activities which he oversaw. He had a Special-Purpose Brigade with a force of more than 20,000 men and women. Intelligence radio officers were sent behind the lines, and in his memoirs Sudoplatov wrote of over 212 guerrilla detachments with some 7,000 men in the rear of the enemy.[126] Sudoplatov estimated that with these detachments some staggering 137,000 Germans were killed, 87 high-ranking officers and numberless collaborators were eliminated. Later, under the name Operation *Monastery*, Beria's Intelligence components managed to create a degree of havoc in the German Abwehr.

There had been a sense of understandable panic as the invasion of Moscow appeared imminent. Beria had ordered the evacuation of all who could not fight, and the need to distribute food.[127] Beria moved his office from the Lubyanka to Dzerzhinsky Street into the basement next to an air-raid shelter. Beria, under Stalin's orders was responsible with others for the scorched-earth policy wherever there was a possibility of German occupation. Beria was responsible for armament production, but the real work was done by Ustinov and a man called Vannikov. Beria at the very best was the manager who applied the pressure. This amount of work was becoming a problem for Beria, and the NKVD had become too widespread. Within the armaments production Beria ensured his own NKVD troops received weapons, and it was claimed that anyone working in that industry walked in the shadow of Beria's terror, and it was the fear of him which made him a driving force. He found most of the necessary labour from the prison camps. From many reports the conditions in these camps were appalling and the number of deaths from overwork will never be known, but it was in the hundreds of thousands, if not millions. Beria never raised questions about these conditions, but human suffering never concerned him.

In the spring of 1942, the NKVD formed another unit responsible for guarding the rear, catching spies and deserters and suspected traitors. They also took on the task of guarding PoWs and became garrison troops in those areas which the Germans had left. The men of the NKVD found they could receive orders from their own superiors and from the Red Army, and this dual control naturally led to internal conflict.

Beria as an individual tended to stay well-clear of any frontline appearances with a few exceptions exaggerated by him for self-propaganda. In the summer of 1942, he visited the Transcaucasian front on Stalin's orders as a member of Stavka, as the Germans were advancing. Beria was accompanied by Sudoplatov, now a commissar of state security and lieutenant general.

Stalin later reprimanded them for being too close to the front line (if that were true) because he needed his spymasters close to home.[128] Sudoplatov accompanied Beria as they oversaw specially trained mountain troops try to block German advances over the high passes.[129]

Stalin was naturally suspicious of the reaction of the local people if they appeared to him as cabals. He was particularly doubtful about the Muslims who had been courted by the Germans, as was Beria. Himmler had created an SS Division from some Muslim areas where there was no love for Stalin and his brand of communism. Stalin was especially worried about the oilfields, warning his agents that they would lose their heads if the oil fell into German hands, and also if they destroyed the facilities too early. Beria's main task according to some historians was 'to stamp out the embers of treason among the ethnic groups', along with more pertinent duties.[130] Later in the early 1950s, when Beria was still in favour with Stalin, it was announced that Beria had led the defence. The truth was that he was only there for a few weeks at the most, and he stayed safe, well away from the frontline.

The military, when they felt safe to express themselves, had a different perspective of Beria the bully, interfering in military decisions, and making blunders. One general was threatened with arrest by Beria, and the whole episode increased the general mutual animosity between the military and Beria. Beria returned to the Caucasus in the early spring of 1943 to check supplies, but he stayed just over a week before returning to the relative safety of Moscow.

The NKVD engaged in the important effort to build up partisan work behind the lines not only to disrupt the Germans, but to gather Intelligence information. They were sometimes referred to as 'destruction battalions'. This effort increased along the entire front especially in the Ukraine and Belorussia, and Beria made much of its success to Stalin. Beria had a special interest in Belorussia where one of his home henchmen Lavrenty Tsanava was working. This relationship was widely known and Lavrenty Tsanava was sometimes known as 'Lavrenty the Second'. However, the partisans were themselves divided, which given the reality of their dangerous task was no surprise, and soon the Red Army took a firmer control over this potential chaos.

Of importance was the Intelligence work with men behind the lines discovering what was happening. This led to a degree of co-operation with the British SOE who sent Brigadier George Hill to Moscow where he met Beria whom, he noted, appeared uncommonly interested in guns which had effectively silenced Beria when they were fired. Hill observed 'all his ruthlessness came to the fore, and I realised the power that he had within him, power that has brought him to, and kept him at the top...the more I saw of him, the less I liked him; an evil, sinister creature'.[131] This came from an SOE officer who had experience dealing with tough and ruthless men.

As the war turned in favour of the Soviets during 1943 the NKVD was divided into two sections. The chief administration of State Security of the NKVD was transformed into the People's Commissariat of State Security (NKGB) and SMERSH (Death to Spies) which was intended for Counterintelligence. On the surface this appeared to diminish Beria's powers as Stalin placed Abakumov in charge, but Abakumov at this stage of events, always listened to Beria, and Stalin took an interest in Abakumov. Stalin with his traditional paranoia was always wary of those with too much influence and power.

Beria never lost the power he had accumulated even when Counterintelligence was transferred to the Red Army. Beria's cohorts held key positions, and Beria obliged them to answer directly to him. Beria's protégés were everywhere, and in May 1944 he was promoted to be deputy chairman of this supreme wartime authority. It is quite possible to speculate that Beria may have been frustrated by these changes, but held onto his powerbase, and no doubt was continuously looking to the future now the war was looking towards a Nazi defeat.

The war was now turning in Russia's favour, but the bitter fighting persisted, and Beria's role once again was a matter of security with increased cruelty at a mass level. Stalingrad had been the turning point followed by the important Battle of Kursk. The Kursk confrontation was gigantic, and for this battle Beria's slave labour had dug 'an unbelievable 3,000 miles of trenches. Over a million men and, including reserves, around 6,000 tanks' were engaged in this deadly conflagration.[132] The Eastern Front war was vast and the sacrifices so immense it was not surprising that the Russians have always considered the Second World War as their victory. Not all Russians were killed or imprisoned by the Germans, and at the end of 1943 as the Red Army were making progress, Beria reported to Stalin that for that year alone, he 'had detained 582,515 uniformed persons, and in addition 349,034 civilians. They ranged from deserters to gangsters and marauders, or those without proper papers. Thousands more died in armed struggles'.[133]

The NKVD functions were extensive, and they controlled a huge number of troops which has been estimated at nearly 650,000 to possibly 750,000. Some historical analysists have estimated the figure to be a million. The troops were to investigate, and if necessary, punish those people who had been unfortunately overrun by the Nazi war machine, because Stalin had become suspicious of them as possible collaborators. Anyone who had been rumoured to have been disloyal was punished by death or sent to the camps, with Beria always taking a tight control.

Thousands were taken in cattle trucks, normally about forty per truck until it was noted children took less space and the number was increased to forty-five, travelling for weeks to places like Central Asia and Kazakhstan. They had no food nor water, there was no sanitation, and typhoid became rife with deaths happening in untold numbers. When the train stopped, they buried their family members in the snow close by the train because to wander more than five yards from the rails meant instant death. Under Beria's supervision the NKVD, NKGB and SMERSH worked together to conduct these barbaric reprisals, most of which reflected a barbarity greater than the normal detritus of war.* Beria not only responded to Stalin's paranoid wishes, but he added his own selections. It was Beria who informed Stalin that in his opinion the Crimean Tatars should be deported. He oversaw the deportations of nationalities considered suspect by Stalin and himself, Chechens, Kalmucks, Crimean Tatars, Volga Germans, and many others. Beria personally wrote to Stalin on 18 August 1944 about the small Caucasus spa towns Pyatigorsk, Kislovodsk, Zheleznovodsk, and Essentuki in the Stavropol district. Still living there, he said, were 'the families of active German collaborators and traitors who had been convicted or voluntarily

---

* SMERSH: 'The counterintelligence men used to love that tastelessly concocted word SMERSH, manufactured from the initial syllables of the words death to spies. They felt it intimidated people'. Solzhenitsyn, Aleksandr, *The Gulag Archipelago 1918–56* (London: The Harvill Press, 1985), p.18.

departed with the Nazi occupiers.' He wanted permission for the NKVD 'to purge these cities by relocating 850 family members'.[134] This information indicated the massive numbers caught up in the Soviet retribution and Beria's sheer ruthlessness. The same attitude applied to Red Army officers who had been captured. Beria branded them as traitors and 'according to the notorious Order 00270, generals and other officials, including those in the NKVD, were subject to the death penalty', and even their relatives were included for punishment.[135] Stalin made no exceptions, and when his son Yakov was captured, his wife was arrested. She was released two years later when Stalin felt satisfied that his son was not a traitor. 'Between 1944 and 1949, a total of 5.45 million Soviet citizens from all countries, including PoWs and civilians, were repatriated to the Soviet Union whether they wanted to be or not'.[136]

As early as late 1943 the authorities began preparing a *Chechevitsa*, which was a total deportation of all the peoples of the Northern Caucasus. Stalin and Beria saw this as a solution to traitors as well as ethnic problems, and Beria travelled to Grozny to supervise the operation. The cleansing started in February 1944 and lasted for weeks. Beria gave the final numbers 'as nearly a half million people, though his figures have a typical phoney exactitude'.[137] Beria sent daily reports and 'liked to observe the process first hand, and he reminded Stalin in May 1944 that there were still more anti-Soviet elements in Crimea'.[138] For Beria 'this suffering had no meaning. It was all part of a day's work: the deportations were a routine, successful NKVD operation for which he [Beria] might receive an additional approval from his leader'.[139] Only Beria and Stalin could believe that whole ethnic groups could all be traitors, and many NKVD officials received awards for their efforts.

After the battles of Stalingrad and Kursk, Stalin relaxed in his own self-perceived greatness at both the national and international level. The following repression had been ruthless in Ukraine where nationalist armies had been fighting the Soviet forces, and both Beria and Khrushchev had retaliated with brutality, as they did in the Causcasus and Crimea. It was during these campaigns that Beria had suggested that major ethnic groups should be deported. 'Stalin's men had to distribute this unwanted human flotsam throughout their empire' and Beria followed this with meticulous care based on the dubious loyalty of the Tatars in the Crimea.[140] Beria's suspicious mind was drawn to ethnic groups, many of whom died in transit, making it no different from the Nazi oppression. Needless to point out the Gulag camps grew exponentially during these years, packed with innocent soldiers and civilians. The great sadness was the way the West co-operated with Stalin's demands, and under the postwar prisoner exchange thousands of victims were returned to the Soviet Union in the certain knowledge that they faced death or slave-labour. This led to some bitter recriminations, and even legal investigations later during the Cold War.

As a sense of jubilation arose as the end of the Nazi war became evident, the Western Allies prepared for a major conference, and Stalin decided to seek a new national anthem and invited composers for their submissions. Voroshilov was put in charge of the contest leading to the strange mix of Shostakovich and Prokofiev with Stalin, Beria and Voroshilov spending time together choosing the right song and music, while more momentous global events were still taking place.

At the same time Stalin's paranoia focused on the very officers who had gained the victory. Voroshilov the deputy commissar of defence was removed, and the extraordinarily successful now 'Marshal' Zhukov knew he was in danger following the fall of Berlin, and he was side-lined to the Odessa Military District. Stalin would have preferred him dead, but he was too popular, so he was put in a back room. It was Stalin's wish to be seen as the only source of Russian victory, and to be hailed as the man who had saved Russia and the rest of the world. Later Khrushchev and Brezhnev would hold the popular Zhukov in the backwaters for similar reasons.

Beria had always detested the military and took great delight in organising Stalin's quiet attack upon the military commanders, who were no longer mentioned in the press, and disappeared from public sight. A repercussion of this policy was that members of the police and security services were given military ranks, and Beria became a Marshal of the Soviet Union, even though he had never been active in military organisation or experienced fighting first hand. It was Stalin's ploy to put his military commanders in their place.* Beria had used slave labour to help war-industry, deported

---

* After appearing to reject his cohorts' efforts to give Stalin the Soviet Union Gold Star award, Stalin eventually accepted the term of Generalissimo though he never liked the title which was used by his enemy Franco. It was for Stalin all to do with public image.

thousands of innocent victims, murdered others, and grown powerful (and rich) because of his machinations. His attack on the military would not be forgotten, and in 1953 when he was arrested it was Khrushchev to whom senior army commanders offered support to bring Beria down, which would have been a pleasure for them.*

As far as the rest of the world was concerned Beria was a mysterious figure somewhere in the shadows of the background. Those who had knowledge of the Kremlin scene knew he held power, was close to Stalin, but he always remained a mysterious enigmatic character. Stalin disliked anyone who held any prominence, and it was Beria's low profile which enabled his survival for so long. Beria attended the Tehran Conference (1943) and the Yalta Conference (1945) but rarely mixed with the diplomats of whom he always held a deep suspicion.** He was ignorant of much of the Western world, and he tended to be xenophobic. It has been astutely noted that 'his main preoccupation was with the Byzantine world of Kremlin politics'.[141] It has been suggested that it was prior to the Tehran Conference that Stalin started to show the first signs of turning against Beria. As with Franco, Stalin disliked flying, but had little choice when attending the Tehran Conference, and his proposed pilot stumbled into a situation in which he found Stalin shouting abuse at Beria.[142] On this occasion Beria had his own plane prepared, but Stalin suddenly swapped planes.***

Beria's sense of self-importance always caught people's attention as he insisted on extreme security whenever Stalin was present. The NKVD had already prepared the Tehran site and Beria arrived and took charge. When Stalin was invited to a meal at the British Embassy Beria led the NKVD on a methodical search of the area for the event. Beria also ensured that rooms were bugged with listening devices in order that private conversations

---

*   Khrushchev always 'held a special place in Stalin's affection: perhaps his irrepressible optimism, sycophantic devotion – and practical cunning made him a useful comrade'. Montefiore, Simon Sebag, *Stalin: The Court of the Red Tsar* (London: Weidenfeld & Nicolson, 2003), p.314.

**   Yalta had been under threat by the Nazis, and this had been followed by Beria's attack on the Tatars and led Churchill to describe the area as 'The Riviera of Hades'.

***   In a curious note Sudoplatov mentions that Otto Skorzeny was ready to launch an attack on Tehran which the Russians thwarted. See Sudoplatov, Pavel and Anatoli, *Special Tasks: The Memoirs of an Unwanted Witness – A Soviet Spymaster* (London: Little, Brown and Company, 1994), p.130.

could be overheard. At Tehran, Sergo Beria (Beria's son) 'manned the recording equipment bugging their rooms and was surprised to overhear FDR [Roosevelt] level a counteraccusation at Churchill for trying to engineer an anti-communist government' in Poland.[143] Beria's son was clever and spoke both German and English which had given Beria a major excuse for not sacrificing him on the frontline.* It appeared Churchill was not fooled by Beria. Various other reports on meeting Beria have surfaced from time to time, and while some found him convivial most felt his coldness and desire for power to be the dominant feature of his personality. For most observers Beria was the dark and unknown side of Stalin and his Kremlin.

Stalin had needed a man like Beria, an obedient servant who would respond to any demand, and who did not appear to have any ambition which would threaten Stalin. During the war years there was hardly an area of activity in which Beria was not involved, and as the Russians had moved into non-Soviet territory, Beria recruited and trained communist bodies which, when they became Soviet-dominated, came under his security forces. Having ensured this happened he established Communist groups in the newly acquired territories, as his priority was to establish a NKVD type structure answerable to Moscow and himself.

The Atom Bomb

(**Editor's Note:** *Much of the Russian atomic bomb scenario will be looked at in the next chapter, but starts here as it involved Beria*)

As he prepared for the Potsdam Conference Stalin liked the image of himself as a revolutionary, but he rode to Berlin like one of the Tsars. On 2 July Beria 'reported to him that all security preparations had been made. Travel would be made by train from Moscow, over a distance calculated at no less than 1,195 miles. Beria was proud to say there would be 'between six and fifteen men' posted for each and every mile. He 'listed in loving detail

---

* Stalin needed a daily appraisal from Beria's son as to what was being said whether it was being said in a way which was genuine or whether Roosevelt was aware that he was being bugged. They later used directional microphones to hear Roosevelt as he was wheeled around in the open areas. Roosevelt always suspected that his conversations were recorded.

all the security steps that were taken and the elaborate provisioning that would be provided on the way to and at the Big Three conference'.[144] The provisioning of manpower and luxury was enormous, even though during the postwar years Stalin's government could hardly feed their population, and his correspondence with Beria later indicated that 'they could not feed their army in Germany, let alone the East Germans'.[145]

It was at Potsdam that the Americans informed Stalin of their atomic bombs, which was an area of mild interest to Stalin from early in the war, based on various rumours from the scientific community. However, it was to become one of the prime seeds for growing the Cold War. Stalin was ignorant of physics and had therefore derided the subject. Beria was aware of his master's views and was caught between being 'Stalin's ideological apostle' and the need for a similar weapon. Stalin's attitudes towards his scientists amounted to 'leave them in peace. We can always shoot them later'.[146]

It has been noted that 'the Intelligence about Western atomic research in May 1945 had come to the NKVD chief Beria, who was slow to react. When Soviet scientists wrote to the Politburo (Stalin) asking to accelerate work on the bomb, they received only a muted response'.[147] It is generally accepted that from the earliest days in 1940 there were rumours and fears that the Germans were looking into the prospect of an atomic weapon. Donald Maclean, the British spy had reported that the British government had initiated the necessary scientific study.[148] Beria was naturally always suspicious, and as early as September 1941 one of his foreign agents had obtained some documents from a member of their Uranium Committee, and the first cryptograms about this very preliminary work on the atom bomb with uranium were sent to Moscow. However, 'Beria had dismissed this Intelligence as disinformation and only after the reports had reached Stalin' was it decided to investigate more deeply.[149] Beria's agent and henchman Sudoplatov, having organised the death of Trotsky, used his own agents to work their way into the company of these atomic scientists. Some of Sudoplatov's work will be explored in the next chapter. This was not a difficult task because 'Sudoplatov realised that the scientists saw themselves as a new breed of super-statesmen whose mandate transcended boundaries; he and his officers exploited this hubris'.[150] Many of these international scientists had moral considerations, and they were only concerned about stopping Hitler;

later they were anti-violence hoping their new technology would produce a balance of power by sharing nuclear technology. For these scientists it had been a matter of defeating Nazism, but they did not want to arrive at today's situation of standing on the edge of international collective suicide.

When Truman told Stalin about the atom bomb, Stalin pretended to show no serious interest, but 'he told Molotov who replied that 'they are raising the price.' Stalin responded, 'Let them. We'll talk with Kurchatov and get them to speed things up'.[151] It appeared their own scientist Igor Kurchatov had already made progress, and by December 1944 he was granted more resources.* In addition to their own progress the Russians had been given plenty of information supplied by spies from inside the American Manhattan Project.

For the Soviets it may have been somewhat patchy, but they were not in the dark. As early as 1941 Kurchatov had raised the question of a chain reaction which could create nuclear energy. Another scientist, Petri Kapitsa, had drawn attention to the possibility of an atomic bomb in the same year.** Information had dribbled through to Beria's desk about this development, but it was filtered by Lieutenant-General Fitin who, being sensitive, 'never presented to his superiors Merkulov, Beria and beyond them Stalin anything likely to incur their anger'.[152] It is questionable as to how much Intelligence information reached the top echelons. During the initial attacks of Operation *Barbarossa*, the early atomic project had been shelved, but it was reactivated when the war started to change in Russia's favour. Beria's Intelligence agents were discovering such vital information about the German, British and American research into a possible atom bomb, that this work should be taken seriously. Stalin eventually reacted and gathered his leading scientists together to pursue the subject's viability.

---

* Igor Kurchatov (1903–1960) was a Soviet Nuclear Physicist known as 'the father of the Soviet Atomic Bomb'. He later advocated the peaceful development of nuclear energy and assisted in the development of the Hydrogen Bomb. In 1949 he was involved in a serious accident caused by entering the hall of a damaged reactor, after which his health declined, and he died in Moscow in 1960 and become part of the Kremlin Wall.

** Petri Kapitsa (1894–1984) was an outstanding physicist with several major studies. He studied in England gaining a PhD at Cambridge and was deep into atomic research but clashed with Beria. In 1955 he became Director of The Institute for Physical Problems (in 1990 the Institute was named after him); he won the Nobel Prize in 1978, and he died in Moscow in 1984.

When Beria was tasked with the atomic project, he used resources overseas to find out as much as possible.* He used his trusted agent Sudoplatov who complained in his memoirs that he was already consumed in activity with the German war. Beria ensured the experts employed in the project were granted extra food and medical care.[153]

It was known as the '*Number-One*' task and Beria had nearly 500,000 people to manage, including technicians and high-flying scientists, but it is claimed that the well-known Klaus Fuchs was his main source for information.** He also made sure his agents had briefed Robert Oppenheimer, informing him that anti-Semitism in the USSR 'was now a dead letter'.[154] As early as 1943 Solomon Mikhoels had been instructed by Beria to make an American tour and inform his contacts that Jews were respected in the Soviet Union. Mikhoels became well-known, perhaps too much, which would explain why Stalin later ordered his death.

'The extent to which the Soviets relied on Intelligence gathering to develop their own bomb has only recently come to light'.[155] The Russian scientists had been given considerable information, which saved them much research and time. During these early years Molotov had been the leader in charge, but Kurchatov took the step of complaining to Beria that Molotov was not allowing appropriate progress. A complaint to Beria was risky, but Kurchatov had correctly worked out that this would reach Stalin, and Beria replaced Molotov, even though Beria was not to become a full member of the Politburo until March 1946. This change to Beria prompted Kurchatov's assistant to claim that 'Beria's administrative abilities were obvious for all of us at that time. He was unusually energetic. Meetings did not drag on for hours; everything was decided quickly'.[156] Beria supplied the necessary

---

* From the ruins of Berlin Beria had managed to secure some metallic uranium, some uranium oxide and heavy water. See Montefiore, Simon Sebag, *Stalin: The Court of the Red Tsar* (London: Weidenfeld & Nicolson, 2003), p.441fn.

** Klaus Fuchs was a highly respected physicist who had emigrated to Britain from Germany and had offered to spy for the Soviets as early as 1941. He continued this effort while working on the Manhattan project in America. 'Fuchs understood the war could not be won without the Red Army. It made sense to him, therefore, to keep the Russians informed…the idea of sharing the bomb secrets did not seem as outlandish at all to his colleagues at Los Alamos' and he declined Russian payment. See Ings, Simon, *Stalin and the Scientists: A History of Triumph and Tragedy 1905–1953* (London; Faber & Faber, 2017), p.330. He continued this until his arrest in 1950.

labour, while the scientists were obsessed with their mission, and worried in seeking a solution for the sake of the balance of power because of their fear the Americans might attack Russia with atomic power. It was the Gulag labourers who produced the essential buildings, laboratories and testing sites. Many of the prisoners were specially trained and worked in highly secretive centres under constant guard.

Stalin's sense of self-assurance, Russia having been a major factor in defeating the Nazi regime, controlled most of Eastern Europe. As a major figure on the world stage he would have been unsettled on hearing the Americans were ahead in this weapon development. Stalin then established a Scientific-Technical Council, and the Special Committee was headed by Beria, with one scientist complaining to Stalin in 1945 that Beria had no knowledge of science and only wanted to copy the Americans, but he was ignored.* Beria had experienced similar hostility from the military, which arose because he was always asserting himself, and assuming he knew better even in areas where he had no knowledge. However, there is evidence that there were some scientists who liked working with Beria, stating he grasped the essential facts, kept meetings to the point, and they found him a first-class administrator.

Beria discovered two German scientists, Gustav Hertz and Baron Manfred von Ardenne, who were to work in a guarded place near Sukhumi in Abkhazia (on the Eastern coast of the Black Sea). They were disgruntled at their living conditions, but they were so necessary in the research that Beria tried to resolve their complaints. Progress was made and on Christmas Day 1946 Beria witnessed the opening of the first atomic reactor.

The first bomb was successfully tested in Kazakhstan in September 1949, but Beria delayed telling Stalin before he was absolutely certain that the bomb had been a success. Only Beria with his ambition could treat all this at a personal level, and when he contacted Stalin, who had gone to bed, Stalin told Beria he already knew and put the phone down. Beria was furious realising that someone had beaten him to his personal announcement of triumph. 'Beria shook his fist at those around him and exploded. 'Even here

---

* The scientist was Pyotr Kapitsa who later became a Nobel Laureate, and according to some he had asked to be relieved from his work, and he was removed to a form of house arrest.

you put spokes in my wheels, traitors! I'll grind you into powder!'[157] Beria seemed to know that during these early postwar years Stalin was possibly turning against him. He had undoubtedly hoped that his atomic activity might re-establish Stalin's favour towards him. The undeniable fact was that much of the necessary information for the new weapons had already been in Soviet espionage hands, but the Russian scientists had pushed the boundaries. Beria was equally concerned when the Americans announced the Russian success before the Russians. There was an immediate suspicion that the Americans had an agent within the system, but the scientists explained that an atomic explosion could be detected by sampling air near the borders. In 1952 America detonated a thermonuclear device in the Pacific, and Russia followed in 1953 with 'Beria again the politician in charge, and by 12 August 1953, they successfully replicated the American experiment', but by this time Beria was under arrest.[158]

The Cold War

The postwar period was consumed by the Soviet domination of Eastern Europe, which was one of the factors which developed into what has been called the Cold War. Democratic elections had been the original and agreed policy amongst the victors, but it was known by Beria and Molotov that this was merely a placatory and temporary phase.[159] The communists were widely supported because during the war it had been the local communist resistance to the Nazis which had been the most effective. Beria was initiative-taking in ensuring the various communist parties took over control, managing most of this from behind his desk.

Sudoplatov in his memoirs also made the point that there was an underlying agreement between the powers to divide the spoils, noting that 'Stalin is bitterly attacked for betraying principles of human morality in signing a pact with Hitler; it is overlooked that he also signed a secret deal to divide Europe with Roosevelt and Churchill at Yalta, and later with Truman at Potsdam'.[160] There were some ironical truths contained in Sudoplatov's book. The Soviets were flexible to start with, simply because they could afford to be. Beria ensured there were agents in all the vital areas reporting back on any events or the people most likely to try and unsettle these long-term plans.

The relationship between the Americans and Soviets appeared cordial if not jovial but was for both sides a charade. Stalin had rejected the Marshall Plan, as the Soviets had been alerted by Donald Maclean, then first secretary of the British Embassy in Washington, that the plan was to ensure American domination of Europe.[161] There were also suspicions that the Plan would be contrary to the Soviet policy of using East German resources as part of their reparation projects.

For his part Beria had authorised thousands of agents to infiltrate overseas, although he personally knew little of matters outside the Soviet Union. All Beria needed to know was that Stalin wanted the consolidation of control in Eastern Europe. From the Soviet perspective the Western support for nationalist unrest in the Baltic States and Western Ukraine was the main cause of the developing tensions. On Stalin's demand Beria and Khrushchev decided to liquidate any resistance to Soviet domination in the Ukraine, but Beria was more concerned about the intrigues and machinations on the home front.

During the time Beria spent on the atomic project there were serious political changes, and in 1946 it was announced that Beria had stepped down as head of the NKVD. It has been widely suggested that Beria's work in advancing his security briefs, not only in Russia but in the new occupied territories, was making Stalin suspicious of his increasing power. However, in early 1946 Beria was made a full member of the Politburo and Deputy Chairman of the Council of Ministers, but more to the point he was replaced as head of the NKVD by Sergei Kruglov.* Not long after all this Beria's protégé Merkulov was replaced as the head of MGB by Viktor Abakumov 'who, like Kruglov, did not belong to Beria's Caucasian mafia.[162] However, it soon became clear that Abakumov had become Beria's lapdog and always reported to him, although some argue that in Abakumov Beria had met his match.[163] Abakumov was needed by Stalin because he demanded total

---

* Kruglov held an honorary British knighthood in recognition of his security services for the Big Three.

secrecy and control, and Abakumov was soon at 'the centre of a complicated, multidimensional game'.[164]

When news of the American creation of the CIA in 1947 was studied in Moscow, it was understood that the CIA's intention of using military and civilian Intelligence could be effective. Consequently, Molotov proposed that it was essential to unify the foreign Intelligence directories of the MGB and the GRU under a single roof.* This 'proposal had the further advantage, from Stalin's view point, of weakening the influence on security of Lavrenty Beria, whose protégé, Abakumov, headed the MGB'.[165] In the machinations of the personal power-play it was not an easy matter uniting the various agencies. The resultant KI (Committee of Information) was unstable from the beginning.** Typical personal jealousies marred the scheme, using the excuse that military Intelligence had been reduced to a subordinate role. There was a major dispute involving Molotov and Bulganin who managed to withdraw military Intelligence from the KI, and 'probably with the support of Beria, Abakumov, the head of the MGB, then embarked on a long campaign to recover control of the remains of the KI'.[166] In late 1951 the KI was disbanded and reabsorbed by the MGB, and the whole picture was both complex and confusing. When the NKVD and NKGB became the MVD and MGB, Beria had not lost his authority. There was no apparent decline in Beria's national status, and during the immediate postwar period he often appeared to be third in the line of ascendancy after Stalin and alongside Malenkov.

Political Tensions in the Soviet Union

The rise and fall of the leading politicians could be compared to puppets on a string played by the controller Stalin, but the political machinations did not seem to have damaged Beria's political standing. He was often close to Stalin giving advice even on foreign matters. According to Khrushchev, who was deeply suspicious about Beria in this power-play, he pestered Stalin about the return of some Turkish territory which was too close to the Georgian

---

* The MGB was the Soviet Ministry of State Security and the GRU was the Soviet Military Intelligence agency.

** The KI was the Committee of Information which was the combined foreign directories of MGB and GRU.

border, this was when Stalin realised the Turkish government had sought proffered American help, which meant the USA had bases in that part of Turkey close to the Soviet border.[167]

Many of the national policies during this period were left to Stalin's leading men, who were constantly entangled in the bickering for personal power. These complex times of power seeking were not helped when speculation arose about Stalin's health, and it had been rumoured he suffered a slight stroke in 1945 and another in 1947. He had started enjoying long summer holidays in his dacha, from where he also conducted foreign policies. His ministers took full advantage and used their policies to forge ahead of one another in the race to be close to the top, and to be seen as the most likely successor for power.

A typical scenario of this situation were the developments in East Germany. Malenkov was responsible for the industrial ministries but there were debates on stripping East Germany of its industry. Andrei Zhdanov fought for the policy of allowing the industries to stay in order that war debts could be paid. Beria was uncertain, tending to support Malenkov rather than Zhdanov, but Beria was also interested in the rumoured uranium and ore deposits in Saxony. Beria decided it was better to stay with Malenkov if only for his own personal ambitions. Beria and Malenkov became closer as they sought support in one another's company, and they often used the same car to return home after a long difficult night at Stalin's dacha, prompting Stalin to describe them as 'that pair of scoundrels'.[168]

Beria had never found Zhdanov easy, and they often clashed, so he was concerned when Malenkov was side-lined in Central Asia. It was a matter of Kremlin politics and during 1946–47 it appeared as if Zhdanov were in the ascendancy. It was all a competition for primacy of position, and Beria had his sights set as high as Zhdanov. This political chess game of seeking a winning position is common in the democracies, but in a totalitarian state it was potentially lethal.

During the war, the ethnic groups had been unified to fight the German military threats, but after the war this unification was forgotten, and whole populations, including Jews, were shifted East, and some prominent Jews at home suffered. Zhdanov produced articles attacking Jewish art, music, and scholarship. The JAC, the Jewish Antifascist Committee, had been established to unite Jewish people against the Nazi threat, but it was not long before it became evident that the Jews were suffering from yet another purge.

As early as 1946 Stalin had called for the dissolution of the JAC, and Zhdanov had the key role. Solomon Mikhoels, a famous theatre director and head of the JAC, was killed in circumstances which bore all the characteristic signs of a Stalin-directed State murder. It appears there was no evidence that Beria was behind the scheme, but it was Abakumov who had probably been ordered by Stalin to organise this murder. Because of his looks there had been a rumour that Beria himself was Jewish, but there is no evidence for this claim. Beria would have been anti-Semitic as and when it promised him political opportunity, but there was no question that Stalin was deeply anti-Semitic.

In her youth Stalin's daughter claimed she suffered because of her relationship with Jewish men, and when her first husband had a Jewish origin, she noted that because 'he was Jewish, my father didn't like it'. Nevertheless, they married, and Stalin accepted it on the condition 'that my husband never set foot in his house…he never once met my first husband'.[169] There were and remain rumours that Stalin intended to deport all Jews, 'but no conclusive evidence has come to light'.[170]

The attacks on Beria happened because they were focused on the tussle for supremacy on the inevitable death of Stalin, and those surrounding Zhdanov and many others, including Khrushchev, were caught up in this anti-Semitic drive which resulted in the infamous Doctors' Plot. It appeared at this time that Beria was under attack, and even in Georgia he was losing some of his support. Many of his protégés had been replaced and the impression was that Moscow was trying to reduce Beria's influence in his home country. It was mainly, once again, more a struggle of internal power cliques rather than a matter of specific policies. The two major contenders for supremacy were Zhdanov and Malenkov, with Beria watching closely.

By 1949 Molotov was out of favour with Stalin and succeeded as Foreign Minister and Chairman of the KI by Andrei Vyshinsky who had been the brutal prosecutor at the show-trials.* It was often noted that Vyshinsky emulated

---

* Stalin had developed a distrust of Molotov early on, and this was probably based on his popularity and power as well as Molotov's Jewish wife of whom he was always suspicious. As noted in the text Stalin always took an interest in his cohorts' wives. Molotov had agreed with Stalin concerning his own wife's Jewish background just to survive. Beria later would whisper

Beria, starting any interview in an accusatory fashion and always abusive. Vyshinsky had 'retained from the 1930s a sycophantic admiration for Beria' and as a result Beria's influence over the KI increased.[171] The First Deputy was Sergei Romanovich Savchenko who was also a protégé of Beria, to whom he appeared to answer rather than to his Foreign Minister. In the battle for grasping personal power many recalled that Beria was the master of events.

As in the 1930s Soviet Intelligence targeted opponents and any who carried the slightest suspicion. 'Like Stalin, Beria and Abakumov interpreted Josip Tito's break with Moscow in 1948 as part of a wide-ranging imperialist conspiracy to undermine the Soviet Bloc'.[172] Zhdanov informed Cominform that he had proof that Tito was in league with the Imperialists; he did this to discredit Tito, but all these machinations chiefly indicated Stalin's paranoid tendencies, and once again the problems of the internal tussle for power.*

Zhdanov had died from a heart attack in 1948 with the usual rumours about his death then and later, but his death from natural causes appeared more likely, given his excessive weight and lifestyle.** Zhdanov's death provided Beria and Malenkov with the way forward, and by 1949 both appeared in good stead with Stalin again. Probably with Stalin's connivance Zhdanov's name was denounced, and there followed a mini purge of his followers. This was dubbed the 'Leningrad Case' as those closest to Zhdanov lost their posts, their reputations and in many cases their lives. This extensive list remains somewhat obscure, but it must have made many nervous. Amongst those to fall during this time of vengeance was Kuznetov (CC Secretary), Voznesensky (Politburo member) and Popkov (the Leningrad First Secretary). Voznesensky was one of the more important ones to be moved and was later executed following the Leningrad Case in 1950.*** At one stage it had appeared that Stalin had intended Voznesensky to be his

---

to Molotov that his wife was still alive even though she was in the interrogation rooms of the Lubyanka. Malenkov also had to extricate his family from their Jewish connections.

* Stalin was especially angry when Tito formed an alliance with the Bulgarian leader Dmitrov without permission, and he was annoyed at their defiance even when confronted by Stalin, Beria and Zhdanov.

** Had Stalin or Beria wanted Zhdanov's death it would have been an easy medical assassination because he had five heart attacks before the one which killed him.

***After the Great Purges life had settled down for the politicians and military after 1938, and Voznesensky was the first major player to find that the purges had re-ignited.

successor.* It was later claimed that Beria hated Voznesensky because he saw him as a possible competitor in the ever-present internal power struggle, but both Stalin and Malenkov eventually distrusted the man. By the end of 1949, the Zhdanov faction had become a thing of the past, and Beria was once again installed near Stalin's seat of power.

During 1949 Beria appeared to have become Stalin's favourite again, and in his social life he was always trying to be as comfortably close to Stalin as possible in his dacha. They all had superior dachas, originally built at government expense by the best architects. It was a luxurious life for those at the top of the political echelon, but for ordinary people it remained a matter of day-to-day survival. Beria held a lifelong passion for football and his NKVD (later MVD) ran the Dynamo Football club (the Trade Unions had their own club called Spartak), and 'an invitation to watch a game in Beria's box for a young Chekist meant entering his circle'.[173] Sudoplatov was thrilled to be invited as will be noted in the next chapter.

Stalin's social habits were nearly always late-night drunken dinners with his closest men, mainly at his dacha which he preferred to the Kremlin. Stalin's daughter wrote that Stalin spent most of his time at his various dachas, claiming 'the idea that Stalin lived in the Kremlin is a false one. I can't imagine who thought it up. It is only true in the sense that my father's office and work were in the Kremlin'.[174] Foul language and drunken pranks were a characteristic of these social evenings as his sycophants pleased him by joining in as he demanded. As Stalin's daughter wrote 'these merrymaking leaders amused themselves with coarse practical jokes, the victims being mostly Poskrebyshev and Mikoyan.** As for Beria, he would just incite my father and others, they would all go home drunk and 'Beria, too, would often go home in this condition, although no one ever dared slide a tomato under him. My father called him the Prosecutor'.[175] One history researcher asked the question as to 'why did Stalin host these nightly orgies? Wasn't it in order to assert his status as Master outsider the Kremlin offices? Here in Kuntsevo, under the influences of drink (just try *not* to drink) the true face of

---

* The same scenario was played through with another would-be successor Kuznetsov.

** Mikhail Poskrebyshev (1891–1965) was assigned to work for Stalin in the Kremlin. In 1930 he was Chief of the Special Section of the Central Committee. He was forcibly retired from the post-1953 re-arrangements probably because of his involvement in the Doctors' Plot.

each of his colleagues was revealed. Just try to ignore the invitation or plead illness'.[176] Khrushchev tried to avoid drinking on one occasion complaining he had a kidney issue, but Beria claimed he had the same problem which left Khrushchev with no excuse. Beria revelled in these occasions acting as Stalin's court jester. On one occasion the *Pravda* editor Leonid Ilichev did not drain his glass in a toast to Stalin. This was not etiquette according to their so-called social rules and Beria announced he would finish it for him. 'The editor was speechless with fear' and only survived by becoming drunk.[177]

By 1949 some observed that Stalin appeared to be drinking less and may have been aware of his declining health, but these parties allowed him to be the grand friendly host while he studied the characters of his drunken guests. It appeared that few of the participants enjoyed these occasions, especially Khrushchev and Beria, and when Beria's wife challenged him, he answered, 'You have to put yourself on the same level as the people you're with'.[178] There is no doubt that Beria used these occasions not only to pander to Stalin but to engage his sharp if not bitter wit on his colleagues. He would often take home his drunken comrades and put them to bed, and Bulganin virtually became an alcoholic. From later reports it was realised that few of the participants enjoyed these occasions, muttering to one another about the boredom of having to listen to Stalin's endless repetitious stories, and Beria even suggesting that Stalin was lying, not that he would ever dare say this outside the peculiar privacy of the urinals.[179] Stalin would insist on telling and re-telling his exploits, even going back to his childhood and the way he was beaten by his father. Stalin would often boast he was a good shot with a gun, but on one occasion in the garden when shooting at some caged birds he nearly shot Mikoyan. His cohorts all dreaded these evenings and waited in trepidation for the phone call summoning them to the dacha. Despite the boredom Beria always remained the perpetual sycophant, always managing the right move to please Stalin or challenge a colleague.

At the personal level Beria was intimately involved in every aspect of the social life surrounding Stalin, causing his daughter to blame Beria for being involved in the arrest of some of Stalin's family members. 'True, [she wrote]'my aunts were inclined to blame Beria for the arrest which had fallen upon our family…Yevgenia Alliluyeva maintained that, as far she was concerned, Beria could not forgive her a personal insult, having a sharp tongue, she had once, in a large company, in my father's presence, made fun of the crude way in which he made advances to women, Beria had felt foolish, everyone had laughed, and this he had remembered'.[180]

She had seen firsthand Beria ingratiating himself with Stalin, his friendship with Georgy Malenkov, then predicted to be Stalin's successor, and 'one could always see Malenkov and Beria walking arm in arm. They always moved as a couple, and as such used to come to my father at his dacha, in appearance as the closest of pals'.[181] However, later in June 1953 when the gloves were off, it was finished, 'no one came to Beria's support, everyone now being as afraid of him as they had been of my father. The government's secret archives were in his hands, and this didn't suit the members of the Politburo at all'.[182] In these later observations Stalin's daughter underlined the nature of the inner-Kremlin politics, where friendships were a political convenience and advancement. This remains true of many politicians in many systems, but in Soviet Russia it was a deadly game of chess.

However, in March 1949 Beria appeared to be in the ascendancy and his fiftieth birthday was marked by the award of the Order of Lenin. The American Ambassador observed these events and machinations, noting the powerful grouping of Molotov, Malenkov and Beria stating that 'no struggle is likely to occur that is in any way commensurate with the battle of the giants which took place after Lenin's death'.[183] The ambassador missed the fact that in 1949 Stalin had turned seventy and was becoming even more paranoid. There is no doubt with the benefit of hindsight that these men, including Beria, were not as trusted by Stalin as many believed to be the case. Stalin could not bring himself to the point of countenancing a replacement for his glorious self. This is a characteristic of many autocratic leaders who find it impossible to contemplate a life beyond themselves. It took years of persuasion to tie down Franco in Spain to accept that one day someone would have to take his place. The irony was that with Zhdanov gone, Beria had made himself a prime target for Stalin's suspicions.

Stalin and Beria

Beria had been involved in nearly all of Stalin's terrors and as his daughter succinctly put it 'he knew too much', placing him in danger with Stalin in the final times of Stalin's life.[184] This moment of anxiety and anticipation undoubtedly concerned the other would-be leaders within the regime. In the early 1950s Beria's reputation and prominent position had appeared secure, but the tide was turning against him, and with his political antennae he would have been aware of the emerging crisis. Before the new decade opened Stalin, always acting on the principle of divide and rule amongst his subordinates, showed signs of initiating further purges. He had elevated Khrushchev from the Ukraine probably because he was becoming increasingly aware of the potential Malenkov-Beria powerhouse waiting and pondering his death.

His paranoia was probably not helped by his loneliness and decreasing health. His daughter noting at this time that 'as he got older my father had begun feeling lonely. He was so isolated from everyone by this time, so elevated that he seemed to be living in a vacuum'.[185] However, according to Beria's son Sergo, his father sensed that Stalin's loneliness was an act, he wanted the company of his closest men to keep an eye on them. Stalin would also have been aware of the various tensions amongst his cohorts as they sought to increase their own personal power. Molotov had noted that Stalin was 'jittery' and 'swung to extremes', and he 'was jealous of Molotov and Zhukov's prestige, suspicious of Beria's power, and disgusted by the soft smugness of his magnates'.[186] If later consistent evidence is to be believed it was clear that Stalin's old cohorts, including Beria were becoming somewhat disillusioned with their master, although they maintained their apparent attachment to him out of mutual safety. One historian noting that 'Stalin and Beria despised each other but were linked by invisible threads of past crimes, mutual envy and complementary cunning', but Stalin still allowed Beria access to power, and Beria manipulated Stalin with his habitual scheming.[187]

Khrushchev began his planned rise to the top with his own purge of the Moscow Party, and he increased his well-known policies of collectivising the farm system, a policy he had long projected. He had pursued this idea of what was dubbed Agro towns, but this concept was not welcomed by everyone. Beria was cautious and at first took a neutral line on this issue because his old friend Bagirov did not want the loss of the small farms of Georgia being amalgamated. However, Khrushchev now had Stalin's attention who ordered an investigation into Bagirov, but with Beria's aid the investigation petered out.

Nevertheless, 'it was becoming clear that Beria's power base in Transcaucasia was no longer secure from attacks by the centre'.[188] This became more apparent when Stalin started the process of replacing Georgian officials with Russians and his favoured Party members. It was clear that Stalin was losing his trust in Beria although he continued to be a regular guest at Stalin's notorious drinking parties, but this was probably to keep an eye on him. Stalin went so far as to order Abakumov to find potential prosecution cases against Beria's Mingrelian colleagues, and to 'go after the Big Mingrelian', namely Beria.[189] Stalin was playing his usual duplicitous game of control by subterfuge, and his cohorts continued to use the principles of state policy (meaning Stalin's wishes) as part of their power play to gain ascendancy over one another. Beria had probably relied too much on his own glory of the atomic project, which would not have pleased Stalin. Stalin knew that Beria would be cautious in his own private premises, aware that he might be overheard, so Stalin ordered listening apparatus to be placed in Beria's mother's household to find out more about disgruntled Mingrelians overseas.

Not wanting any one man holding too much dominance, Stalin suddenly removed Abakumov from his post but this was only a minor relief for Beria who knew he was losing Stalin's favour. It had been Malenkov and Beria's 'goal to remove Abakumov, and they were prepared to use whatever means were at hand', but they were never safe themselves.[190] New appointments were made by Stalin, and Khrushchev tended to appoint only Party people who were nearly always ethnic Russians, including the later leader Leonid Brezhnev who was brought to Moscow to work within the MGB. It could be argued that Stalin wanted to ensure that Party members were preparing for the future, but it was also a full attack upon his traditional comrades. Despite this Beria was a constant guest but aware of his diminishing status. When Stalin went to dinner with Beria, he made much of Nina and ignored Beria, often refusing to speak to him in Georgian, and damning him with the faintest praise.[191] Beria's enemies assisted Stalin, especially Vlasik who gave Stalin what he considered necessary information.*

---

* Nikolai Vlasik (1896–1967) was a Soviet security official and a general. He headed Stalin's personal security from 1931–1952 when he was falsely charged with involvement in the Doctors' Plot. He was sentenced to ten years in the camps but in 1956 this was reduced to five. The sentence was annulled in 2000. His wife always maintained that her husband was convinced that Beria was responsible for Stalin's death.

As noted, Beria's dacha was of the best quality and he enjoyed life in Georgia, but his reputation was under attack, and often not helped by his personal behaviour. His biographer Amy Knight related an incident at this time when he took some official out in a boat, spotted a female swimmer whom he picked up and, deciding to force his attention upon her, threw the official into the sea. This was by Amy Knight's own reference, and it is curious that Alan Williams in his novel about Beria starts off with a remarkably similar story.[192] Many legends and stories surround Beria, and it is a difficult path for the best researchers to know whether there is any truth in the account or not. There is little doubt that his reputation for abusing women had substance, but some individual incidents are often questionable as legends tend to proliferate about many major figures, good and bad. However, there is no doubt that by the end of 1950 Beria was under attack. During 1951 the first signs were emerging from Moscow that Beria was being undermined by many senior figures within the regime.

In late 1951 Stalin demanded a purge of the Georgian Party and the state machinery. Almost immediately several important heads rolled, all of whom were Mingrelians and members of Beria's network. A few months later more officials were fired or sent elsewhere, giving the sense that the purges were part of daily life. In March 1952 Stalin pushed through another resolution to give momentum to his new Mingrelian conspiracy. There was considerable talk of corruption, cabals, and bribery which may have been true, but the real target remained Beria. Khrushchev later claimed that Stalin was afraid of Beria and wanted him destroyed. He also claimed that Beria was no Marxist, and he used Beria's wife Nina and her connections to the Menshevik émigrés in Paris to undermine him.[193] He ordered Beria to hold an assembly of Georgia's Central Committee who obeyed and feigned shock at the revelations of corruption. Beria managed to weather the storm, but 'he emerged with a renewed sense of the fragility of his political and physical existence'.[194]

Few leaders now supported Beria in public, as most of them knew he was out of Stalin's favour and despised by many others. The general attack was on what has been described as 'localism and patronage' which was used to implicate Beria. This hostility deepened because the Americans had moved close to their borders in Turkey, with Khrushchev blaming Beria for this development. Another aggravation was that in the Transcaucasian area nationalistic and ethnic feelings always ran high, giving Stalin the opportunity to link Mingrelian nationalism with sympathies towards Turkey.

It was a complex time in the politics of power within the Soviet Union under Stalin. At this moment in time, it was curious that Stalin appeared to surround himself with the four men, Beria, Khrushchev, Malenkov, and Nikolai Bulganin and rejecting other comrades. These men were mutually careful with one another, as they were concerned for their own well-being, living in a small world of mutual suspicion, and accepting that they had to please Stalin by obeying his frequent demands. When Sudoplatov described Bulganin as 'a man without any political principles, only the obedient servant of any leader', he could have applied this description to any of the four cohorts including himself, such was the nature of Soviet power.[195] The Khrushchev and Malenkov dachas were near one another, and Beria's car was always waiting to pick them up. They all knew they were in potential danger from the erratic behaviour of their declining dictator, and these last 'four men standing decided, according to Beria's son, not to let Stalin set them against each other', prompting Stalin to ask whether they were forming a bloc against him.[196] This indicated that Stalin intended to stay in power until he died, which he eventually managed.

During October 1952, at the time of the Nineteenth Party Congress, the purges in Georgia were as notorious as the mid-thirties as all the speakers attacked what they called 'bourgeois nationalism', but Beria always responded with carefully prepared responses. There were some elements of resistance against the tide of stated official opinion which was most unusual.[197] To defy Stalin was a dangerous road, and Beria would have been aware of his vulnerability. Many understood that Stalin could be even more dangerous as his paranoia was increasing. He had openly made his suspicions of Molotov and Mikoyan clear, claiming they were Western infiltrators. This may have been the reason Stalin disbanded the Politburo and created the twenty-five-man Presidium, with an informal group in the Presidium which significantly included men like Khrushchev, Malenkov, Kaganovich and even Beria. He may have done this in Beria's case based on his old premise that 'one keeps one's enemies close', as well as his habit of being seen as comfortable with men he intended to eliminate.

Khrushchev continued attacking Beria's hold and influence in Georgia and moving closer to Stalin in this silent battle for power. Despite the purge Beria managed to keep many of his supporters in place including some with the MGB. However, Beria had alienated most of the military command apart from a few, one of whom was Marshal Shtemenko who had once accompanied him to the Caucasus during the war years. It was therefore significant when some of Shtemenko's closest supporters were dismissed in late 1951, because it was risky to have any connection with Beria. These dismissals cast a shadow over Shtemenko because gone were the days when Beria could influence Stalin.*

During the war Stalin and his cohorts had supported Jewish people and other ethnic groups because their efforts were required to fight the Nazi threat. After the war, this policy vanished, and Stalin's growing paranoia became focused on so-called Jewish plots. Although anti-Semitism had been a Russian tradition it has been claimed that Stalin was not fixated on it as the Nazi-type liquidation policy.[198] It has been believed that because some of his one-time comrades who had turned against him such as Trotsky, Kamenev and Zinoviev had been Jewish, this had turned him into an anti-Semite. Nevertheless, although hating the Poles even more, there seems little question that Stalin was anti-Semitic especially against those of the male variety. Sudoplatov, the major obedient agent was married to a Jewish wife and one of his closest associates was Leonid Eitingon also Jewish, tended to believe that Stalin's anti-Semitism was a façade for stirring up political conflict to his own ends, which may or may not be true.[199] Beria had instructed Sudoplatov to sound out the American Averell Harriman on the idea of a Jewish settlement, with Sudoplatov later writing 'I could not imagine at the time that to be associated with such discussions would turn into a kiss of death'.[200]

As early as 1949 some prominent Jewish leaders had been detained, and in late 1951 the general secretary of the Czechoslovakian Communist Party, Rudolph Slanksy had been arrested.** This action had been taken on the grounds that he had helped organise military support for Israel over its

---

*   After Stalin's death Beria had Shtemenko re-instated for him only to fall again after Beria's arrest.
** Slanksy survived Stalin, but after the fall of Beria he was then denounced for the crime of being a 'Beria man', and having introduced Beria methods within his area of responsibility.

conflict with the Arabs. It had also been rumoured that Beria and the MGB had supported this effort. Abakumov had been instructed to investigate (or fabricate) this subversion against the State, and the nine culprits were executed; they were later termed the 'apprentices of Zionism'.[201]

This episode arose from the infamous and well-known Doctors' Plot referred to earlier. All of Stalin's plots and purges 'required a generic character: kulak or bourgeois social origins in the 1920s, Trotskyism in the 1930s, and now Jewish nationalism'.[202] The background of this plot seemed to have its origin in a letter written by Dr Timashuk about Zhdanov's death, stating that he was killed by Jewish doctors, based on the treatment not being the best possible, as the ECG revealed he had needed constant bedrest. There was no doubt that Dr Timashuk was one of many agents working in the Kremlin Hospital, and unfounded claims have been made that she was anti-Semitic. It was about four years before Abakumov drew Stalin's attention to the letter, but it was not Zhdanov's death which worried Stalin. At the time when Zhdanov had suffered his self-evident heart attack, he had been more than aware that Stalin was turning against him, probably because he was gaining too much prominence. He and Stalin had also fallen out in 1942 during the siege of Leningrad, which Stalin would never forget or forgive. As in the previous purges 'those who had risen to governmental positions of great eminence before and during the war now found themselves being pushed aside', and all this was a sign of a new purge in Stalin's paranoid mind.[203] This letter from Timashuk was a distraction for Stalin's deeper purposes, in so far that her complaint about a patient's treatment had suddenly involved major state interest. There is no question that Stalin was anti-Semitic, but his intentions ran beyond his personal bigotry to domestic and foreign policy. Jewish people had suffered under the Tsars and the new Communist system had allowed many to rise in power. Jewish people held many prominent positions, and amongst the best known were Trotsky, Litvinov, Kamenev, Zinoviev, Yagoda, Kaganovich, to name just a few. In the post Second World War years Stalin was aware that the USA was the major rival and a potential enemy. He was annoyed and uncertain when the new state of Israel sided with the West, deciding that Soviet Jews could not be trusted, and on 1 December 1952, 'at a dramatic meeting of the Presidium of the Central Committee, Stalin declared that 'every Jew is a potential spy for the United States'.[204] As far as Stalin was concerned, America and Zionism were linked, and the Doctors' Plot, the attack on the Jewish Anti-Fascist Committee, the Leningrad affair and the purging of the MGB (from July 1951 to September 1952 some 42,000 individuals were purged from the MGB) were all part of Stalin's singular way of finding enemies to exterminate. There is no doubt that Beria would have cooperated but much of it remains a mystery, because after Stalin's death Beria destroyed any information. Beria and members of the MGB were worried because the plot may have implicated them. Beria had some association with the workings of the JAC (Jewish Antifascist Committee) and this was enough for Stalin who may or may not have believed the information was correct.* 'If certain facts were not empirically true, they became functionally true to suit political purposes that, in Stalin's universe, represented a higher reality', which made life dangerous for his supporters and many others.[205] It was impossible even for Stalin's cohorts to know what was going on, and equally difficult for historians. This plot implicated many other people including his doctor and his own bodyguard Vlasik of many years.**

It has often been suggested that Khrushchev was one of the instigators not just because of his anti-Semitism, but his wish to destroy Beria. It has long been established that Khrushchev was anti-Semitic even in public statements then and later, but his desire to rid the Soviet system of Beria, although secret at the time, is now well understood. One well-known historian of the Soviet Union, Robert Conquest, has suggested that Stalin did not necessarily believe the case against the Jews, because during the purges he happily sent men to their deaths or captivity not believing the charges at all.[206] It has also been suggested that Stalin was degenerating with the hardening of his cerebral arteries causing irrational judgement and increasing his inbuilt paranoia. This leads to the view that 'having suffered some kind of major physical collapse – either a heart attack or a stroke – immediately after the war, which caused him to recuperate for long periods of time in Sochi, Stalin had to demonstrate that he was still the "master of the house",

---

* It had been under Stalin's direction that Beria helped form the JAC.

** Because Vlasik had been so close to Stalin he 'became Beria's venomous rival' but because of his loyalty Stalin started to suspect him as an enemy in his last days, Kotkin, Stephen, *Stalin, Vol II: Waiting for Hitler, 1928–1941* (London: Allen Lane, 2017), p.526.

able to control foreign policy, domestic policy, the security services, and the military, as well as Soviet agriculture'.[207]

What is certain is that Khrushchev needed to crush Beria, who was influential in too many parts of the state apparatus. During the previous year, these followers of Stalin had started to prepare for a future without him, the unmentionable possibility. According to a ruling of 10 November 1952, the Presidium, and the Bureau of the Presidium of Sovmin (Council of Ministers) were to be jointly chaired by Beria, Saburov and Pervukhin.* 'Beria took advantage of Stalin's distractions elsewhere to hijack the Council of Ministers for his own ends. Organising sessions of the Sovmin Presidium and the Bureau of the Presidium without consulting either of his co-chairs. Beria structured the agendas, cancelled voting, and steered pecuniary rewards, in the form of prizes, pensions and the awarding of flats and country houses, towards his own clients', basically usurping all bureaucratic authority and investing in those he believed he could trust.[208]

During what are now seen as Stalin's end-days, Khrushchev with many others were becoming aware that Stalin was preparing another possible purge not just of Jews, but his own political advisers. In December 1952 he dismissed Aleksandr Poskrebyshev who had been head of the secretariat for some twenty-five years, then ordered, as mentioned, the arrest of MGB General Nikolai Vlasik the long serving chief of his bodyguard, and his personal physician Dr Vinogradov who was obliged to confess his involvement in the fictious Doctors' Plot. To the Stalin watchers the signs of another irrational attack appeared to be imminent as Stalin announced 'what will happen without me is that the country will die because you can't recognise your enemies'.[209]

'The evidence suggests that Beria discovered, in the winter of 1952–3, that Stalin was planning to remove him', and 'on the night of 1 to 2 March Stalin suffered a stroke. Beria immediately began planning the succession'.[210]

---

* Mikhail Pervukhin (1904–1978) served under Stalin, Khrushchev and Brezhnev. He was Chairman of the Council of Ministers (First Vice-Premier of the Soviet Union) from 1955–57. In 1959 he was Ambassador to East Germany. Maksim Saburov (1900–1977) was a Soviet engineer, economist and politician. In 1921–26 he was Secretary to the Bachmut Komsomol Committee and headed Gosplan (State Planning Committee) three times. In 1947 he became a member of the Supreme Soviet of the USSR, and First Deputy Premier in 1955. He was a member of the failed effort to depose of Khrushchev in 1957.

It has been suggested that because Beria recognised the personal threats he had organised Stalin's death.[211] This is very unlikely and Sudoplatov saw this claim as totally unfounded.

Beria later, when it was safe, brought the anti-Semitic drive to an end although it re-emerged later at various times. As 1953 opened it was clear that those hoping for the highest power were planning their futures, making useful connections with others who might help, namely those who could be either useful or jettisoned when required. Beria was the one individual who most potential leaders feared the most. Stalin prior to his physical and mental collapse had made it clear that his successor was very much 'in the air' and he would reject Beria out of his distrust of the man, and because he was not Russian. Kaganovich was Jewish, Voroshilov was considered too old, Mikoyan was an Armenian, and Khrushchev he considered 'a country boy and Russia needed a leader from the intelligentsia', leading to each candidate for succession feeling nervous for a variety of reasons.[212] They had speculated that Stalin had fancied someone from the new generation and were slowly reaching the conclusion that only 'a collective' leadership could succeed the great leader, probably a decision arrived at for personal safety.

Stalin's Death and Tussle for Power

On 1 March 1953 an assistant warden found Stalin on the floor and 'Malenkov and Beria, who were the first to be informed, arrived followed by Khrushchev at 7.30 am, and a group of doctors an hour later', although it was often claimed there were problems in finding Beria's whereabouts.[213] When the somewhat astonished daughter of Stalin was brought to the scene she stated that she saw the attendant doctors and that the 'Academician V. N. Vinogradov, who had looked after my father for many years, was now in jail – were making a tremendous fuss, applying leeches to his neck and the back of his head', making the scene appear almost perversely bizarre.[214]/* The doctors who arrived were terrified of the prostrate body of the leader

---

* 'Leeches were preferred for bloodletting, because the sharp fluctuations in blood pressure that would have resulted from bloodletting were considered undesirable'. See Brent, Jonathan and Naumov, Vladimir P., *Stalin's Last Crime: The Plot Against the Jewish Doctors, 1948–1953* (New York, Harper Collins, 2003), p.318.

and the presence of the others, especially Beria. The dentist called to remove Stalin's false teeth dropped them on the floor in his state of nervousness, and his shaking hands could hardly undo Stalin's shirt.[215]

The precise circumstances remain a mystery, but 'new documents have recently turned up, but there will never be enough information to quieten doubters who insist that Beria or someone involved in a plot may have poisoned Stalin'.[216]/* The fact remains that of the survivors of that day only Stalin's daughter and Khrushchev have left memoirs of the occasion, and neither are entirely trustworthy about this episode.

There were many unanswered questions about the nature of Stalin's death, and the various versions, 'despite their discrepancies, suggest strongly that members of the leadership may have deliberately delayed medical treatment for Stalin – probably for at least ten or twelve hours – when they knew he was seriously ill'.[217] There is no written evidence available, only personal observations which in this conspiracy of silence can be unreliable. Most involved on the fringes would have had sound personal reasons for wishing Stalin dead, not least Beria who had been under suspicion for a long time. Out of the senior men, Beria was the one who had the most reason to be concerned, because he knew that Stalin was probably finished with him. This will always remain mere speculation to the delight of conspiracy theorists because even post-Stalin documentation cannot necessarily be trusted. Despite a degree of openness after *glasnost* in trying to find the details of what happened in Stalin's last hours, the details remain obscure and confusing. Khrushchev and Stalin's daughter, with others have offered conflicting reports, but each with a personal agenda. Stalin's daughter hated Beria noting 'there was only one person who was behaving in a way that was very nearly obscene. That was Beria. He was extremely agitated. His face, repulsive enough at the best of times, now was twisted by his passions – by ambition, cruelty, cunning and a lust for power and more power still. He was trying so hard at this moment of crisis to strike exactly the right balance to be cunning, yet not too cunning'.[218] Later she observed 'all of them except

---

* One of the more recent attempts to assess the medical evidence that Beria was involved can be found in Brent, Jonathan and Naumov, Vladimir P., *Stalin's Last Crime: The Plot Against the Jewish Doctors, 1948–1953* (New York, Harper Collins, 2003) but they admit that 'no hard empirical evidence supporting this has been unearthed to date', p.314.

the utterly degenerate Beria spent those days in great agitation, trying to help yet at the same time fearful of what the future might bring'.[219]

Stalin who had needed company in the evenings tended to watch films to the early hours, because as Khrushchev noted 'the main thing was to occupy Stalin's time so that he wouldn't suffer from loneliness. He was depressed by loneliness and feared it', giving the impression of a haunted man.[220] On the night when he fell fatally ill Malenkov, Beria, Bulganin, and Khrushchev had been present; Molotov and Mikoyan were absent being under a cloud. When they had left Beria travelled with Malenkov, and it was Malenkov who had later suggested that Beria was with some woman when during the hours of panic no one could find him. When Stalin's so-called supporters arrived, no one summoned medical assistance, and no one could be certain as to how long Stalin had been in a state of collapse, whether medical assistance was required or whether it was drunkenness or tiredness or even a trick to test them. In the event Beria, Malenkov and Khrushchev returned to their own homes, but on returning it was noted that Beria and Malenkov had left together, and it was presumed they were discussing the future. Khrushchev, according to his memoirs 'was well aware of Beria's energy and his thirst for power'.[221] Beria's behaviour during Stalin's death hours was described by Stalin's daughter as obscene, and Khrushchev claimed Beria was cursing Stalin until he thought he might recover, kissing his hand when there was a glimmer of life, and cursing him again when the hand felt limp. How far this was accurate is impossible to know because it is now well-known that Khrushchev hated Beria. Molotov later claimed that Beria told him he had been responsible for Stalin's death: 'I did him in', Beria boasted, 'I saved all of you!'[222] However, Khrushchev never mentioned this which he unquestionably would have done if there had been the slightest possibility of this outburst being true. The biographer Amy Knight's suggestion that the surrounding company had just let him die sounds more reasonable, though, because of Beria's nature, it is always possible he could have slipped some poison in his drink, but it all remains speculation. Later an official report was made called *The History of the Illness of J. V. Stalin from March 2 to 5, 1953* which tends to favour the account by the doctors.

One curious aspect was that inside Stalin's desk there were only three items he kept locked away. The first related to his relationship with the Yugoslavian Tito, the only so-called communist leader who had openly challenged Stalin's leadership. The second was Bukharin's letter pleading for mercy, and the third a letter of admonition from Lenin. It was noted that 'he would not have conserved [these items] in the desk unless it had echoed round the caverns of his mind'.[223] There was an autopsy report, but it has never come to light, and it was clear from other evidence that his comrades had been right in the assumption he had been planning another purge. It transpired that Beria had his son Sergo trained as a pilot in case they needed to escape as a family.[224] Following Stalin's death the contenders for power were worried about Beria, because 'each member of the Presidium knew that Beria held a potentially embarrassing dossier on him'.[225] Even as Stalin's death was being accepted, the possible battle-lines were taking shape with Malenkov closer to Beria, and Khrushchev moving alongside Bulganin. Apparently, Stalin's residence was emptied in hours with a frantic house clearance and all his staff were dismissed.

The main issue was that Stalin had not named any successors, and there were no known procedures for such an appointment because Stalin had transformed the ideals of communism into a totalitarian leadership. The bureau of the Presidium nominated by Stalin, consisted of Beria, Bulganin, Voroshilov, Kaganovich, Pervukhin, Saburov and Khrushchev, who promptly met during the night of 4 March making changes to Stalin's latest so-called reforms, and deciding to do away with the enlarged Presidium. Khrushchev was concerned because it appeared that Beria and Malenkov were taking charge, Beria nominated Malenkov as Chairman of the Council of Ministers, and Malenkov proposed that Beria be named as one of the first deputies. It was an almost medieval type of tussle for power, and Sudoplatov noted that in April 1953 'I noticed certain changes in Beria's behaviour. He openly criticised his colleagues in the Presidium while making telephone calls to Malenkov, Bulganin, and Khrushchev in my presence and that of other senior officers'.[226] However, these leaders were aware of a wider reaction and moved with caution in this play for power. During Stalin's lifetime any form of opposition would not have arisen out of personal fear, and so the tussling would-be leaders tried to present the image of unity, but it was a cunning charade.

Khrushchev was obliged to stand back and watch the dismissal of Brezhnev, and during these months it began to appear that Malenkov was the leading contender. Beria promptly ensured his control over his old security empire which added problems for others because Beria had considerable armed support. He installed a close friend Vasili Stepanovich Ryasnoy as a new head of the Foreign Directorate, although this man had no experience, and the contenders had good reason to be nervous of Beria's machinations.

Khrushchev loathed Beria without explicitly stating as such, and consequently Khrushchev's well-known reminiscences must be treated with caution. Beria was clever enough to know he was being observed, but his error was in his personal sense of importance and underestimating Khrushchev. Many observers believed that Malenkov was going to take Stalin's place. In *Pravda's* article on the funeral arrangements, Malenkov received the most coverage and pictures, whereas Beria's and Molotov's contribution appeared side by side on page two. To all outward appearances Malenkov was the clear front-runner. The leadership team were allotted new tasks, and it was announced that Beria would head the Ministry of State Security and Ministry of Internal Affairs which had now become amalgamated. It has been noted that 'Beria was now grabbing the most powerful levers of domestic coercion', and because of his wide-reaching powers he was a challenging presence.[227]

Khrushchev headed the organising commission for Stalin's funeral, introducing Malenkov who gave the major eulogy with Beria and Molotov following. It was claimed that both Beria and Molotov spoke without much reference to Stalin and more about the future, and it was noted that Beria's speech, 'with his accent and his sharp, sometimes croaking intonations, displayed this absence of grief the most obviously'.[228] Stalin's funeral became a political platform, with Beria hinting at possible reforms, and stressing the multinational nature of the Soviet Union.

By mid-March the press, including *Pravda*, was playing down the cult of potential leadership and placing the emphasis upon the Central Committee. It was all a form of power-brokering which the outside world and the public watched with anticipation. Most knew that Stalin's regime had been oppressive, and Malenkov, Khrushchev and Beria all realised this had become counterproductive.[229] Beria suddenly surprised everyone by suggesting a series of reforms, a novelty, which given his past was incredulous, but without being too cynical it was clearly a case of Beria expanding his public awareness to improve his public image. Many of his proposed reforms prefigured

Gorbachev, but Beria was well-known, and the others recognising his widespread powers still made them nervous. However, it is worth noting that Sudoplatov in his memoirs argued that Beria was an innovator who would have brought about the unification of Germany in the 1950s, which may well have avoided many of the future international tensions.[230] Sudoplatov's views are merely curious, as Beria's intentions may well have been reformative, but his motives were his cunning way of securing power. Beria conducted a purge of the foreign Intelligence directorate and made his own appointments within the MVD (MGB). He needed to be regarded as a person who could de-Stalinise the system to win popular support. Khrushchev had similar ideas about de-Stalinisation, but Beria forged ahead with longer-term ramifications than the others thought necessary.

He suggested sensible economic reforms by putting a stop to many of the gargantuan building projects which had been started for the purpose of Stalin's personal historical glory. He also attacked the continuous problem of agricultural collectivisation and the Agro town policy, which had been a Khrushchev policy, and was much resented by the rural community. For some observers this may have appeared as hopeful, and curious to others as Beria was presenting a vastly different image of himself. It has been argued that Beria was in an advantageous position to reform the State because he had already proved to be strong and determined. However, to most people, past and present, this was a clever manoeuvre by Beria who wanted to be regarded as the man of the future.

Beria had cunningly after Stalin's death established five commissions to review cases within Stalin's last years, with a special emphasis on the death of Solomon Mikhoels and the Doctors' Plot, establishing it as a vile plan by Stalin, and presenting documentary evidence to those prepared to read them in the guarded privacy of the Kremlin. There was the distinct impression that as Stalin blamed the past, so now Beria was now accusing Stalin. Beria turned to reforming the Gulag system, proposing a transfer of the Gulag economic enterprises to civilian ministries. He convinced his colleagues for a form of limited amnesty to release some Gulag prisoners. It may have been a limited amnesty, but it was the first time anything like this had been suggested. However, none of these proposals applied to political prisoners. In Sudoplatov's observations this made some areas risky with the return of the criminal element, and 'no doubt the amnesty and possible disruptions weakened his standing in public opinion'.[231] Beria took the next step and named the killers of Solomon Mikhoels who had been awarded medals, demanding the medals should be removed and they were to be arrested. He was trying to make himself the proposed person for necessary reform, making himself the central figure. He also promoted himself by reminding all that he had ensured the success of the Soviet hydrogen bomb, and reminding everyone it was he who had instructed Sudoplatov to coordinate possible plans for sabotaging NATO bases.

All these potential leaders including Khrushchev, had been Stalin's compliant servants and they had committed brutal acts, and it was unbelievable that they were seeking some form of personal redemption, but it was more a political *volte-face* by casting blame onto Stalin, as they propagandised their credentials for their own good. This helped explain why a man like Beria needed to be seen as a reformer and the same reasons applied to his colleagues. The leaders appeared to back Beria to show the public and the world that Stalin's police state was ending. For a brief time, following Stalin's death, an effort was made to show that a collective leadership would reform the Communist State. Few of these would-be leaders, if any, were true communists in the proper sense of the Marxist ideals, and most of the emerging so-called collective leaders were waiting for their moment to seize power either individually, or as a selected cabal. In the immediate post-Stalin weeks, there is no doubt they were all watching Beria who held the most power and who had promptly moved with speed and purpose.

Immediately following Stalin's death Beria involved himself with foreign policy, and by early April rumours abounded that Soviet Russia was seeking a peaceful solution to the war in Korea with better relationships with the USA.* The Western powers were aware and curious about this apparent change of direction, and there was even a possibility of some form of reconciliation with the difficult Tito in Yugoslavia, with the curious twist that just two days

---

* Stalin had made a blunder in withdrawing from the UN over that body's refusal to accept China. It was during this time Truman had managed to persuade the UN to fight in Korea. Beria and Khrushchev had worried about America's reaction to the unpredictable Stalin, especially when Stalin ordered that Moscow be surrounded with anti-missile sites. Ironically it was to be Khrushchev who nearly brought on a global war during the Cuban crisis.

before he died Stalin had been discussing with Sudoplatov the possibility of having Tito killed.[232]

Beria suddenly appeared as the defender of the rights of the various nationalities, and denounced Stalin's attack on the Mingrelian people (the so-called Mingrelian Conspiracy) without, significantly, consulting with the other leaders, even when officers of state in that region were replaced by those of Mingrelian blood. The Moscow politicians towed Beria's line as he spread this policy across the USSR's various republics. The usual rhetoric was employed, and Beria started to attack what he called Russian chauvinism and found support from those who wanted to hold the USSR together. This brought him back into conflict with Khrushchev who was angry that this new policy touched upon the Ukraine, where Khrushchev had a lifetime's involvement.*

At surface level it had appeared that Beria and Khrushchev were amiable with one another, but both had always disliked and distrusted the other. Sudoplatov recalled a time during the early war years when Khrushchev had threatened him over the phone following an unpleasant conversation with Beria, who then turned on Sudoplatov berating him 'with language I did not expect from a member of the Politburo'.[233] As mentioned above the subject of the Ukraine was always sensitive for Khrushchev and this was not helped when Beria proposed changes whereby Ukrainians took over the leadership roles. He even started the promotion of religious freedom releasing the Primate of the Uniate Church Yosyf Slipyi from his prison camp.** This was a total reversal of Stalin's and Khrushchev's policies and reflected a liberal approach which was never normally associated with Beria. His sudden reversal of policies and most especially his pro-nationalistic support was not confined to Georgia and the Ukraine but was being initiated in the Baltic states and Belorussia where they were encouraged to assert their culture and language. The other leaders, even Khrushchev, were compelled to support Beria's reforms because he held too much power to contradict,

Many of the Party leaders would have had reservations about these changes, but Khrushchev took the cautious approach, claiming in his own

---

* Khrushchev had been born on the Russian side of the Ukraine border and saw the Ukraine as his personal responsibility as Beria regarded Georgia.

** After Beria's fall Slipyi was returned to his imprisonment.

words to Malenkov, in the full knowledge that Malenkov and Beria supported one another, 'Don't you see where this is leading? We're heading for disaster. Beria is sharpening his knives'.[234] Beria was cunning and understood human passion, and to win over any opponents he suggested they all had dachas built at government expense in Georgia. This was naturally met with approval, but Khrushchev, who was as crafty as Beria, warned Malenkov that this was a Beria plot because to build these dachas other people would have to move, causing resentment. Malenkov at first would not believe this, but as Khrushchev noted in his memoirs 'this conversation started Malenkov thinking'.[235] Khrushchev was trying to drive a wedge in the Malenkov-Beria alliance. Khrushchev cannot be entirely trusted in his memoirs any more than Beria could had he had the time to write his, but it seems Malenkov started to move away from his quiet political alliance with Beria.

The Fall of Beria

The post-Stalin government appeared to have taken a new shape with a five-man Party Secretariat, which had followed the surprise announcement that Malenkov had resigned as secretary of the Central Committee. Khrushchev was slowly emerging as the leader when he was listed first and not in the proposed alphabetical order. Malenkov remained premier, but he had no leadership within the Party, and although Beria was the first deputy premier and head of internal police, he had no formal role among the Party leaders. This new development made it abundantly clear that Khrushchev was being generally regarded as the leading man.

Among the key issues for the new Soviet leaders were the growing problems in the GDR, the Soviet portion of Germany. The East German economy was in sharp decline, there were few consumer goods for sale, and food was reaching an all-time low even by the last war's standards. Walter Ulbricht the Party leader and deputy prime minister and head of the Socialist Unity Party (SED) was activating some hard-line policies in the economic sphere, and in the first four months of 1953 some 120,000 had risked crossing the border to the better-off pastures of the west.* Following

---

* 'Close to 500,000 East German citizens had fled to West Germany since 1951', see Knight, Amy, *Beria: Stalin's First Lieutenant* (Princeton: Princeton University Press, 1993), p.191.

Stalin's funeral, Ulbricht had sought help from the Moscow leaders, as he was a determined Party hardliner.

Beria reported what was happening in Germany to the Presidium, and he even proposed that the policy of the forced construction of socialism should be set aside. This argument naturally raised considerable concern and was sharply criticised by Molotov. Sudoplatov made the interesting claim that the original policy of a united Germany never originated with Beria, and that Stalin had considered this as an option in 1951, (which seems highly unlikely) but Sudoplatov agreed it was probably Beria's interference which caused many of the Soviet problems in East Germany.[236] Beria had argued for a democratic and independent Germany, stopping the agricultural collectivisation, reducing the policy of eliminating private capital, improving the financial arrangements, and suggested a system to reform the judicial procedures and examine injustices. It is not difficult to imagine the response of the Presidium members listening to Beria of all people proposing such far-reaching western type changes.

There was a momentous controversy, indicating that Beria had taken a step too far. It was just what Khrushchev needed, who along with Molotov accused Beria of turning against Socialism. Ulbricht was called to Moscow where a shouting match between Beria and Ulbricht ensued. Moscow had already announced that the military command in East Germany was to be recalled, however, a civilian administration was established under Vladimir Semenov, who was politically close to Beria. Moscow had eventually accepted what was dubbed the Beria document, and preparations were set in place to oust Ulbricht. Reforms were instantly announced despite protests from Ulbricht, and farmers who had fled West were promised their farms would be returned if they came back. The cost of consumer goods would be reduced, and this along with other promises raised the expectations of the East German populace. It did not proceed as rapidly as the East German public had anticipated, and on 16 June there were street protests which soon spread beyond East Berlin. This turn of events led to a clash between Moscow and East Germany, and the failure to manage the overall problem was clearly evident.

'Beria's rivals for power did not applaud his efforts to moderate the Stalinist system', as many of them had learnt to be suspicious of his motives.[237]

When the revolt broke out in East Berlin the Russian military were called in, resulting in the deaths of some twenty-one demonstrators, and Beria flew there to take control. He soon heard that the Presidium had been unexpectedly called, and he became aware that East Germany was causing serious problems which could impact on his ambitions. He gave a sharp appraisal as to what had happened in Berlin, and Molotov protested at 'such an attitude to a friendly country'.[238] Beria had become too accustomed to his assumed political power and failed to recognise the potential personal danger he was in. He found himself accused of permitting a policy which might result in abandoning East Germany, at a time when many Russians felt that Germany remained a potential threat. Beria in his haste had reacted too rapidly. Some observers and historians have tried to evaluate Beria as a reformer, but while his intentions may have appeared worthy, his motivations were, as always, based on personal ambition. As often stated, Beria belonged to the Machiavellian and Byzantium type Kremlin cliques trying to grasp power. He had, without realising the facts, given the opportunity to his political contenders to claim that he was restoring capitalism, but his sudden bout of liberalism failed for East Germany and for him. All it did was provide Khrushchev with a pretext for rallying opposition against Beria and his clique.

Khrushchev had been planning a move against Beria, but he later insisted his actions against Beria had moral foundations and not just for self-preservation. Khrushchev 'had survived Stalin and now he had to outlive Beria'.[239] The details of Beria's downfall are obscured by various accounts based on self-serving memories of those involved. More information has since come to light and there are some minor deviations between Amy Knight's account written in 1993 and Rubenstein's book written some twenty-three years later.[240] Such was the confusion that the belief that Beria was arrested at a meeting of the Presidium was challenged by Sergo his son, who claimed he was arrested at home. Later Khrushchev would claim that although Malenkov chaired the meeting it was Khrushchev who stood and denounced Beria. What occurred remains a puzzle, but it is generally assumed that Beria was making a bid for total power and lost. Sudoplatov noted that 'it has now been established that Beria never plotted to seize power and overthrow the collective government. He had no power base within the bureaucracy', later adding that this belief was confirmed by Kiril Stolyarov, a scholar who saw Beria's file.[241] The truth is impossible to establish with certainty. In 1991 *Izvestia* published the minutes of the plenary session regarding Beria, indicating from the speeches of the others such as Khrushchev and Malenkov, that it was all intrigue by Beria's so-called comrades. It appears possible that if Beria were not planning to take total control, he was ensuring that he remained important within the collective leadership with his own formidable powers. Khrushchev was aware of Beria's immense powers within the security services; when Beria attended the Presidium, he tended to arrive with his own bodyguard. When Khrushchev started this *coup*, it was in total secrecy. Beria was aware that he had enemies, and he suspected that Malenkov was changing camps. Nevertheless, Voroshilov and Mikoyan were amongst Beria's supporters and Khrushchev kept them in the dark, and as with many others, Beria's arrest took them by surprise.

Khrushchev worked with Bulganin, and they enlisted the help of General Moskalenko commander of the Moscow Air Defence and the famous Marshal Zhukov, who being military men had little time for Beria. Khrushchev had to move with care, ensuring Beria could not summon help, and so a special Presidium was called for 26 June and Khrushchev claimed he had arrived with a gun in his pocket. According to Khrushchev, when Malenkov lost his nerve in answering Beria's question as to what was on the agenda, 'I jumped up and said, "There is one item on the agenda: the anti-Party, divisive activity of imperialist agent Beria. There is a proposal to drop him from the Presidium and from the Central Committee, expel him from the Party, and hand him over to the court martial. Who is in favour?"'[242] Others joined in the denunciations and Malenkov was supposed to have pressed a secret button which summoned Zhukov with armed soldiers, who had already brought into Moscow an armoured division in case of problems. This version was probably coloured by Khrushchev. It was Malenkov who had opened the proceedings by announcing that Beria's activities were to be examined, as it was claimed that Beria had tried to set one Presidium member against another, and he had caused problems in Hungary, and in East Germany with his innovative approaches to the problems.* Malenkov asked other

---

* Beria had wanted to reshuffle the Hungarian leadership and put forward Imre Nagy as a candidate for prime minister: Nagy had been an NKVD agent.

members to voice their opinions and several commented on how Beria had often tried to promote himself at their expense. Khrushchev weighed in with his habitual invective, accusing Beria of the amnesty for criminal inmates, stating that 'Beria was trying to legalise arbitrary rule, and that no honest Communist would ever behave the way he does in the Party'.[243]

It was at this point Malenkov then pressed a secret button, and Beria was led away at the point of a gun. He was taken under escort to a military cellar under an orchard, his belt and trouser buttons had been removed, and in this humiliating situation he had to hold his trousers up with his hands. Stalin's daughter wrote that 'General A. A. Vishnevsky, Chief Surgeon of the Soviet Army, told me that Beria, after his arrest, had been kept for a few days in the basement of the General Staff Building in Moscow, and had been shot there ten minutes after sentence was pronounced'.[244] The room under the orchard was probably the same place.* There was still a genuine fear that the *coup* would fail because many in the Presidium were taken by surprise, and there were angry objections from General Maslennikov (a first deputy chief of the MVD) and Vlasik (Stalin's old guard recently released from prison), but they were persuaded to go away, and later others complained but were shut down. 'Beria's arrest was, then, a highly risky operation that succeeded more by luck than anything else. The *coup* plotters, improvising as they went along, were in considerable danger for the next few days, until the Beria forces could be subdued, and any potential challenges resisted'.[245] Beria suddenly disappeared and Sudoplatov realised the next day that the picture of Beria which normally hung in the reception room had been removed.[246]

Beria's family and other supporters were locked up, and his wife Nina spent nearly a year in prison. The CC Presidium met again on 29 June to decide the next step, making it clear they were holding Beria under political charges. Beria had been given many prestigious awards including five Orders of Lenin, Hero of Socialist Labour, two Orders of the Red Banner and others, and he still had supporters who were swiftly identified and, in many cases, locked up. Their main fear, beyond Beria's supporters, was that Beria in a public defence could also involve the conspirators in their own murky

---

* It seems from most accounts that they took Beria to the garrison guardhouse at Lefortovo prison, then for safety reasons transferred him to an underground bunker under the apple orchard mentioned to Stalin's daughter.

past, not least during the various purges. They organised that the judicial machinery should be in their favour, and Marshal Moskalenko was appointed for the investigations, and the Procurator-General who knew Beria well was replaced by a friend of Khrushchev, Rudenko, who had held this post in the Ukraine. Beria's closest associate Merkulov was permitted his freedom if only to cooperate in the initial stages by revealing all he knew about Beria, to stay alive and free. From his cell Beria wrote a series of letters asking for mercy, apologising, and requesting that he be allowed to work in some minor post where he would prove his worth, but his paper and pencils were removed.

His Trial and Execution

The conspirators knew that the Central Committee members were needed to give a formal sanction to be regarded as legitimate. They could have followed Beria's methods, such as the excuses that he had been killed trying to escape, or he had died from an illness, or committed suicide, but they were well aware that the rest of the world was watching this sudden upheaval. To overcome this problem a carefully planned offensive was prepared when the Central Committee met in a secret session between 2 and 7 July. The proceedings were noted but held in secret and the records were not seen until decades later in 1991. These papers revealed a picture of events 'surrounding Beria's arrest, making it clear that Beria's opponents were still on very shaky ground [given their own behaviour] at this point and were thus pulling out all the stops to contrive a criminal case against Beria, and persuade the Central Committee members that they had done the right things'.[247]

Khrushchev chaired the session, but he cleverly left Malenkov, Beria's one-time friend, as the lead-man in the proceedings. Malenkov raised the issue that Beria had used the MVD for his own political ambitions, had collected information on Party members, and had misused his power in East Germany and Yugoslavia. The point which probably gripped the attention of many of those listening was the fear that Beria had many personal files on those present. Malenkov explained the reason for the meeting was the necessity for the leaders to keep a sense of Party unity. Khrushchev covered the same ground but with added barbs, even raising the old rumour that Beria had spied decades before on behalf of the

Musavat, but this time in a tone of absolute authority. He explained his one-time friendship with Beria with his sense of humour, explaining how on the surface all seemed like a happy family, and describing how he and Malenkov shared a car with Beria and 'saying goodbye, he squeezed my hand, and I responded with a warm handshake: well, I thought, you fraud, this is the last handshake. Tomorrow at two o'clock we will be waiting for you. [laughter] We won't shake your hand, we'll put your tail between your legs'.[248] It was clear to the conspirators and the listeners that the situation was a politically delicate issue.

Beria's accusers examined his life and there were even charges relating to the war, and he was accused of trying to consult with the Germans to overthrow Stalin.[249] Molotov was more measured and focused on Beria's foreign policy which Molotov had been genuinely concerned about in this his field of expertise. Molotov was angry about Beria's intrusion into East Germany and tampering with the difficult relationships with Yugoslavia. Bulganin offered the possibility that Beria was a spy and asked why it had been necessary for Beria to have armed MVD troops with Russia already having a well-equipped army. Kaganovich used the powerful word 'counter-revolutionary' implying treason. Shatalin, a CC Secretary painted a sensational picture of Beria's sexual appetite and behaviour, including that he had syphilis and illegitimate children. For personal safety many of Beria's old friends and supporters spoke against him, but his oldest friend Bagirov, part way through his speech was interrupted because some claimed he was trying to save himself. Bagirov was later executed in April 1956 following his trial.

By the end of the trial on 7 July 1953, the Central Committee agreed that Beria was to be expelled from the Party and to stand trial on criminal charges. Beria was portrayed as amoral and a person with no human compassion, claiming his recent calls for reform were based on his ambition for power. His role in the purges was never mentioned, as this would have involved his accusers who were also immersed in this Stalin crime. Beria's arrest had not been announced until 10 July, and it was before Christmas before anyone heard that Beria and six co-conspirators had stood trial, announcing he had worked for British Intelligence, but no reference was made of mass murders which would have been too embarrassing for many of his accusers, having been involved.*

The first signals for the more interested, was that Beria's name suddenly disappeared, and then the political onslaught started with claims that Beria had been prepared to hand East Germany over to the Americans, planned a return to capitalism. Beria was not helped by the fact that just after his arrest Russian tanks had been used to resolve the East German riots.

The news of Beria's arrest caused astonishment, especially among the Western powers, with some wondering whether it portended the end of the regime. In a Gulag prison camp Solzhenitsyn said the news came like a 'thunderclap', and pictures of Beria once everywhere in the prison camps suddenly disappeared.

Khrushchev and others were aware that it might cause some unrest, and he ordered that the various reactions were monitored, but it is known that there had always been a high degree of public scepticism about official announcements. There were rumours that a military coup was under way, but everyone soon relaxed and regarded the whole incident as another power struggle amongst the leading echelons.

The reaction in Georgia was slightly different where Beria had made many supporters and enemies in his home territory, but his pictures were removed, and streets and avenues named after him were changed and often replaced with Malenkov's name.** There followed a purge of Beria's supporters, although the conspirators took their time not wanting to create problems.

The MVD's foreign Intelligence agency had a change of chief which worried many of Beria's agents abroad. Foreign diplomats and those watching Beria's agents noted this sudden change. In Australia, the MVD agent Vladimir Petrov defected, noting that 'what is certain is that Beria was the loser in a naked struggle for supreme power which is not yet ended'.[250] There were other defections as in Japan, and a sense of relief in the East German Communist Party under Ulbricht who was returned to full power. The

---

* 'Beria thus became, following Yagoda and Yezhov in the 1930s, the third head of the KGB to be executed for crimes which included serving as an imaginary British secret agent'. Christopher, Andrew and Oleg, Gordievsky, *KGB: The Inside Story of its Foreign Operations from Lenin to Gorbachev* (London: Hodder & Stoughton, 1990), p.351.

** Later in 1956, when there were riots against Moscow rule, pictures of Stalin and Beria were waved in demonstrations.

collapse of Beria created headlines in the West especially amongst those who had hoped that Beria had started a more reconciliatory era. There was a great deal of ignorance of what was happening, with many giving Khrushchev little attention believing Malenkov would be the new leader.

It was not until 17 December that the announcement was made that Beria and six of his accomplices would be on official trial, the chief prosecutor was Roman Rudenko who had served on the Nuremberg Trial during the prosecution of Göring. The trial was held in secret and presided over by a Second World War military commander called Ivan Konev on 18 December. Others were tried at the same time including Merkulov, Dekanozov, Kobulov, Goglidze, Meshik and Vlodzimirsky, all accused of being part of Beria's network. The charges were far-ranging and included Beria's attack on the collectivisation policy of the farm system, creating food shortages, and generally raising dissent within the country. These were followed by the old charges of spying for the Musavat, working for the Mensheviks, contacting enemy Intelligence agencies, and working with Georgian dissidents living abroad. He was also indicted for working with counter-revolutionary elements during the civil wars.

Once these various charges were made public there followed a national denunciation and newspapers joined in the condemnation. There were many real reasons why Beria should be condemned for his work under Stalin, who in postwar legal terminology was guilty of crimes against humanity and genocide, but these charges were a trumped-up political agenda for the safety of the accusers, and to justify their actions. Whatever the feelings about the man Beria he was condemned by men who had participated in the same or similar evil deeds. As noted, the trial was held *in camera* for obvious reasons, and only the results were reported to the press on Christmas Eve with the news that Beria would receive the highest criminal punishment, namely death.

Rumours abounded that Beria had been dead for some considerable time, even his son Sergo had remained convinced his father had been killed earlier in the year. It is, however, most likely that he attended the trial. Khrushchev himself muddied the waters of speculation later, but it is generally believed that after the trial ended on 23 December Beria was taken to a cell, handcuffed to an iron ring where he was shot by the senior officer and then by four others. The American Ambassador Charles Bohlen pertinently reported that 'there is of course elementary justice in the fate of Beria and his associates, but it would have been more fitting if retribution had been meted out by his victims rather than his accomplices'.[251]

Unlike Stalin's policy, Beria's family survived after a brief imprisonment, but restrictions were placed on them. After his death and 'as a symbol of his non-personhood, the editors of the Great Soviet Encyclopaedia sent out a discreet notice to all their subscribers recommending that they cut out with a small knife or razor blade the entry on Beria'.[252] They offered a replacement article on the Bering Sea, in an attempt to make the exorcism retrospective as if Beria had never existed.

The Person of Beria

Beria had always been obsessed with following Stalin's orders, including the execution of Trotsky and countless others. Beria was clever at organising executions from a distance even if they were in foreign lands, as he was an expert in such matters. On one occasion he asked an NKVD officer called Boko if he could kill with a single blow; following the affirmative answer, a Soviet ambassador in the Middle East, whom it was rumoured was about to defect, was killed by one blow from an iron bar. When the ambassador's wife asked about her husband's whereabouts, she was told he had been recalled to Moscow, and she and the children were to return, but only as far as a prison camp for enemies of the state.

Beria often did the killing himself when younger, but mainly operated through his selected henchmen, especially his main agent Sudoplatov, who will be noted in the next chapter. It was this man who, on Beria's orders from Stalin, had organised the elimination of Trotsky. If it meant incarcerating innocent women and children into Gulag camps, on Beria's orders this was arranged without hesitation. Stalin had recognised Beria was a man who would do anything without objection. Beria recognised Stalin needed him, and he always pandered to Stalin as he was aways driven by his own personal ambition. Stalin was always rude and crude, often teasing Khrushchev and Malenkov for their flabbiness, and Bulganin's beard was a point of laughter for him.[253] He would laugh at Beria for not wearing a tie which he seldom did, probably because Stalin never wore one.* Beria never allowed Stalin's ridicule to dissuade him from his habit of being in the right place to exhibit his obsequious support of the master.**

Beria was always deeply suspicious like Stalin, and at one stage he even suspected that the infamous Cambridge spies in England were working for the British or the Germans.[254] However, when Donald Maclean in March 1942 sent news of the atomic research Beria, out of necessity, believed him, and passed the information on to Stalin. He trusted very few, and it was generally known that Beria looked after his own interests, and even Sudoplatov's Jewish wife Emma (also an agent) warned her husband 'that there was something evil about Beria and that he was a man without feeling'.[255] Sudoplatov was Beria's trusted agent, but he and his wife always suspected their apartment was bugged.

Beria's moral depravity was widely known, as he had women and young girls taken from the streets for his own sexual gratification. How far he was a sadistic rapist, or the level of his debauchery will never be ascertainable, but there is no question that there was considerable veracity in these claims. His bodyguard Sarsikov gave the number of assaulted women as thirty-nine, another bodyguard called Nadaraia spoke of these habits, and American diplomats living in his vicinity were aware of the women coming and going from his home.[256] Beria's name occurs in many personal reminiscences such as Tatiana Okunevskaia an actress, who claimed that Beria raped her repeatedly in 1947.[257] Even at Stalin's death it proved difficult to find Beria because it was rumoured he was with some woman.[258] Beria later referred to them as mistresses, but his sexual predatory nature was widely known. It has been suggested that this sexual predation was deliberately enhanced after his downfall, but the evidence is too consistent to be brushed aside. As noted by one historian, the evidence of witnesses is extensive and 'reveals a sexual predator who used his power to indulge himself in obsessive depravity'.[259] His power as the police chief and politician allowed him to carry through

---

* When Sudoplatov first met Beria, he recalled he was not wearing a tie. Sudoplatov, Pavel and Anatoli, *Special Tasks: The Memoirs of an Unwanted Witness – A Soviet Spymaster* (London: Little, Brown and Company, 1994), p.39.

** Sudoplatov noted that Beria himself was always rude to high-ranking officials but polite to those of a lesser rank. See Sudoplatov, Pavel and Anatoli, *Special Tasks: The Memoirs of an Unwanted Witness – A Soviet Spymaster* (London: Little, Brown and Company, 1994), p.113.

these appalling acts to a 'mind-boggling' and gross level of debauchery.* Even now 'Beria's illegitimate children are well known among Moscow and Tbilisi society…'including a highly respected Georgian Member of Parliament'.[260] His family always denied such rumours, his wife believing the women were his agents, but his son Sergo admitted his father had a child by another woman.** Later his marriage with Nina had been under strain because his then mistress, Lilya Drozhdova had given birth to a daughter who shared the same cot with Sergo's baby. The denials were probably based on the need for family unity.

At first his public reputation appeared good, especially after the much-feared Yezhov. This image changed as his reputation developed to become more menacing than that of his predecessor. As one historian wrote, 'The appointment of Beria is usually taken as a convenient date to mark the end of the Great Purge. Of Beria! – that is, of a man whose name, even in official Soviet circles, is now the very embodiment of terror and torture. And yet there is some sense in the convention'.[261]

Because of his ambition Beria swiftly adapted to changing situations, and he quickly made comrades from men such as Mikoyan, Molotov, and Voroshilov. He drank and socialised with those whom he deemed important, and especially when he was in the company of Stalin. He had the advantage over others because it was possible for Beria and Stalin to converse in their home language of Georgia, alien to most other guests. Stalin, as noted, used dinner-parties and drunkenness to keep an eye on his minions as they revealed themselves through alcohol, and with this life-long habit he found in Beria the ideal colleague as a person who used the same crafty techniques. Stalin even tried competitive drinking at an international level but met his match with Churchill.

Stalin's daughter Svetlana Alliluyeva described Beria's habits of target shooting, his enjoyment of films, sport, and his overall comfortable life-style.[262] In all her writings Stalin's daughter exposes a deep hatred of Beria, recalling

---

* Even now 'Beria's illegitimate children are well known among Moscow and Tbilisi society… including a highly respected Georgian Member of Parliament'. Montefiore, Simon Sebag, *Stalin: The Court of the Red Tsar* (London: Weidenfeld & Nicolson, 2003), p.450fn.

** Sergo became well educated, gained a doctorate in physical mathematics and married Maxim Gorky's granddaughter.

as a youngster she called him 'Uncle Lara'.[263] Beria enjoyed photography, volleyball, and swimming and he 'attracted everyone back then by his inner power, his ineffable magnetism, the charisma of his personality' thereby following Stalin's habits of gathering admiring followers.[264]

Beria always obeyed Stalin's instructions or listened to what he was hinting, but he also pursued some personal vendettas. One was against the Komsomol First Secretary Kosarev who had, according to one of Beria's many informants, suggested that Beria was not the best of leaders. Beria's personal interest went so far to make him want to attend the arrest, and when Kosarev's wife protested he ordered her to be taken prisoner. This was supposed to be part of the Military-Fascist plot, but when the interrogators failed to find any evidence, the trial was held *in camera*. His predecessor Yezhov had virtually wiped out the military command and its officers, but Beria pursued the remnants and took a personal interest in the interrogation of Marshal Bliukher, even including the man's helpless wife. The list of men subjected to Beria's brutal interrogation techniques were innumerable, but it included many from the arts and the general intelligentsia, including scientists. He deviated from his Lubyanka tradition at one stage to establish an NKVD entertainment group for song and dance to entertain troops fighting in the Finnish war, but it was politics and policing which dominated his time. The Lubyanka and the Foreign Commissariat (which Beria soon dominated) were geographically close together and nicknamed 'the Neighbours'. The name Lubyanka still instils a sense of fear, and even Solzhenitsyn confessed to confusing the two buildings.[265]

By 1939, when it was clear that Europe stood on the brink of war, Beria's attention was drawn away from local developments after nearly two decades, and he took an active interest in foreign affairs. This was initially directed by Stalin who had decided to purge the People's Commissariat of Foreign Affairs, which he considered necessary in the light of foreign tensions. It was probably based on Stalin's annoyance for being unable to establish any agreement with the Western democracies. Litvinov conducted these negotiations, he had an English wife, he was Jewish and an anti-Nazi, causing Stalin to wonder whether this was the safest route to a negotiation with Germany. He decided that for this purpose Litvinov was not, in his opinion the best man for such hopes. Litvinov was given another post,

The Aral Sea's sources were diverted for industrial purposes, and in time became a toxic salt desert. (*Adam Harangozó via Wikimedia Commons/CC BY-SA 4.0*)

Lavrenty Beria, an ambitious man who was ruthless, sadistic and feared as much as his master Stalin. (*Public domain*)

Vladimir Lenin and Stalin, September 1922. (*Public domain*)

Pavel Sudoplatov (left) and his enemy Viktor Abakumov, who even accused Sudoplatov's young children of planning to kill Stalin. (*Mil.ru via Wikimedia Commons/public domain*)

Stalin – for some Uncle Joe, for others a ruthless tyrant, pictured here at the Potsdam Conference in August 1945. (*US Library of Congress/public domain*)

Building in a Gulag camp with picture of Yezhov and a smaller picture of Stalin at the top. This was taken a few weeks before Yezhov was removed from power. (*Public domain*)

Nikita Khrushchev in 1924. (*Public domain*)

Khrushchev with Stalin in 1936. He hated and feared Beria, but following Stalin's death in 1953 succeeded in the struggle for power. (*Public domain*)

Khrushchev pictured in October 1962 as First Secretary of the Communist Party. (*Dutch National Archives via Wikimedia Commons/ CC BY-SA 3.0 nl*)

J. Robert Oppenheimer, often called the father of the atomic bomb. (*Public domain*)

The Red Terror (1918–1920) was a time of brutality as the Bolsheviks imposed their will.

Operation Barbarossa turned the tide against the Nazi onslaught after Stalingrad, but it was a bitter battle with millions of casualties on both sides. (*Bundesarchiv, Bild 183-R76619/CC-BY-SA 3.0*)

The Manhattan Project: building the atomic bomb, which was a top secret stolen by the Russian secret agents known as illegals. This picture shows Norris Bradbury, group leader for bomb assembly, shortly before the Trinity Test. (*Public domain*)

In the Gulag camps inmates were worked to death.

The railway tracks leading to the entrance of Auschwitz-Birkenau. (*Dieglop via Wikimedia Commons/CC BY-SA 4.0*)

Leon Trotsky, assassinated under Stalin's orders.

Ramon Mercader, who as a young man killed Trotsky.

Genrikh Yagoda was noted for his cruelty, personal habits, and he was feared by everyone.

Churchill and Stalin. Friends only when necessary.

The Lubyanka building, headquarters of the KGB. (*Adobe Stock 15110374*)

Churchill, Roosevelt and Stalin at the Yalta Conference, 9 February 1945.

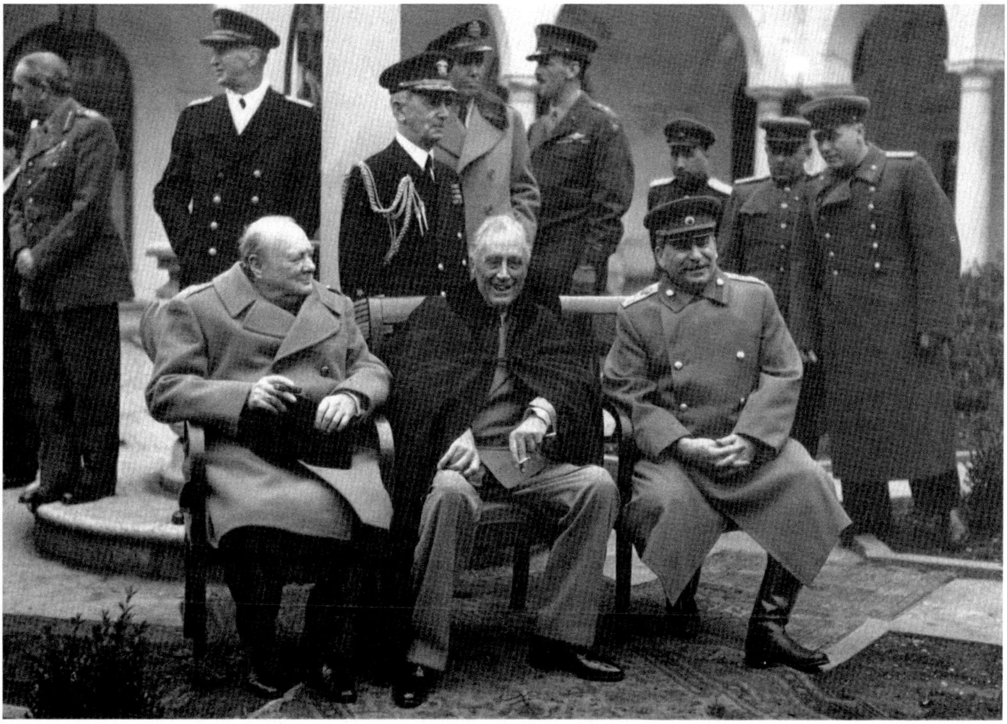

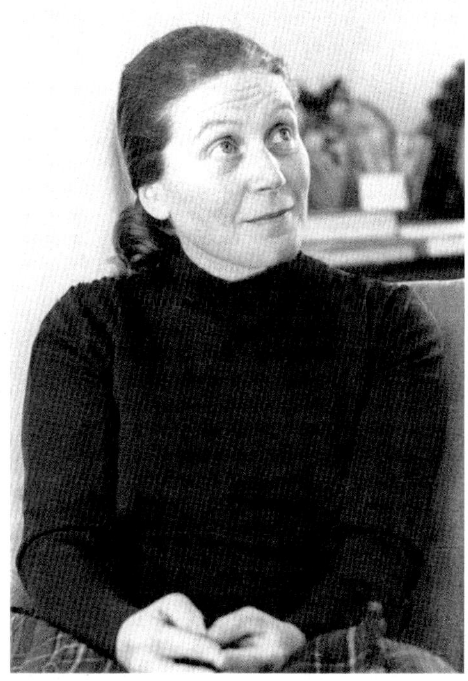

Svetlana, Stalin's daughter, who changed her name several times.

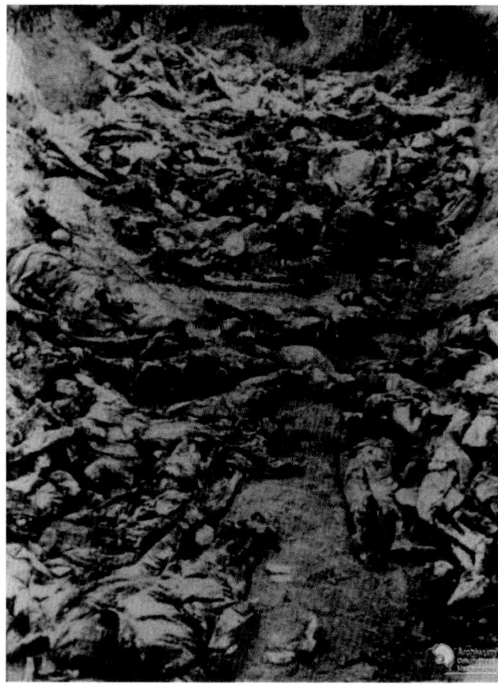

Katyń massacre mass grave, uncovered by the Germans in 1943. Ordered by Stalin, probably on Beria's suggestion.

Vyacheslav Molotov, pictured in 1917 and 1945 – a significant component in Stalin's Regime.

Stalin's dacha, more like a palace than a comfortable home.

but his foreign affairs' offices were taken over by Beria's NKVD. Many of Litvinov's underlings were interrogated, but they found no incriminating evidence, and although Molotov took over the reins, Litvinov survived. This was unusual and various speculations have been raised, the least likely was that Stalin was concerned about his international image, the most likely was Litvinov was reliable, intelligent, and would be of use in another situation as these difficult times unfolded. Litvinov who had worked long and hard at collective security was rapidly displaced by Molotov but survived. As it was Litvinov became the Soviet Ambassador to the USA. It had been a difficult and tenuous time for Litvinov who not only lost his Moscow apartment, but Beria had surrounded his dacha with NKVD troops. His phones were tapped but he managed to contact Beria who jovially replied that 'the goons were stationed there for his protection'.[266] Beria's involvement would have been worrying for Litvinov.

As a result of Stalin and Beria's machinations the NKVD moved into the Foreign Office, and like a spreading virus controlled everything. Beria had brought one of his special henchmen with him, a man called Vladimir Georgievich Dekanozov, who was already infamous for his sadistic behaviour during the purges. He was promoted to head of the Foreign Intelligence Service (INO) and passed on information about British connivance, which was entirely false, prompting a purge on possible Western sympathisers. 'At the very moment when the NKVD's foreign Intelligence was at its least reliable, its influence on Soviet foreign policy was simultaneously at its peak'.[267] It was a serious problem because the very diplomats who were the most informed about the West, were subject to Beria's suspicions. As troops built up in on the western borders Stalin later told Marshal Timoshenko 'We are starting a panic for nothing'.[268] Whatever mistakes and blunders Stalin was making he always had the unstinting support of his faithful and ruthlessly ambitious servant Beria.

If any person is asked to name the most notorious blood-thirsty known leaders, there is a considerable list of potential candidates. Springing to mind are such names as Pol Pot in Cambodia, Kim Il Sung in North Korea, the Turkish Enver Pasha for killing Armenians, the Pakistani Yahya Khan for genocide in Bangladesh, the Japanese leader Hideki Tojo, Chiang Kai-Shek, but the three most common on their lists would be Hitler, Stalin and Mao

Zedong; all belonged to the twentieth century. When Stalin attended the Yalta Conference, he had amongst his cohorts Lavrenty Beria whom he introduced to Roosevelt and Churchill as 'my Himmler'. This was probably more accurate than either of the Western leaders would have liked to believe, as they were becoming aware of his atrocious crimes and inhumanity. Beria's son later claimed this must have hurt his father who was becoming excited about stepping onto the international stage, rather than being regarded as the secret and sadistic policeman.[269] Nevertheless, Lavrenty Beria was as ruthless as Genghis Khan, as cruel as Vlad the Impaler, as manipulative as the best Niccolò Machiavelli, and a sexual predator of pitiless proportions. Like most bullies he was a coward, and when he was eventually executed it is alleged his executioners had to stuff a rag in his mouth to stop him pleading for mercy.[270] As Solzhenitsyn wrote 'those who have condemned many others to be shot often wilt at the prospect of their own death'.[271] After his execution Beria's name was carefully expunged from Russian history, and although Himmler's name remains well-known little is known about Beria. There are few adjectives strong enough to describe his cruelty, sadism, and lack of compassion. He was a criminal working for a criminal leader.

Chapter Two

Sudoplatov the Agent

This chapter is a brief summary of one of Beria's major secret agents who produced his own memoirs, written postwar but with a sense of honest revelation. He was the major agent who helped organise Trotsky's death, gained the top secrets about atomic bombs. It includes his work during the Second World War, his relationship with Beria and Stalin. His last conversation with the latter was the projected assassination of Tito. He played a role during the Cold War, participated in the dispute with Ukrainian nationalists, and like Beria stood trial, was imprisoned but survived to offer his reflections. He offers many insights into the criminal type of State which at first, he had admired.

Writer's Note: *This chapter is based on the memoirs of Sudoplatov (Sudoplatov Pavel and Anatoli, Special Tasks, The Memoirs of an Unwanted Witness London: Little, Brown and Company, 1994) and to avoid increasing endnotes unnecessarily any direct references are contained in the text in brackets.*

Introduction

Sudoplatov was an Intelligence agent, a specialist in assassination, and recognised as a professional in overseas work, organising the death of Trotsky. The historian Hastings summarised Pavel Sudoplatov as one of the 'principal puppeteers of the Kremlin's *danses macabres*'.[1] After Beria's death he was imprisoned and survived as an embittered man, later writing his memoirs, which form the basis of this chapter.[2] He could be described as a criminal working for a criminal system, very much like a gang member for a mafia boss, totally obedient, ruthless, cold-blooded with a loyalty which propelled him to risk his own life for the master. He soon became well known for his proficiency in his cruel work and caught the attention of both Stalin and Beria. He was, as will be seen as his life is unfolded, a person who could make a close almost affectionate friend of someone with the purpose of later blowing him up with a gift of a box of chocolates. He was for Stalin's regime the ideal agent, clever, good at his craftwork, obedient and prepared to do anything which was required.

When doing any research into the clandestine services of any country finding documentary evidence is often difficult if not impossible, and even those papers which become known cannot always be trusted. It must not be forgotten that in some regimes some orders are given which are initiated by word of mouth with no follow up accounts required. There are also similar problems with diaries and autobiographies, where some matters are concealed or changed. Sudoplatov was a resolute servant because he thought that Stalin was the perfect communist, and he was prepared to kill and put his own life at risk for the cause. This was for him and others a gross error seeing Stalin as the Marxist ideal and not the tyrannical totalitarian leader that he was in reality. However, because Sudoplatov viewed Stalin as the rightful leader he therefore regarded his work as justifiable. He started his 'secret-life' as a minor official, caught Stalin's attention and was given the task of State murders. He came under suspicion for a time, as everyone in Soviet Russia did, and was Deputy Head of the Foreign Department, then called in for tasks in the Spanish Civil War and became trusted by those at the very top, Stalin and Beria. It could be stated with some certainty that during Stalin's reign he was regarded as one of Stalin's best agents.

Sudoplatov had worked in the administration of a department called 'Special Tasks', which was a title implying the elimination of the enemy by whatever means necessary. Despite his total allegiance to Stalin, he still held some personal values, not least he was not anti-Semitic as his life will indicate, he knew that Beria could be monstrous but also saw him as a reformer, which, as noted above, was an image used for the sake of personal ambition. It was because he worked closely with Beria that he eventually landed up in a Soviet prison.

Early Life

Sudoplatov was born in 1907 in Melitopol in south-eastern Ukraine from a Russian mother and a Ukrainian father who worked as a miller. He was baptised in the Russian Orthodox Church as Pavel Anatolievich and was taught the scriptures. He spoke Russian as in Tsarist times Ukrainian was forbidden in schools. He had a brother called Nikolai who joined the Red Army in 1918 and who two years later joined the Cheka Battalion. Sudoplatov as a mere early teenager joined a Red Army unit at the time it was retreating from a White Army surge. The Ukrainian nationalists at this time demanded independence and would not achieve this ongoing demand until 1992. Sudoplatov was a mere boy but educated enough to read and write and found work as a telephone operator and cipher clerk. His unit was given the task of trying to penetrate the Ukrainian nationalist forces. It was at this stage his brother was killed near the Polish border.

Sudoplatov's life was starting on a course of a clandestine nature, as on his return to Melitopol he became a junior case officer looking for informers. He was promoted in 1927 working for the Secret Political Department of the Ukrainian OGPU in Kharkov whose principal task was to seek inside information about the Ukrainian nationalists (p.10). It was during this time he met the Jewish girl Emma Kaganova who was working for the OGPU and later became his wife. Sudoplatov was also appointed as a commissar for homeless children resulting from the civil war.

It was during these years that under Soviet instruction he became involved with Yevhen Konovalets, who was a major military and political leader of the Ukrainian nationalists, meeting him in Finland and playing the role of an ardent supporter, and to all appearances managing to make it feel like a genuine and loyal friendship between the two of them.

While this was ongoing, Sudoplatov under instruction was left free to wander around Nazi Germany, attending the Nazi School in Leipzig. In 1936 Konovalets suggested that he and Sudoplatov should travel together between Paris and Vienna to meet their national supporters. Konovalets had financial support from the Nazis who were promising the independence which Ukraine craved. Sudoplatov explained how he grew so close to Konovalets that on one emotional occasional he was hugged and kissed by the man whom he considered the enemy (p.19). It was no easy task moving around Europe during the 1930s, and on one occasion trying to cross borders he was arrested for a brief time in Finland. His adeptness at moving around Europe as a courier and lookout was making him noticed, and in 1937 he was summoned to meet Nikolai Yezhov the dreaded head of the NKVD, but Sudoplatov was unimpressed by the man. Sudoplatov may have thought little of Yezhov, but he was taken to the Kremlin where he met Stalin for the first time, later writing that he was so excited that he felt overwhelmed by his emotions. The point of the meeting was that Stalin was determined to find a way to close down the Ukrainian Nationalist movement as soon as possible. Sudoplatov later came up with a plan to infiltrate three more agents deep inside the movement, especially in Germany where they had been welcomed, but Stalin, in his usual pattern wanted the head of the organisation liquidated as soon as possible. They talked about this, and Stalin asked questions about Konovalets' tastes and weaknesses. Sudoplatov was able to point out that Konovalets adored chocolates and soon a meeting was held and Sudoplatov was given the task of assassination. A specialist produced a bomb which looked like a box of chocolates. Sudoplatov travelled as a radio operator with a Czech passport on a ship to the Netherlands where it was known Konovalets happened to be at that time. As a matter of interest Sudoplatov's code name was Andrew. The chocolate box had been re-designed so that the detonator would activate thirty minutes after the box was turned from a vertical to a horizontal position. He presented Konovalets with the chocolates and after leaving his victim bought a new mac to help in disguise, soon hearing the bomb exploding several roads away. Later he would write that he felt this killing was justified, claiming he was pleased that no innocent people were hurt (p.38), and always believed his 'killing work' was the right thing to do.

After this he made his way to Barcelona on forged Polish papers to work in Spain in a guerrilla warfare group run by the NKVD. His life working for the Stalin regime was the consuming part of his life. In his work Sudoplatov also spent considerable time commenting on the Stalin years and the various agents he knew. He stated that in the 1930s Stalin was preoccupied with what he considered two key issues, the first was his prime enemy Leon Trotsky and then the Spanish Civil War. While in Barcelona Sudoplatov met Ramon Mercader who had been behind Franco's lines on a guerrilla mission whom he would use later in the assassination of Trotsky. In the same place he met Leonid Eitingon, later an important colleague, also operating behind Franco's front lines of battle. He outlined Eitingon's background including his Jewish origins, and who after Spain went to France, participated in running Guy Burgess, then off to Turkey where he was involved in a failed assassination attempt on Franz von Papen who was then the Nazi-Germany Ambassador. Later in life Sudoplatov found that Eitingon had become cynical if not critical of Russian leadership, by which time Sudoplatov was having similar views, no doubt because after Beria's downfall both these agents found themselves locked up as well.

Meets Beria

On his return to Moscow, he met Beria for the first time in a four-hour meeting, who pleasantly grilled him about his work in Western Europe, asking detailed questions giving Sudoplatov reason to believe that Beria was experienced in tradecraft. He also felt Beria was testing him for yet further work in the western zone. Sudoplatov was a trifle embarrassed because he was in a tailored suit whereas Beria was in everyday work clothes, and he assumed Beria dressed like this not to stand out in a crowd; others noted, as mentioned above, that it was more likely imitating Stalin who never wore a tie.

In 1937 Spanish gold and treasures had been shipped to Russia, but somehow suspicion arose as to whether the transfer had signs of corruption, and Sudoplatov was asked to check the books to discover if these accusations were founded. During this investigation he came across the name Nikolsky Orlov (his real name was Aleksandr Feldbin) their agent in Spain who was their man to look after security, but while in Spain he had helped in the guerrilla warfare. Orlov was, like so many, caught up in an affair with a female agent who dramatically committed suicide outside the Lubyanka when Orlov refused to leave his wife; this, along with Sudoplatov's investigation left Orlov with the impression that he was on the wanted list, and consequently he fled to America. This raised many concerns because Orlov knew too much including the British spy ring in Cambridge. According to Sudoplatov, Orlov remained safe because he wrote a letter to Stalin telling him that if he felt he was being pursued or his old mother in Moscow hurt, then he would not let go of his secrets including the Cambridge spies. As Sudoplatov noted, it was not a matter of loyalty to the Soviet Union, but personal safety and it seemed to work. These reminiscences of other agents offer insights into the lives of Russian agents, not only in danger while working overseas, but in more danger at home once they fell under the slightest suspicion.

Sudoplatov claims it was not until 1938 that he became more aware of the home front war instigated by Stalin by killing or imprisoning any internal opposition, frequently identified as Trotskyites. This pursuit of so-called traitors was widespread involving family members. It was the years of the purges when Stalin was determined to rid himself of anyone who was evenly mildly critical of his regime. To demonstrate the chilling setting of these days, Sudoplatov raised the death of Sergei Kirov the Leningrad Party leader in 1934. It was generally felt that Stalin wanted this old colleague off the scene, but Sudoplatov also suggested that it was Stalin who started the rumour that it was a Trotsky plot. Most tended to believe that it was an enraged husband Leonid Nikolayev whose wife had an affair with Kirov. It was Sudoplatov's wife who investigated Kirov and discovered he had many mistresses (p.51), but this was kept secret for the sake of a Soviet leader's reputation. One way or another, Stalin accused Trotskyites as causing this death. For some it has been thought, Sudoplatov later added, that it was a myth that Stalin had opposed the unhealthy elements in the Party, especially Kirov who would have been a better replacement for Stalin. The speculations on this particular death continued long after the Second World War into the 1960s, and in 1986 at Moscow University when on the subject of rewriting history, it was claimed that all it did was 'reveal dirty linen in Kirov's personal affairs'. As late as 4 November 1990, '*Pravda* published a report from a commission [still] investigating the Kirov affair, charging that the motive for Kirov's murder was personal' (p.53). Generally, the overall opinion was that it was important to keep Kirov's memory sacrosanct. However, most believe that Stalin manipulated the whole affair; though there is no evidence that Stalin ordered the death, it seems highly likely. Now, well into the twenty-first century, the details behind Kirov's death remain a mystery lacking any certainty or reliable evidence. By raising this issue Sudoplatov inadvertently brings to light not just the nature of living under Stalin's rule, but the fact that in this secret world so much has to remain speculation, because there is no reliable evidence, and had it ever existed, it has long disappeared.

Known as the period of the purges mentioned above it was a time of mutual suspicion even amongst the ranks of the NKVD from the clerks at the front desks to the upper reaches of power. Rumours, according to Sudoplatov, abounded that a commission from the Central Committee was checking all personnel for any involvement in subversion or corruption. Sudoplatov was soon summoned at four in the morning for an interview, and both he and his wife were rightly concerned as to where this would lead them. His nervousness was misplaced this time because in the purges others had fallen, and Beria told him as a result, he was to be the acting director of the Foreign Department. Here he learnt more about how operations were run, especially the Special Tasks (known as the *Yasha* group) with networks in Germany, France, and Scandinavia. He soon discovered there was no sense of ongoing stability as leading personnel were often changing, often through denunciations or general suspicion, and in this complex race for power it was impossible even to trust old friends. Later, he wrote, that it was only in 1963 that he learnt that behind this reshuffling was the figure Beria taking selected gossip and news to Stalin for his own benefit. It was at this stage, as mentioned in the previous chapter, when his own wife Emma warned Sudoplatov to be wary of Beria as 'he was a man without feeling'(p.60). Sudoplatov soon heard he was also under investigation, interviewed by a man he considered a good friend only to find that he was seen as a 'Trotskyite double-dealer'. He knew the recommendation was made that he should be expelled from the Party and the date was set for this to be examined and acted on, leaving Sudoplatov sat at his desk doing nothing but waiting a phone call. He admitted this whole episode left him in doubt about the system and the way it was controlled, and the dangers, as his wife pointed out of living and collaborating with jealous colleagues. The date of January 1939 had been set for the committee to confirm his expulsion, but it was suddenly postponed, and in March he was suddenly summoned to Beria's office thinking his final moment had come.

Assassination of Trotsky

Instead, Beria took him to the Kremlin to meet Stalin for the third time, and he was surprised when Beria suggested to Stalin that Sudoplatov should be appointed a deputy director of the NKVD Foreign Department. Stalin seemed only interested in one thing which was eliminating the Trotskyites, and to complete this action it was decided that Sudoplatov's new appointment was to organise the assassination of Trotsky, as without his figurehead the rest of his followers would fall apart. It was decided that Sudoplatov would head the team of *buyeveke* (shock troops) to kill Trotsky. Sudoplatov pointed out that he had no Spanish, but Stalin simply told him he could have all the necessary resources and personnel he needed, and Sudoplatov was given a new office in room 735 of the seventh floor of the Lubyanka.

It was Beria's usual way of working, choosing the right man to do his work so it reflected well on him, and it was through his main agent Sudoplatov, who arranged for Ramón Mercader (his code name was *mother*) to eliminate Trotsky.* As Stalin was wily in organising his personal henchmen, Beria as noted used the same methods, and his choice of Sudoplatov was astute. Sudoplatov was a natural secret agent, known as an illegal, and had first met Ramón Mercader during his devious machinations in the Spanish Civil War, and he later trained him for this task which had obsessed Stalin for years (p.30).

A day later his old colleague and friend Eitingon contacted him wondering whether he too was under investigation. Sudoplatov told him he had no idea, but the next day asked him to join him in killing Trotsky, which with Eitingon's wide experience was a sound move. Trotsky had moved to Mexico in 1939. He had left Russia in 1929, lived in Turkey, then Norway, followed by France moving to the relative safety of Mexico before the war started. Sudoplatov had already believed that Trotsky was to make the communist movement chaotic and weak, not the more measured approach that he thought Stalin was making, even though Stalin was moving away from Marx towards an autocratic regime. It was Eitingon who suggested the code name for the operation should be *Utka* (Duck) which apart from the bird itself, indicated disinformation.

The main issue was being able to become trusted enough by Trotsky to infiltrate his circle, and because he knew Stalin so well, Trotsky was more than aware of the possible dangers, and Sudoplatov wondered whether Orlov had possibly warned Trotsky of the dangers. The various means and

---

* Stalin was later overjoyed at the news of Trotsky's death, and Beria was pleased that his agents had proved more successful than Yezhov's men. Trotsky, Stalin claimed, was the victim of his own intrigues.

people that could be deployed were the basic problems, but Eitingon knew of some who would be able to help. These connections were essential, and they decided to use a task force led by David Alfaro Siqueiros, a Mexican painter who knew Stalin and was a veteran of the Spanish Civil War. They also turned to Caridad Mercader, a Spanish aristocrat, one of whose sons was Ramon. In 1938 Ramon and his mother were living in Paris for safety reasons, both willing agents of the Soviet Union. Another agent was code-named Harry and was English. He had stolen the Trotsky operational records in December 1939, proving to be reliable in obtaining necessary forged documents. Sudoplatov informed Beria of their intended plans who added some ideas which Sudoplatov did not think were sound enough. Either way, Sudoplatov was ordered by Beria to go with Eitingon to Paris, so they sailed via Odessa to Athens, changing identities before arriving in Marseilles, took a train to Paris to meet Caridad Mercader and her son Ramon. Sudoplatov also decided they needed to be taught some tradecraft. Caridad and her son sailed to New York in August 1939, Eitingon was supposed to follow but was prevented because of his false Polish passport.

The amount of work to carry out their plans was vast, but they eventually arrived, setting up an import-export company as their cover. There were various strands within their squad, one was known as the Siqueiros task force, and Ramon Mercader who was going to use his charm and personality to infiltrate Trotsky's villa, with a home loaned to him by a Mexican painter called Diego Rivera. Ramon had made it clear he was a businessman not interested in politics. There was a third reserve team under Joseph Grigulevich who cooperated with the Siqueiros group.

It was Grigulevich who by befriending a guard managed to have the gates opened in the early hours of 23 May 1940, allowing the Siqueiros task force to storm inside. It was claimed to be somewhat amateurish, because although they heavily machine-gunned Trotsky's bedroom he survived, as he had been fast enough to 'duck' under his bed, a seemingly obvious place had the attackers had the sense to blow the door open.

It was embarrassing for Beria, not so much because it failed, but because of the general state of nervousness and badly used codes, and more to the point Stalin heard of the failed attempt from the news agency TASS. Sudoplatov considered it essential to keep everything in place, so they had informants planted who could let them know what was happening in Trotskyite circles. Stalin, Sudoplatov believed, wanted Trotsky eliminated as the Trotsky-movement would lose momentum without him.

Ramon Mercader on social grounds found his way into Trotsky's room and managed to plunge a small pickaxe (normally used in climbing) into Trotsky who screamed for help. Trotsky was rushed to hospital but died the next morning. Mercader was arrested as Frank Jacson, a Canadian businessman, and persuaded his captors the attack was not political but a tangled love relationship with a person in Trotsky's household. Mercader spent the next twenty years in prison and 'kept the Stalinist faith throughout his years'.[3]

It was not until 1969 that Sudoplatov met Mercader again, and he learnt more details and how eventually Mercader's real identity and motives were later revealed, though Mercader always refused to admit he had killed Trotsky on orders from Soviet Intelligence. Later when Trotsky's son Lev Sedov died, the blame understandably was placed on the NKVD, but Sudoplatov always claimed it was not the case (p.83).

Following this operation, many of the operatives went into hiding and became useful as hidden sitting agents wherever they chose or were sent, and they were generally known as 'illegals'. This was useful for the NKVD Intelligence as many 'illegals' became trusted and became part of the fabric of various communities which could provide essential information. Eitingon in the USA was used to find out more about potential American communists and looking for Japanese and Chinese emigrants who might make useful recruits.

This amounted to a careful infiltration into many western communities constantly viewed as potential enemies by looking for sound information, not just about policies but also critical information. Sudoplatov mentioned Viktor Liagin working in the San Francisco area of the USA, who, for example, sent Moscow information on anti-magnetic devices to protect ships against mines.

This was the start of a vast development of having illegals learning to be acceptable to their community and trusted, being seen as 'one of us'. It was clever, professional, and much more widespread than any other activities carried out by other nations. The British, once famous for their knowledge of home and information from overseas, known as the SIS or MI5/MI6, appeared almost amateur, they tended to rely on diplomats and 'gentleman travellers' were asked to keep their eyes open. The NKVD was doing more than just watching, they were infiltrating areas of interest and were more acceptable than most because they could find, even if they were known to be Russian, some sympathy because of having fled Communist Russia, while for some contacts being communist was relevant. It was also a long-term programme as the illegals were often in place for years before they were needed or activated. Over such a long time of settling in they were frequently regarded as friendly and kind neighbours or colleagues, giving them sufficient time to garner considerable trust and confidence. Those who had been in Mexico slipped out of that country after Trotsky's murder, moving over the border into California and New Mexico where they settled down in various professions or businesses, and as planned became accepted as part of their selected communities and workforce. It was by these means the first contacts were made with Robert Oppenheimer and others involved in the experiments of the atomic bomb.

The Military Purges

Meanwhile in Moscow, Sudoplatov was watching the purges of leading military commanders taking place, most notably the most famous Marshal Nikolayevich Tukhachevsky, one time Red Army Chief of Staff and chairman of the Revolutionary Military Council, a highly significant figure. Years later when he wrote his memoirs Sudoplatov realised that the charges against Tukhachevsky and many other military men had been a total fabrication, and with the benefit of hindsight from a man who lived through this era, he came to several reasons why they fell from power. Sudoplatov felt they may have been compromised by German and Czechoslovakian disinformation, which did not take long to convince Stalin's characteristic suspicions of those of any standing. During the immediate post-First World War era when both Germany and Russia had been regarded as pariah states, they had worked together, especially when General von Seeckt was trying to restructure the German military after the restrictions of Treaty of Versailles. There had, almost inevitably, been a growing relationship between German and Soviet commanders. The second reason Sudoplatov suggested, and probably closer to the mark, was that Stalin felt that he had better theories and strategies than these commanders. The final reason he considered, was that Stalin and Tukhachevsky had a history of conflict over who should carry the blame over mistakes made during the Civil War and against Poland (p.88). Having reviewed the three possibilities and given thought to these denunciations, Sudoplatov claimed that at the later time of writing his memoirs, he believed none of these reasons. He recalled that Tukhachevsky had often disagreed with Marshal Voroshilov, a commander totally subservient to Stalin, and he further remembered that Beria had underlined a sentence in a document which read, 'the fall of Tukhachevsky decisively shows that Stalin rightly controls the Red Army' (p.89). Sudoplatov also adds that there was evidence that the files relating to Tukhachevsky seem to indicate that he was attempting to reshuffle the military leadership, but there was nothing about illicit contacts with the Germans. In summary, Sudoplatov appeared to have accepted that it amounted to a series of fairy tales of a more sinister nature with power cliques tussling while Stalin was ensuring he was the leader in total control, and no one should dare oppose his status. The questions and issues over these military purges continued for decades and have never been truly resolved apart from being able to identify Stalin's influence, and Sudoplatov later acknowledged there were probably no military plots at all.

In the meantime, Stalin was becoming pre-occupied with Soviet influence and control in the Baltic states, and he sent Boris Rybkin to bypass normal channels looking for a treaty, but it was turned down despite the offer of bribery, causing some disruption in the Finnish leadership. The Finns were trying to avoid becoming a Russian buffer state and leaned more towards the West and Germany. At this stage, a major war was becoming likely, and Sudoplatov in August 1939 heard that Donald Maclean then working in Paris, had reported that the British and French were not that happy to support Soviet Russia in a war against Germany.

Sudoplatov was surprised on hearing that Ribbentrop was in Moscow, learning that it was no sudden decision that these talks were taking place, which given his position should not have been a surprise. However, he wrote that 'the Kremlin leadership was ready for a compromise with any regime, provided it guaranteed stability for the Soviet Union. The first priority of Stalin and his aides was the fulfilment of their geopolitical aspirations to transform the Soviet Union into the largest superpower of the world' (p.96).

When Sudoplatov used the word 'superpower' it was because he was drafting his book well past the end of the Second World War. In 1939 Stalin was probably only looking for European domination, and Sudoplatov admitted that the secret protocol with Germany over the invasion of Poland came as a complete shock.

Stalin wanted to work with Germany while securing a Russian hold in the Baltic states. Sudoplatov was more reminiscent of the petty politics of the scheming within the Intelligence Service than the overall geopolitical situation. Secret messages were sent about progress in the Baltic region by Gukasov who had once challenged and suspected Sudoplatov's reliability. When Beria asked Sudoplatov's opinion about some of these messages he had no answer because he had not seen the scripts. Beria, being Beria was furious with Sudoplatov but when learning why turned his threatening vitriol on Gukasov. This whole episode underlined a weakness within the Soviet Intelligence system, where suspicion of closest colleagues led to machinations of intrigue. Sudoplatov became personally involved being flown directly to Latvia where he could work as Molotov's secret messenger, but eventually Soviet troops took control of that country as Russian and Germany worked out their delineations. Sudoplatov compared these agreements to the later situation in the Yalta Conference, when victorious leaders divided the spoils of war. When he returned Beria suddenly asked Sudoplatov to accompany him, which always caused most people some concern, but it was to a football match between Spartacus the trade union team and the NKVD team Dynamo. He accompanied Beria to his box to watch the match and found it full of the leading Party members. Sudoplatov kept his distance and out of conservations in such imposing company, but later realised it was Beria's way of telling him and others that Sudoplatov could be trusted, and a warning to men like Gukasov that the leading men trusted Sudoplatov.

The Molotov-Ribbentrop Pact had also facilitated the takeover of Western Ukraine and Soviet troops moved into Poland's Galicia. Sudoplatov's wife Emma was part of the team sent in to identify some of the more extreme nationalists. Ukraine was to be a long-time problem because Khrushchev was always identified with that area and believed he had a personal stake in its command and all operations. Sudoplatov rightly believed that the Molotov-Ribbentrop Pact had put an end to the Ukrainian Nationalist movement, but Khrushchev persisted in seeking possible culprits and telling Stalin that he was resolving the problem. This eventuated in a major clash between Beria and Khrushchev, with Sudoplatov overhearing a rampant and angry argument between these two senior Party members over the phone. This animosity between Beria and Khrushchev would last until 1953 when Stalin died, and Khrushchev emerged as the new leader eventually having Beria shot, but as noted in the previous chapter, both managed to conceal their mutual contempt even appearing as friends during the time of Stalin for mutual safety.

These internal machinations reached from the top of command down to the prison cells. Sudoplatov reminded Beria of a jailed agent called Pyotr Zubov imprisoned for failing to carry out a coup in Yugoslavia. While in prison he had been so badly tortured he had become a cripple, yet Sudoplatov convinced Beria to have him released because he could be useful in gaining the trust and information from Polish Colonel Stanislas Sosnowski, who was head of Polish Intelligence in Berlin. When the director the of Investigations Department heard of the request he objected until Beria threatened him. The plan worked, yet once again the internal conflict was almost unbelievable, as was it that an agent who had been so badly tortured was still willing to cooperate. The one decent event from these conflicting machinations was that Pyotr Zubov started work again outside prison and was allowed to retire, indicating that the quip of 'it's who you know that counts' was just as important in the Soviet Union as in any other form of society.

It emerged from Sudoplatov's memoirs that Chekhov's niece Olga reported to the NKVD, she was known to Göring, and the idea was floated of trying to assassinate Hitler by a team led by Boris Miklashevsky an illegal, who had arrived in Germany in December 1941. Miklashevsky was a boxing champion and posed as a defector from Soviet clutches. This was easily accepted as his uncle had arrived before but as a genuine defector, and this helped make him acceptable. It was not only a difficult mission, but Stalin suddenly turned against the mission on the grounds that if Hitler were killed his main Nazi cohorts would be purged by the military and there might be treaties signed with western powers. Boris Miklashevsky left for France after killing his uncle, and he spent the war years looking for possible leftovers of the renegade Russian army led by Colonel General A. A. Vlasov (p.116).

The Russian Failure over German Intentions

Even when he wrote his memoirs many years after the Second World War, Sudoplatov tended to ignore the general criticism that it was Stalin's fault that Operation *Barbarossa* caught him by surprise, having constantly ignored warnings from his own agents, and even from Churchill and others. Instead Sudoplatov placed the emphasis more on the failure of the Intelligence Service both in terms from where the Intelligence emanated, their failure to note the power of the German forces, as well as their policy of speed warfare now known as *blitzkrieg* war with its novel tactics. According to Sudoplatov, Stalin had even invited German commanders to view their military resources in order to drop a massive hint that they would survive even a long war. In April 1941, a German attaché accepted this invitation. Even their English spy Kim Philby reported that the British were virtually encouraging conflict between Germany and the Soviet Union.

Stalin suddenly turned his attention to Yugoslavia thinking it would be a useful move to overthrow their pro-German government, but Hitler soon attacked and as is well known was promptly successful in this Balkan region, which, as Sudoplatov noted, shocked everyone. Sudoplatov noted that it now dawned on some that Hitler never felt bound by any agreements even when they were signed. Stalin had believed because of his personal correspondence with Hitler that he could be trusted. It had been the same problem in Britain where the moral appeasement effort had floundered because few had managed to grasp the reality of the warped psyche of Adolf Hitler, and his driven passion to dominate Europe if not beyond at any cost. It is easy to project this view with the benefit of hindsight, but a British ambassador in Berlin, Sir Horace Rumbold (1928–1933), had bothered to read *Mein Kampf* and sent out the necessary warnings but was ignored. Sudoplatov later concluded that Hitler's idea of the Axis alignment of Germany, Japan, would include the Soviet Union, again making it clear they had either not read or had ignored *Mein Kampf* and Hitler's plan for *Lebensraum* (living space) in the east.

Sudoplatov recalled the time in May 1941 a German Junkers 52 had entered Russian airspace and landed in Moscow undetected, which caused a few heads to roll, but Stalin remained convinced that Hitler would not attack, and if he did the Russians had the forces to throw them back. The fact was, as Sudoplatov pointed out, that military conscription had not started until 1939, and the purges had eliminated many of the leading commanders. Nevertheless, Sudoplatov was aware that there was much coming and going to and from seeing the *Hozyain* (the master) and looking back at the various machinations prior to the sudden surprise of the Germans launching Operation *Barbarossa*, there were many fabricated accounts and reports to cover the embarrassment of being caught by surprise.

Operation Barbarossa

Sudoplatov was promptly appointed director of the Administration for 'Special Tasks' by Beria on 5 July 1941. He successfully asked for Eitingon as his deputy, not least because he was better acquainted with military matters, and he knew of the need to look into German occupied areas, organising illegals, disinformation units, and guerrilla warfare. As the months rolled by his department grew in size, always reporting back to Beria on every detail. Sudoplatov knew they needed as much professional help as possible, and he approached Beria about the release of some ex-Intelligence men then locked away in prison. Such was the sense of gathering urgency Sudoplatov noted that Beria's response was 'yes if he thought they were needed', the question of guilt or innocence was never raised, but a few he looked for had already been shot. Sudoplatov also took advantage of this by looking for those prisoners who had once been amongst his closest friends. Sudoplatov mentioned a few such men by name and some who died because of the nature of their work. When after the war Beria started to lose a grip on power and came under direct attack and arrest, he was accused of releasing friends, but he had managed to find someone higher up the ladder to sign for their release. Typically, in the Soviet system prisoners were released because they would be useful, as today it is rumoured that Russian prisoners can be released if they are willing to fight against Ukraine in Putin's war, and President Trump in his second term of office released those men who had stormed Capitol Hill after he lost the election. As is often the case it was swapping one danger for another, and Sudoplatov's accounts of these released men indicated they managed to work well for the state. They were, however, not only in danger from being caught by the Germans, but in severe risk from their own side even if they escaped, following Stalin's policy of being suspicious of men who surrendered and who then managed to return.

On 26 June 1941 Sudoplatov was made deputy chief of the NKVD for the role of combatting the German parachutists, who had played a role in the stunning move forward into Soviet territory. Sudoplatov arranged with others to dispatch guerrilla groups behind the lines and according to Sudoplatov they had some '212 guerilla detachments and units comprising 7,316 men to the rear of the enemy' (p.129). It was not just a matter of destroying enemy communications and resources, but seeking information for the Red Army. In one single scathing sentence Sudoplatov summarised the times when he wrote that 'this chapter in NKVD history is the only one that was not officially rewritten, since its accomplishments stood on their own merit and did not contain Stalinist crimes that had to be covered up' (p.130).

According to Sudoplatov their information sources discovered that Otto Skorzeny had been given the task of attacking the Allied conference in Tehran They claimed they had discovered this operation thanks to having infiltrated one of their agents (called Kuznetsov, code name *Pookh* [Fluff]) who had managed to pass himself off as a senior Lieutenant. He was fair-haired and blue eyed, which gave him a Germanic appearance which had proved useful. Later it was rumoured that he committed suicide with a hand-grenade when it appeared he had taken a step too far. They also had a Fourth Directorate dedicated to the railway war to block or hinder this form of communications. Another even more delicate and formidable task for Sudoplatov was for being responsible for laying mines in critical installations in Moscow itself, in the event of the Germans occupying the city. This task transpired to be ultra-delicate because when he was associated with the fall of Beria, it was proposed that some mines which had remote control facilities might still be used to kill those proposing to take Stalin's place as the Master. It must have been like working for an organisation which demands total obedience then condemning that person for supposedly working against them. There were two networks involved in this project in the event of German success. Again, the idea was mooted of assassinating Hitler if he ever arrived for a victory parade in Moscow.

Unlike most, Sudoplatov never detected a sense of panic in Stalin when Operation *Barbarossa* suddenly surged forward towards Moscow, but at this stage only the very top men knew what was going on, and they had to find Stalin in his Dacha and convince him to return to the leadership in the Kremlin. To enforce his point, Sudoplatov later entered into detail the way the well-known annual military parade took place in central Moscow even though the Germans were on the outskirts of the city, less than 30–50 miles away. Sudoplatov realised there was little danger of a Luftwaffe attack as the sky was heavily laden with heavy clouds and it was already snowing. Sudoplatov believed this performance ordered by Stalin revealed his sense of calmness and was giving the right message that the Germans would be stopped, indicating there would be an eventual Russian victory.

In terms of agents, they found a new and surprising candidate. This was Count Neledov who had been an officer in the Tsar's army, and he had been an agent for Canaris. He had been sent just before the war to Poland where he was captured with the Soviets finding him in Lvov prison. Neledov had worked for the Germans on testing how far their 'lightning war' tactics would be successful. Now advising the Soviets, Neledov was able to inform them that they knew this type of attack would only work if it were successfully rapid, which meant the seizure of 'Moscow, Leningrad, the Donbas, Kiev, and the Northern Caucasus, including the essential Baku oil fields' otherwise the operation would be deemed a potential failure (p.136). The reasoning, Sudoplatov noted was simple, that for a prolonged war the Germans had insufficient resources especially in terms of oil and gas.

Sudoplatov's next task was planting as many illegals in Western Europe as possible, running a network under diplomatic cover. Many of their previous efforts of this nature had disappeared for a variety of reasons, and there were even fears the Cambridge Circle of Five may have been compromised, but they were wrong. Sudoplatov set up the new system under difficult circumstances which became known as the Red Orchestra, but the German Gestapo and Himmler's SD were efficient in their work, and Sudoplatov had to admit many of his efforts were destroyed.

For some reason, undoubtedly built on long-term memory meant that Stalin found it difficult to trust the British, even though some of their Intelligence information was both accurate and informative. Sudoplatov and his 'comrades' were curious as to how the British were obtaining their accurate information, wondering where they had placed their illegals, whether they had a source in the heart of German command. Later in life, still uncertain, but he came to believe (correctly) that they had broken the Enigma code, and naturally they had needed this kept a total secret which they managed until long after the war. The Soviets had an agent called John Cairncross, associated with the Cambridge ring of spies, who might know something vague about Bletchley Park, but they still had doubts about the British wish to assist the Soviet Union, as they seemed to be 'rationing the information' (p.142), even though the Soviets had guessed the British were only protecting their source.

When their own Red Orchestra failed it was put down to the defection of an agent called Gurevich, who hotly denied this to be the case, but they badly needed a scapegoat. Even in 1958 Gurevich was re-arrested, and in 1990 it was still a point of contention. In 1991 his innocence was generally accepted, although he was not given any compensation and denied all rights to a pension. The sense of accusation and suspicion raised by Sudoplatov and many others, clearly demonstrated the lack of trust and personal suspicion of all operatives, which was pervasive within the services. Sudoplatov had to be the master of creating rumour and counter-rumour, even using the Bulgarian ambassador to spread the false rumour that Moscow might be seeking peace with Germany. It was for Sudoplatov, a matter of using disinformation to gather time for finding more resources. Such were the varied machinations of these fraught times that in 1953 some rebounded, and Beria was even accused of attempting to overthrow Stalin. Creating rumours needs nothing to be written or recorded, only word by mouth, total silence, absolute secrecy, and always potentially dangerous. As such, later Beria was not believed when he claimed that these rumours were demanded by Stalin himself, and Sudoplatov also found himself implicated.

During the war years Sudoplatov had been given a major task of finding the best 150 mountain climbers, and then Beria ordered Sudoplatov and Merkulov to fly with them to the Caucasus, with the idea of blocking mountain routes to hinder German troop movements, all these efforts being connected with the battle for Stalingrad. The operation worked to a degree by blowing up oil tanks and blocking passes, and the mountain climbers were good at the task, but they were not trained fighters. On his return Sudoplatov had to admit he lacked military training which made Beria angry, though he himself was in the same boat, and after the war Sudoplatov had to go on a military training course, and Merkulov was reprimanded by Stalin for being too close to the fighting. Whichever course one seemed to take, irate criticism still flooded in. Either way, after the battle of Stalingrad the Soviets knew that the tide had turned in their favour, and according to Sudoplatov, theatres opened again and life was more cheerful, and he and his wife and young family were able to move into Moskva Hotel because the heating in their home apartment was not working.

Sudoplatov noted that under Operation *Monastery* they started to play a counterintelligence operation against the Abwehr. It was a matter of finding an agent who could convince the Germans that he was trustworthy. To accomplish this, they thought of setting up a fictitious pro-German underground known as the Throne (*Prestoll*). If they could manage this, apart from disinformation, it was hoped it could help expose Russian collaborators. They had a man called Aleksandr known as Heine (and later Max) who pretended to be a Russia deserter. At first the Germans did not believe him, but after a few months they suddenly changed their minds and recruited him into the Abwehr with the task of setting up a spy ring in Moscow. They probably changed their minds because minimal research revealed he was a Russian émigré. Later American researchers believed that Max was a plant through German Intelligence via the émigrés, however, as Sudoplatov noted, Max was all the Germans' own work.

Despite the confusion, the Germans parachuted him back into Moscow, where he made prompt contact with NKVD Intelligence. He pretended that he had destroyed some railway connections near Gorky, and it was arranged in the Russian press to support this claim, which bolstered his value as far as the Germans were concerned. With one of those strange twists of fate, Max was given the German decoration of the Iron Cross, and the Soviets presented him with the Order of the Red Star (p.158). Max was given information to pass to his German masters, which was seen to be accurate to ensure they would believe him. One such example would have been considered immoral by many other Intelligence services. This occurred on the eve of the battle of Stalingrad, when the Germans were informed the Russians were about to launch an offensive in the North Caucasus, and even Marshal Zhukov leading this offensive was kept in the dark. Thousands of his men died under this order of Stalin transmitted by Max, and Sudoplatov saw this act of deceit as one of the main reasons for the Soviet victory at Stalingrad. It was also noted that the British, through the enigma machine, knew Max was in contact, and Blunt, Cairncross, and Philby played the messages back to the NKVD Intelligence, which for them was good news because it showed their disinformation operation was proving to be successful. It was not just Max, but by various radio tricks there were many deception games played.

It was at this stage the head of SMERSH Viktor Abakumov, proposed these operations had to be handed over to his organisation by higher command, with Sudoplatov agreeing once his own bosses permitted. Beria accepted this, but not with *Monastery* and some of their current ongoing deception games known as '*Couriers*'. This had involved Archbishop Ratmirov of the Russian Orthodox Church in Moscow, who had used novices as a means of infiltration. It was at this juncture that Stalin realised how important the Church could be, and in 1943 he permitted for the first time under the communist regime the election of a patriarch at a ceremony which Sudoplatov and his wife attended in person.

This had all worked to the Soviet advantage, but inhouse fighting continued with Abakumov warning Sudoplatov he would not forget this action which he had taken personally. This was the start of yet more friction, especially when Abakumov suddenly arrested Viktor Ilyin the Commissar of State Security without first referring, as was the Party Custom, to Ilyin's boss who happened to be Beria. This arrest destroyed Ilyin's career which may well have been a mere matter of inhouse fighting between major figures such as Beria and Abakumov. The complex intricacy of these leadership tussles involved many who were innocent. As Sudoplatov noted 'even in the war years, Stalin was obsessed with exercising his personal control over any institution he headed, in this case the Ministry of Defence' (p.163). These tensions were not just the bickering and interpersonal frictions common to many organisations, but they were vicious and dangerous to those caught up in these confrontations. Ilyin, according to Sudoplatov was caught up in interrogations from 1943 until 1947, constantly beaten in trying to force him to confess, and in 1951 he was transferred to another jail where he persisted in avoiding taking any side except to argue his total innocence. During this protracted interrogation and isolation, he gathered the war was over but never understood the changing of times, and later discovered his wife had married again because she had been under the impression he was dead. Without family, home, money, he found his way to work as a freight loader on the railways. After Stalin's death and Baria's fall he was 'rehabilitated' but with no pension, he retired in 1977 and died in 1990, a life torn apart by seniors in the Intelligence network he should have been able to trust.

The origin of Ilyin's disastrous life was Abakumov's effort to take personal control of Operation *Monastery* as part of SMERSH. Stalin felt obliged to step in and called Abakumov and Sudoplatov in to see him, instructing them to work together to give the Germans the impression that they were still able to hamper Soviet supply lines. It was at this time in Byelorussia, that the Red Army surrounded the Germans. This was Stalin's effort to encourage the Germans to try to break out, and with the help of Max mentioned above, managed to create a successful radio deception, and captured German Intelligence agents. Sudoplatov even toyed with the idea of recruiting Grand General Erich Raeder, then a prisoner of war, who was staying in Sudoplatov's dacha, but this came to nothing, and Raeder was required in Germany for the Nuremberg Trials. As for Sudoplatov he believed at the end of the war that Stalin had been the necessary and outstanding leader required.

Atomic Bomb Secrets

Sudoplatov admitted in his review concerning the Russian pursuit for a nuclear weapon, that much of the information came from scientists working on the subject in America, mentioning Robert Oppenheimer, Enrico Fermi, and Leo Szilard. He knew that they were working hard at this deadly weapon because of their fear that the Nazis should build one first with unquestionable consequences. He noted that Niels Bohr felt the same way and encouraged their concerns. When the Soviet scientists were asked their general opinion, it tended to be that a uranium bomb was possible, but only in theory. Some of this information occurred during 1940, but in 1941 Intelligence reports started to identify a wider interest in nuclear weapons not only in America, but Germany, Britain and even in Scandinavia. They also heard from Donald

Maclean (code-named *Leaf*) that the British were showing considerable interest in the research, and that it might well be developed within two years, and Maclean in September 1941, sent the NKVD Intelligence report of some 60 pages from the British Cabinet Committee on the 'Uranium Bomb Project' (p173).

In California Soviet Intelligence had Gregory Kheifetz, a resident in San Franscisco, busy recruiting agents who were ordered to make contact as well as neutralise the influence of White Russians within the American community, as they were an influence against the interests of the Soviet Union. It was Kheifetz who sounded the first warning of the amount of interest the Americans were showing in the proposed atomic bomb, not least the gathering together of many of the world's leading scientists, and Sudoplatov read all these Intelligence reports. Kheifetz also pointed out the huge financial resources the Americans were spending on this programme, which caught Beria's immediate interest. Kheifetz had the sort of attractive demeanour and personality which made it easy for him to make contact. He met Oppenheimer at a party and already had contact with Enrico Fermi. He discovered from Oppenheimer that as far as he and the team were concerned, the main issue was producing the bomb before the Nazis. He also revealed the fact that Albert Einstein had written to Roosevelt urging him of the necessity of using nuclear energy to make a bomb. Sudoplatov noted that Kheifetz knew better than trying to bribe a man like Oppenheimer, and so he befriended him as a person of similar thoughts and leanings. As a consequence of these reports the NKVD recruited another agent called Semyon Semyonov known as Sam with the code-name *Twain*, to pursue this matter further, and he proved able through his established connections to identify most of those who were involved in the project, later known as the Manhattan Project.

Sudoplatov was mainly engaged in guerrilla activity, but he was instructed to use his agents to try and discover whether the Germans engaged in nuclear research. Using Swedish contacts, they knew that the Germans were mainly occupied with rocket research, especially the V2 version, but they had an interest in 'heavy water', which Sudoplatov was told had something to do with nuclear research, but he found it all, understandably, confusing. It was a growing concern for the Soviets, especially when they learnt that

Niels Bohr had been joined by Lise Meitner who confirmed the feasibility of a uranium bomb. As early as March 1940 Beria had talked to Stalin about establishing a scientific consultative group to pursue this issue. This Special Committee on Atomic Energy was headed by Beria in 1942, and soon Sudoplatov was attached to this group as its director of Intelligence. It proved to be a contentious gathering, but Sudoplatov noted how Beria kept it under control.

It was known that the British were advancing their own project under the code-title of the *Tube Project*. The Soviets knew they needed Western help and even asked Bohr, then in London to help in Moscow. This did not work, but they knew he had already spoken to Roosevelt about sharing the project with the Russians (p.181). By the end of January 1943, they heard through their various reports that the first nuclear chain reaction had been successful, and within two weeks Stalin signed an order for a new committee to organise another to develop an atomic weapon as fast as possible. In many of the histories written about the Second World War many refer to Roosevelt's reaction to Stalin's lack of surprise when he told him of the successful Manhattan Project at an international conference, and perhaps Stalin should have pretended to be amazed instead of playing his usual power games.

Molotov was to be in charge of this committee, with Beria as his deputy looking for Intelligence. Molotov later gave way to Beria as he lacked the administration skills. When they told their own senior scientists, the team members promptly recognised it as Fermi's work even though Sudoplatov had hidden the name. It dawned on Sudoplatov, without him writing as such, that this was another closed world of science, and he explained this to Beria who agreed that for once they were reliant on the brains and experience of another type of profession. It was decided that there was no point in holding back information from them and to make a deliberate effort to treat them as friends. It was deemed critical that information from America would be invaluable, and Sudoplatov noted that by July 1943 their agents had provided them with some 286 classified documents on scientific research, but more was needed on the fission process and the reactors. In February 1944 Sudoplatov was ordered to report to Beria's office where he was appointed director of a new Department S, checking, and looking for Intelligence, and for a brief time it was known as the Sudoplatov Group, but not for long. He was also appointed as the Head of the Special Second Bureau of investigating a possible weapon through uranium fuel. Sudoplatov had never been a soldier, and he was certainly no scientist, and his involvement demonstrated the need for the Soviets to uncover what was happening elsewhere, especially in America. Sudoplatov was aware of this, even though he was still busy on guerilla activities. Nevertheless, some progress was made as they tried to penetrate Los Alamos and its various research laboratories. They had a theatre actor tour America with the purpose of pointing out that anti-Semitism under communism was outdated, which was important to a civilised person like Oppenheimer and many of his colleagues.

There is no question that these Soviet illegals or agents were excellent in their work, one agent's wife (Elizabeth Zarubin) was sociable, beautiful, and attracted attention and managed to attract many to the Soviet cause. She and others managed to convince Oppenheimer from not being seen as openly sympathetic to communism or even left-wing politics. They also persuaded him to share information with 'antifascists of German origin' (p.190) which enabled Klaus Fuchs (a German communist who had sought refuge in Britain in 1933) to go to Los Alamos, and with Fermi they even planted moles there and other valuable areas, which increased the amount of information being found. Sudoplatov spent a considerable time in his reflections regarding the diverse types of agents they were able to use. After the war many had to flee as soon as possible once the FBI became curious about the leaks, the classic example well known today, was that of Julius and Ethel Rosenberg who settled in London running a bookshop and still assisting Russian Intelligence. They were arrested (with another agent Gordon Lonsdale) in 1950, having been given false New Zealand passports which had enabled them to make it to London, and were sentenced to 20 years.

The Soviet agents were also able to point out that not all was well within the American venture, with sharp divergences of opinion. There was political infighting among some, clashes between some of the scientists, and also within the American bureaucracy. Oppenheimer and some others wanted scientific knowledge and discovery to be made public and not a hidden private asset, coming into conflict with a General Groves. Oppenheimer was therefore becoming aware of the gathering storm of political interests, and he suggested that a way had to be found to transit the information in a way that it could not be traced back to anyone involved directly with the Manhattan project. Thereafter much of the information came through oral sources who eventually sent five classified reports. It was and is still generally believed that Oppenheimer had no sense of nationalism but always thought on a global scale, that science was not a hidden or occult movement and should be shared. Sudoplatov claimed, probably correctly, that Oppenheimer saw both the good and bad sides of nuclear power. Fermi and Bohr also stood against violence, hoping if all nations had access to the knowledge, they believed it would create its own sense of a balance of power which has worked to this day (2025), but with most human beings hoping they were still right. Bohr remained constant in his views. Sudoplatov was also noticing that some of the Russian scientists were thinking along the same lines, and it was conjectured that perhaps the time had come for overtures to be made to the Western Powers to agree to work together on such a formidable weapon. As noted above Bohr had already mentioned this issue to the American President, but Sudoplatov had been informed that Churchill was bitterly opposed to such an idea.

Meanwhile Russian Intelligence was gaining American information and wider knowledge, but in producing the Soviet bomb, the Soviets were suffering from the usual inhouse fighting problems. A useful agent was Zarubin, and his wife mentioned above, but a subordinate Lieutenant Colonel Mironov wrote to Stalin denouncing him as a double agent because he had been following him and seen him talking to American contacts. Zarubin was recalled to Moscow and underwent a trial in which he could show that all these American contacts were part of his team. It was Mironov's turn to be recalled when it was decided he was schizophrenic, discharged from the service and sent to a hospital. When another agent (Vasilevsky) went to the Russian embassy for a specialist to transmit his coded message he was not there, but he turned up later in the hands of the local police for being drunk. Not everything ran to plan with human fallibility from the bottom to the top of any structure.

Despite these human 'ups and downs' by January 1945 Soviet Intelligence had a description of the first atomic bomb. The next step of looking to the future was where to find the invaluable commodity of uranium. Thanks to captured German documents, a site was found not far from Sofia in Bulgaria, and a Soviet Bulgarian mining company was soon formed, and as Sudoplatov noted, it gave a steady supply for their first bomb in 1949.

In February 1945 Beria was supplied with an up-to-date summary of all the progress made, including details about all the American centres. Sudoplatov and Beria were made aware from two sources of the first assembly of the atomic bomb, increasing Stalin's sense of urgency for the Russians to have the same weapon. Sudoplatov noted that 'the information we received from our sources in America and Britain was extremely valuable in enabling us to develop our own atomic programme' (p.200). When the Americans dropped their bomb on Hiroshima (6 August 1945) the Soviets rapidly reorganised their atomic project with Beria appointed Chairman of the new Special State Committee. Sudoplatov recalled there were two Russian schools of physics, one led by Ioffe and another around Kaptisa, and Beria ordered everyone to stay friendly with both units. Sudoplatov's closeness to Beria opened his eyes to the fact that Soviet policy was looking beyond the war with Nazi Germany to the postwar future in terms of foreign policy and national security. By November 1945, the first Soviet reactor had been built, but it was hindered by various problems, not least an accident with the plutonium, and it felt that more help or information from abroad was essential. They decided to seek Bohr's help who was unsure to start with but proved willing to talk with the Soviet scientists.

By 1946 Beria decided the time had come to halt contacts with their American sources as the FBI appeared to be becoming too close to their various contacts. It was, Sudoplatov noted, a time of change as Germany was no longer the threat, and he believed the Americans wanted to keep the atomic secret to be used as a form of political blackmail. There were political differences between the scientists about nuclear power being used as a weapon, the need for a balance in this power, and the need for science to be shared. Some of the leading atomic scientists such as Bohr, Fuchs, Fermi, Oppenheimer, and many others shared this view. It was a significant moment as this new research was not only a different study area for science but was potentially world changing. It was, as Sudoplatov noted, a 'new era' (p.209).

A new form of undercover activity took place as the Soviets tried to work out the production of uranium which led to calculations about how many bombs the Americans had, later how many missiles, and the new balance of power was based on whether America had sufficient atomic weaponry to destroy Russia which was always difficult to verify. Sudoplatov pointed out that when Truman thought of the possibility of using the atom bomb to resolve the Chinese Civil War (1947–48), Stalin provoked the Berlin Crisis (the famous airlift) to divert attention from China so the Western powers knew they would be contending with Russia and China. It was clear that Stalin was interested in a Sino-Soviet axis to thwart the West.

There was still anxiety because when the Russians had exploded their first bomb in 1949 the Western press announced it before the Soviet Union, and it caused problems with the possibility of Western moles. As it transpired, it was by measuring the level of radioactivity in the air which caused the news to break which, as Sudoplatov noted, was almost a relief. The bomb was successful, but as Sudoplatov wrote, 'without the Intelligence contribution there could have been no Soviet atomic bomb that quickly' (p.211). Typically, of the Soviet system, Sudoplatov recalled that during these early years of postwar tension there were investigations and court trials about mistakes made by the agents and even charges of betrayal. They had the information to enable them to make a bomb because of the Intelligence network, but distrust and suspicion remained a major feature, often looking for scapegoats when some of their informants were exposed by the Americans and British. There were investigations as to how codes had been broken. It was believed the British had broken Enigma, the famous German code – supposedly an impossible task – and a Soviet code clerk called Igor Guzenko had defected in Canada in September 1945, it was also known that some of their code books had been seized by the Germans: they were early codes, but could reveal the methods of thinking and the necessary system processes.

The Soviets played the vital role in the destruction of Nazi Germany, the Americans gave them essential resources, the Royal Navy transported them across the dangerous Arctic waters, but it has to be admitted that Russian numbers, determination, and cunning in the bitter Eastern War, known by the Russians as the Great Patriotic War, was decidedly significant. The war was won because Russia, America, and Britain became allies against a common foe, and although on the surface all appeared well, there was still the mutual political distrust. Churchill might sit, smoke, and drink with Stalin and all appeared amenable in photographs, but the Cold War already had its roots in the closing years of the Second World War. Sudoplatov had noted that America could use the atomic weapon as a threatening means to gain dominance. There is no doubt that Stalin also wanted the same means to be a superpower. The atomic age had arrived, and due to Soviet Intelligence, the Soviets soon caught up with the Western powers.

The Cold War

Sudoplatov claimed the Cold War started when Soviet Russia freed Eastern Europe from occupation and the Yalta agreement for multi-Party elections. Sudoplatov recalled both Beria and Molotov claiming that coalition governments would not last long. Sudoplatov also noted that while Stalin had long been attacked for aligning himself with Hitler in 1939, the same principles of dividing other countries happened at Yalta with bargaining processes constantly under discussion. Roosevelt through his well-known confidant Harry Hopkins was insisting Russia rid itself of Comintern and have some form of rapprochement with the Orthodox Church. Nearly all these requests were met as the new World Order was planned. Sudoplatov believed Roosevelt and Churchill to be naïve in these particular matters, as he knew that their demands for Poland and other areas would be more on their minds and decided by power structures. Sudoplatov knew that the Red Army, and in many areas the local communists already had a powerful grip because of their determined resistance and guerilla war against the Nazis. Sudoplatov noted the Soviets could be flexible because the various governments in exile could achieve little. He even met Averell Harriman the American Ambassador in an attempt to ascertain American thinking, while also knowing the Soviets were already carrying through various machinations in Poland to ensure it came under Soviet control. He had private meals with Harriman which were all taped so they could listen later to try and detect any necessary information, later making the interesting comments that 'some 80 per cent of Intelligence information of political matters comes not from agents but from confidential contacts' (p.230).

Curiously, Sudoplatov noted that originally it had been Soviet Russia's intention to participate in the Marshall Plan. The first news of the Soviet rejection which Sudoplatov picked up was on hearing of a warning sent by Donald Maclean, claiming the first goal of the Marshall plan was the American economic domination of Europe, which Sudoplatov explained as the future disparity between the economics of Eastern and Western Europe. As always, another concern was that they were still slightly suspicious about the Cambridge Five wondering and concerned that Aleksandr Orlov had influenced them. As far as the Soviets felt, the Marshall Plan was supposed to be a substitute for the repayment of reparations by Germany, which Russia desperately needed to restore their economy.

In the meantime, Moscow was deeply concerned in manipulating communist power bases in Eastern Europe, some more easily coped with than others. Sudoplatov quoted Bulgaria with General Ivan Genarov (who had worked for Sudoplatov) telling him in the 1970s 'that Bulgaria is the only Socialist country without any dissident in the West because we ourselves learned the lesson from you and wiped them out before they were able to escape to the West' (p.233). It was not the same in other countries, and Sudoplatov was sent to Prague where he had to ensure that Edvard Beneš took himself off to London transferring power to the communist Klement Gottwald, all under the instructions of Molotov.

Times were rapidly changing not only in Europe but in the Soviet Union. Sudoplatov headed the Fourth Directorate but circumstances and even names were being changed. The NKVD became the MVD, the Ministry of Internal Affairs, the MGB, People's Commissariat for State Security, and the Cold War were all taking shape. Molotov was basically trying to tidy up the various and many departments and wanting a more centralised Intelligence system, but Sudoplatov was disenchanted by these moves. People were suddenly moved for the slightest reasons, such as in June1946, Merkulov was dismissed as Minister of State Security based on the extraordinary excuse there had been traffic jams during a May Day demonstration in Moscow. The traditional in-house fighting for power status was still prevalent, and Abakumov summoned Sudoplatov and Eitingon and informed them that Stalin had ordered him that he had to work with these two, which he had once promised himself he would never do. This attitude pleased Sudoplatov, but he was soon summoned with Eitingon in a study of criminal mistakes made and they were both accused of 'criminal manipulations' which Sudoplatov hotly denied. In July 1946, when he took his first holiday with his wife and children in Riga, he was aware that when he returned, he would still be a target of Abakumov. In September 1946, the Central Committee appointed him 'Director of Special Bureau Number One for Diversions and Intelligence, under the Ministry of State Security' (p.248) and he hoped that he and Abakumov could now keep out of one another's way. He was wrong as Abakumov suddenly phoned and demanded to know why Sudoplatov's sons were planning Stalin's murder. Sudoplatov must have experienced a sense of joyful reaction when he told him about these would be assassins, that his youngest son was three and the eldest five. The phone was slammed down the other end and he did not hear from Abakumov for another year. In reading this account it seemed to underline the dangers of organisational fragility caused by power-seeking causing venomous personal animosity.

Sudoplatov's main tasks of investigations were by penetrating military bases in Norway and France and even looking into their old Soviet networks in the Western world, to see if they were worth re-activating. The Soviets were mainly concerned as to how rapidly American forces could appear in Europe if Cold War tensions inside Europe erupted. Everything had to be handled with delicate care and Sudoplatov recalled arguing against supplying their agents with explosives made in the USSR. He also clashed with Abakumov who, with Molotov, wanted Orlov tracked down, with Sudoplatov reminding them that Stalin had not pressed this matter, and the Central Committee had therefore forbidden such an action. However, during the years of 1951–2 they were instructed to look into subversive plans to destroy American ammunition warehouses and infiltrating as many military bases as possible, everything was based on the perceived dangers or threats of NATO.

Closer to home the Ukrainian issues had returned vigorously. Khrushchev had demanded the 'liquidation' (murder) of A. Shumsky and other leaders of the Ukrainian nationalists. Abakumov, knowing Sudoplatov was an expert in this area, and a Ukrainian, demanded he traced the whereabouts of Shumsky, and it had to be a medical death or accident. Sudoplatov spent time in his memoirs on the Ukrainian Uniate church as it was subordinated to the Vatican, reminiscing on the role of the church in Ukrainian history. He was under the impression that the Vatican was trying to arrange British and American support, leading Khrushchev to call for some ecclesiastical liquidations. There was a scurry of Soviet activity to try and bring Ukraine more fully under the Soviet umbrella, which under a fresh style of Russian government is still ongoing in 2026. Khrushchev was a leading figure but concerned that Stalin's demand for Ukrainian independence had to be fully investigated. Sudoplatov as a Ukrainian noted that 'the Ukraine had never been an independent state, but I still think of myself as a Ukrainian who contributed to the buildup of this partnership within the union', adding that 'the Ukraine's strength within the union was the prelude to its ability to become an independent state after the collapse of the Soviet Union' (p.259).

He also became involved from as early as 1946 with the Kurdish issues, contacting the Kurdish leader Mullah Mustafa Barzani, with the Kurdish background being one of rebelling against Persia, Iraq, and Turkish rule always offering the Kurds help from Russia. The Soviets, Sudoplatov admitted, were happy to continue with help because it was a means to destabilise Western influence in the Middle East. Sudoplatov recognised that the Kurdish leader Barzani fully understood that their influence and progress depended on their opportunities to manipulate the superpowers with their various interests within their geopolitical areas. As Sudoplatov recalled it was never seen as a humanitarian issue but their access to the oilfields was a dominant factor, and often the Kurds were manipulated, as they were just a pawn in the complexities of Middle East politics.

Sudoplatov Reflects

As his massive tome of recollections drew to an end, Sudoplatov started to look back at events in a more reflective style. He referred to the well-known figure of Raoul Gustaf Wallenberg the Swedish diplomat. Today he is regarded as a well-known major humanitarian who saved thousands of Jews in German occupied Hungary, by offering protective passports and giving them shelter and means of escape. During the siege of Budapest by the Soviet Army, Wallenberg was arrested. Wallenberg was widely known, and much admired for his courage and humanitarian attitudes, but while under Soviet arrest this highly moral man simply disappeared.

Sudoplatov knew the Soviet Intelligence had been interested in the Wallenbergs, as they were looking for influential contacts, but the man Raoul meant little to him at the time. From this Sudoplatov rightly started to see that Wallenberg's arrest was no accident, not least because of the Swedish diplomat's helping of Jews, because Stalin was 'playing' with the idea of settling Jews in the Crimea as part of his political balancing game with the Western powers. During the postwar years Wallenberg's disappearance became a matter of interest and embarrassment for the Soviets because he was widely becoming known as a 'good man'. Sudoplatov from the nature of his contacts and inside knowledge knew that he had been in two prisons in Moscow, Lefortovo and the cells of the Lubyanka. The particular cells Wallenberg had been in were almost luxurious, but as Sudoplatov noted, they were dangerous, because the inmates were either recruited or murdered, in Soviet language liquidated. Sudoplatov explained that behind these rooms was a toxicological laboratory run by Professor Grigori Moiseyevich Maironovsky, a biological scientist, and it was believed by Sudoplatov that it was this man who killed Wallenberg with a toxic injection, easily administered on the grounds that it was for medical health.* There was no autopsy, and the body was cremated in Moscow's only crematorium (Donskoi) where Sudoplatov speculated Beria and Yezhov also disappeared. Long after the war various documents have come to light, many of the documents however were officially lost, and the excuse was the usual one that no one had any idea of his fate, trusting it would be lost in the vagaries of war, and accepted that he had perished unnoticed in Hungary. Later it was announced that Wallenberg had died from a heart attack, then Khrushchev suddenly announced he had been unlawfully arrested by the Minister of State Security Abakumov, who had been removed from office in 1951, and after Stalin's death was executed in 1954. In 1991, President Gorbachev demanded an investigation which indicated that Wallenberg had died in prison, but the files were missing. In the following year Wallenberg's diplomatic passport and his other personal files were accidently discovered in the KGB archives.

It was an appalling national embarrassment, but Sudoplatov also raises another national embarrassment over the Katyń massacres near Smolensk,

---

* Maironovsky was arrested in 1951 on charges involving the Zionist conspiracy, sentenced to ten years, he hoped Beria would have him released after Stalin's death, but Beria was shot, and he was kept in jail until 1961. He had admitted that he had 'liquidated' many people under Stalin's orders.

and it was, according to Sudoplatov, in 1992 that Beria's letter to Stalin was found suggesting that Polish officers and other potential leaders should be executed. From before the Nuremberg Trials many suspected that this had been a Soviet and not a Nazi massacre, but like the problems of Allied carpet bombing it was sidelined and not mentioned in public. The writer of this book when travelling as a guest of the Soviet government in Russia in the late 1970s when Brezhnev was holding power, mentioned the Katyń massacres causing a busy room to virtually fall silent, necessitating a diplomatic change of subject. It took another twenty years before the truth was admitted. Sudoplatov claimed he knew nothing of the incident at the time, only the commotion which followed years later.

In terms of Professor Grigori Moiseyevich Maironovsky (mentioned above) acting as a scientific killer on orders, Sudoplatov mentioned several occasions when he was called in by the professor to ensure some deaths were seen as accidents or medical issues, assuming no blame for his part because like others he had only been obeying orders, not making the necessary decisions. He had ignored the Nuremberg Trial evaluation that blind obedience to a criminal order was wrong. However, in reflecting on these problems, he wrote 'the legacy of these tragic events must be taken into account in the making of future policies. History shows that no top-secret decisions, no secret crimes, or terrorist plans, can be concealed forever. This is one of the great lessons of the breakdown of the Soviet Union and Communist Party rule. Once the dam is broken, the flood of secret information is uncontrollable' (p.284). He does not however, refer to the fact that many of these deeds were illegal and by most estimates immoral, and that the attempt to keep them secret was an acknowledgement of this viewpoint.

Sudoplatov moved onto his recollections of Stalin's sudden bout of postwar anti-Semitism, in which he provided some interesting insights, and because he was married to a Jew with some of them being close friends and agents, not least Leonid Eitingon, this obviously felt much more personal for him. Despite these factors he wrote that 'contrary to widespread reports that anti-Semitism was Stalin's main reason for the persecution of Jews, I regard anti-Semitism as Stalin's weapon but not his determining strategy' (p.285). Later Sudoplatov heard that Stalin's strategy was to stimulate a plan for creating a Jewish homeland in the Crimea, and in March and April 1944 some 150,000

Crimean Tatars were moved to Uzbekistan. Sudoplatov painted a confusing situation of the motives behind this, which was not surprising given that Stalin's main consultant was Stalin himself, and he was prone to switch directions at any moment. Sudoplatov picked up from Beria that the idea came from American organisations. The war against Germany had helped Soviet Jews because their individual expertise and labour was required, and as with the Church, any bias was placed aside to ensure Nazi destruction. This was the origin of the well-known Jewish anti-Hitler campaign and the Jewish Anti-Fascists. Sudoplatov added that the Crimean Jewish Republic was really a lure to find American capital, leading to the term 'California in Crimea'. Averell Harriman (American Ambassador) and Eric Johnston of the American Chamber of Commerce met Stalin and rosy pictures of the future were painted. However, once the fall of Nazi-Germany was clear Stalin switched his approach from a Jewish Republic to just another administration district, and many American approaches were rebuffed.

Stalin was changing his strategy and therefore his tactics. His approach this time was more global and being aware that Britain held a mandate over Palestine, he pretended the idea was to help his British Allies over the problem of settling Jews in Palestine, but the British and Americans, probably detecting Stalin's changes of mind, worked together without Russia, which the Soviets found irritating, making them determined on creating problems for the Western Powers in the Middle East. Sudoplatov's task was to find the necessary agents for infiltrating the Stern organisation which was an anti-British terrorist group running since about 1937. Stalin was setting a pattern of causing disruption in the Middle East and stimulating dissension and challenging Western influence.

Sudoplatov suggested that because Stalin was annoyed by being dropped by the Western powers over Jewish discussions, it was probably this factor which turned him towards his anti-Semitic campaign, which eventually became the infamous Doctors' Plot with investigations into supposed Zionist conspiracies. Abakumov as Minister of State Security accused the Jewish Anti-Fascist Committee of their own nationalist propaganda. Eitingon, as noted Jew, told Sudoplatov that he had seen his Jewish relatives dismissed from their posts, even those who worked in the upper echelons of the medical world, and that anti-Semitism was an essential ingredient of Stalin's policy, with Sudoplatov later in life admitting that his friend's perceptions were better than his own.

There was, as Sudoplatov noted, some shifting on internal powers once again as Stalin played his manipulative games. Malenkov was demoted and Beria stripped of his position on state security. The war, for Stalin, had changed from beating Nazi Germany to opposing his one-time Allies, consolidating his grip on Eastern Europe, and undermining British influence in the Middle East by helping the Arab states. Later in life Sudoplatov wrote that one of Molotov's assistants claimed that Stalin had said 'Let's agree to the establishment of Israel. This will be a pain in the ass [sic] for the Arab states and will make them turn their backs on the British. In the long run it will totally undermine British influence in Egypt, Syria, Turkey, and Iraq' (p.296). Stalin then turned his venom on those who knew too much about the original idea of a Jewish Republic in the Crimea, and some were killed (Mikhoels) and dressed up as accidents. At a personal level, Sudoplatov had been more wrapped up with the Berlin crisis and working on a Kurdish guerrilla network, but he was pleased that his Jewish wife Emma had been ill and he therefore retired with the rank of Lieutenant Colonel.

These 'Stalinesque' machinations resulted in the anti-Semitic Doctors' Plot transforming into a power struggle and settling the old scores of the leadership, which was a prelude to the tussle for power on Stalin's death. The Doctors' Plot supposedly started with a letter to Stalin from Lydia Timashuk accusing Jewish doctors of mistreating Party members. It was known that this letter was rejected by Stalin, but resurfaced years later as providing an excuse. It must have seemed like living in a minefield and not being able to trust even those who worked in the same office, let alone the same department. It is now known that Malenkov and Beria's main goal was the removal of Abakumov by whatever means possible. The rising figure of Mikhail Ryumin (MGB Investigation Department later Deputy Minister of Security) found criminal charges against Abakumov who denied any guilt, and when Abakumov resisted under torture he was still held while others confessed readily about him hoping for release or a quick death. In the meantime, Stalin ordered the arrest of all senior ranking Jewish military from colonels to generals. It was developing into a major purge directed by the MGB. At one stage Ryumin was on the point of charging Eitingon, but

Sudoplatov took his friend's file of activities from the death of Trotsky to the current day which helped for a time, but Beria himself was being explored because of his possible Jewish ancestry. Ryumin was eventually fired by Stalin (12 November 1952) for not being thorough enough in his job.

It took Stalin's death before it could be said the Doctors' Plot ended, but it had created damage, a sense of fear, and later Khrushchev continued the policy to a more limited extent. It was an excuse for Beria's loss of power, but looking back clearly indicated that the communist Stalin was as cruel, manipulative, power driven, and as a totalitarian leader was as dangerously autocratic as Adolf Hitler.

Sudoplatov's recollections drew to a close as he commented on Stalin's final years, starting by pointing out that the leader was determined to put new people into power 'to maintain his supremacy by setting up rival groups' (p.310). This included denigrating military commanders who had been successful during the war years, including the famous and popular Marshal Zhukov. Investigations were started to seek out why mistakes had happened, why accidents occurred resulting in many executions as advised by Abakumov. Zhukov was a main target on the grounds of his popularity with Stalin accusing him of 'lack of modesty' and 'overweening personal ambition' (p.311) which from Stalin's perspectives were danger signals, as it intimated a possible rival. Abakumov busied himself arresting Zhukov's generals in Germany on all sorts of charges often based on theft. Some senior men were even shot having been taped by hidden listening devices, with two generals (Grigori Kulik and Nikolai Rebalchenko) being shot as late as 1950. The whole atmosphere during these years was, in Sudoplatov's words 'a sea of suspicion' (p.318).

During Stalin's final years Sudoplatov wrote of the gathering of a small circle of leadership with such figures as Malenkov, Bulganin, Khrushchev, and Beria, with Stalin stimulating rivalry between them. Sudoplatov noted that Beria came under suspicion as early as 1951, his mother's house was monitored for conversations, and as always, his Mingrelian origins and his early years continuously came under suspicion, and evidence was slowly accrued under Stalin's orders. When Beria's son Sergei was considering marrying Stalin's daughter Svetlana, Beria was unhappy about the prospect because in the event of Stalin's death, which for the more astute was on the near horizon, this possible marriage with ties to Stalin would not help him in his future.

The moves against Beria started on the fringes with people close to him, and because of his popularity in helping to organise the Russian atomic bomb, Stalin was even more wary of his once closest confident. Beria was still being feted and admired, but he was shrewd enough to know that he was becoming a target, especially when many of his friends were arrested, and the so-called Mingrelian plot was being investigated. Many of Sudoplatov's personal observations, especially the so-called Leningrad Case have been noted in the chapter on Beria, but are mentioned again to indicate how much Sudoplatov knew what was happening. Nobody was safe in these closing years of Stalin's life, even Abakumov was coming under suspicion, probably because he was seen as being too powerful. Both Sudoplatov and his wife were becoming concerned for their own safety as they were continuously surrounded by senior people being arrested, and this was happening to all grades of officialdom around them.

Nevertheless, Sudoplatov appeared safe as he was engaged in looking into Intelligence strongholds in America and wherever their military bases were. However, his later memories tended to focus more on internal matters, his shock on seeing Stalin appearing old and tired, the movement of personnel around him, and the arrest of many contemporaries. There were rumours that the sickening Stalin already had suffered two strokes, and Sudoplatov was well aware of the tussle for power even during his work of seeking Intelligence on both American and Chinese moves. He was called to meet Stalin where in a lengthy interview and discussion Stalin made it clear he wanted the wayward Tito assassinated as soon as possible, but before Sudoplatov could make plans he heard that Stalin had died. Sudoplatov decided his main task was for him to now stand clear and find work in safer areas outside the Security Ministry.

The curious aspect is that Sudoplatov tended to admire Stalin, writing that 'at the time of his death and funeral, my grief for Stalin was sincere; to my mind, his atrocities were merely mistakes committed with the participation of his incompetent ministers' (p.340). He stated this even with the knowledge that his trusted friend Eitingon had been arrested on charges relating to the Zionist conspiracy along with others who had served Stalin with total obedience.

Beria had survived Stalin and was now amongst the trusted leading cabal, at least on the surface, and ordered Sudoplatov to start freeing many who had been unfairly arrested, especially over the so-called Doctors' Plot. Sudoplatov quoted Russia's chief archivist, Rudolf Pikoya, who wrote in 1993, 'Russian historians do not know postwar history. We lived in the epoch but had no idea what was going on. Even specialists in this period did not know much' (p.346). This was an accurate summary of the postwar years as secrets were kept and either taken to the grave for the sake of personal security or those involved were executed before having the chance to speak or write. There were no written official reports kept of such meetings, and even when the KGB archives were opened in later years much had already disappeared or had not been deposited in the first place.

Sudoplatov had a kindlier view than most of the new emerging Beria. He tended to see Beria as a reformer trying to correct some of the misdeeds carried our during the Stalin regime. To others, Beria was proving to be as cunning as usual and was setting out a platform which offered a better future which meant sharp changes, not, it has been argued, for the betterment of the world, but to ensure Beria stood out in the world as the man who should either lead or be amongst the top leaders. Later in life even Sudoplatov had to acknowledge this viewpoint was valid, writing 'we now know that even this wave, which seemed to us like a benign correction of past mistakes, was motivated by a reshuffle of the leadership balance of power, in Beria's favour' (p.351).

This power now rested in the Bureau of the Presidium and its last session with Stalin present was in October 1952 with Stalin, Malenkov, Beria, Khrushchev, Bulganin, Saburov, Pervukhin, and Ignatiev. In April 1953, after Stalin's death on 5 March 1953, Beria exposed Stalin and Ignatiev for their role in fabricating the Doctors' Plot, mainly because Ignatiev had been one of Beria's major enemies, but rumours continued to circulate in this torrid atmosphere of Beria's Jewish background. Sudoplatov recalled during these years how Beria's personal behaviour changed, with him talking rudely and personally to his colleagues in the Presidium, especially Khrushchev, which was quite different from the Beria of Stalin's time. During the critical year of 1953 Sudoplatov's personal position was unclear, finding he was being suggested for a series of posts, which he thought was due to some simply wanting him out of the way. Speculatively this may have been because it was known that the dreaded Beria and his closest cohorts had files on everyone, and Sudoplatov because of the nature of his work may for many have been seen as knowing too much. Various old colleagues and friends were suddenly being interrogated, causing Sudoplatov a degree of growing concern as these undercurrents of rife suspicion in the tussle for power grew, and even Abakumov found himself in jail. Meanwhile Beria in his effort to be seen as a positive reformer released those who had been caught up in the Doctors' Plot, and gave an amnesty for minor criminal offenders, the latter of which, according to Sudoplatov did not help his effort to be seen in a better light as street criminality suddenly increased. Beria did, however, manage to close the lid on the Mingrelian persecution and released those who had been arrested.

Meanwhile Sudoplatov was working more closely with the military over what they deemed to be the major threat of American power, with Sudoplatov arguing the key for success was cutting supply lines and disrupting communications. He even consulted Marshal Golovanov as to how the various NATO bases could be attacked. He noted that in May 1953 Beria ordered the first test of an American hydrogen bomb, solely on his authority as first deputy prime minister. He did this without consulting his government colleagues, and for them he appeared to be stepping out of line with his suggested policy of German unification, suggesting that Germany would offer a balancing act between the two superpowers. However, there was a growing feeling of discontent and rebellion in East Germany, mainly caused, according to Sudoplatov by Beria's policy. This was highly unlikely because the unrest was basically caused by the economic misery and many, including farmers and other critical members of that part of Germany, were fleeing west in their droves. The Red Army crushed the revolt (on Beria's orders according to Sudoplatov) and Beria's policy was seen as a failure, as was his attempt to win over Yugoslavia by a form of reconciliation with Tito. Beria was also looking into a change in the Hungarian leadership. He was trying to show himself as the main policy holder of many areas, including control of what was called the Eastern European Bloc.

His Arrest and Trial

Sudoplatov on returning from a family holiday found tanks and soldiers everywhere and wondered what was happening. He met Leonid Eitingon and felt there was another purge happening, then heard that Beria had been arrested for anti-government actions. He later realised this had all been the result of the power struggle by the leading members of government, the Presidium, in trying to confirm their top man. Sudoplatov heard from his brother and sister that the purge was wider than the top men who were being arrested, and he and his wife became concerned for their own safety. Later he realised that Khrushchev was the key 'string puller' (p.372) in all that was suddenly happening. Sudoplatov pointed out much later that Khrushchev's memoirs concerning Beria were not convincing, as Beria had not set out to seize power and overthrow the collective government. How far Sudoplatov's judgement on this issue is true remains somewhat doubtful, not that Khrushchev was any better, as in 1952 the post of General Secretary of the Party was abolished leaving Khrushchev first amongst equals with the greater ability for manipulating power.

As the charges against Beria were building, even going as far back as his activities during the civil wars, Sudoplatov was doing his best to continue as if none of this was his concern. He went to work every day, mainly sitting at his desk, but was soon called for interviews, many concerning his work with Beria, and the question of whether Beria had sought peace negotiations with the German Nazis based on territorial concessions. Sudoplatov was questioned on NATO bases, but then suddenly the clock was turned back, and he was asked about secret liquidations, which Sudoplatov answered by pointing out that Stalin had directly ordered all such events. The interview appeared to end favourably with the plan that he would be given the task of liquidating the Bandera leadership of the Ukrainian fascist movement in Western Europe. However, his younger brother (Konstantin) soon told him his name had appeared on notes to do with the interrogation of Beri and others, but Sudoplatov decided that whatever he would fight to the end.

This was his end days in terms of serving the Soviet government as he was arrested and sent to Butyrka jail where he was told he was there because of his complicity with Beria's attempt to seize power. He said he had no such involvement, was unaware of this plot and complained that a guard had stolen his watch. Slowly he came to realise he might be heading for elimination because of whom he knew, which in the eyes of the accusers amounted to conspiracy. He fell ill and was fed intravenously and was soon in a semi-conscious state. He gathered from a kind nurse that Abakumov and probably Beria had already been executed. Emma was confined to one room with her children in their apartment, but he accepted this because he knew his wife was a strong person in her own right.

His next prison was in Leningrad in Kresti prison which from Tsarist days had an infamous reputation. They kept giving him spinal taps in the lower lumber region, a supposed effort to discover any health issues. It proved to be a painful procedure and nearly crippled him. It was only in 1957 he was allowed to see Emma a few times, but he felt unwell, and his front teeth had been broken by forced feeding. By 1958 he had started to recover as his conditions improved, and he was told he was fit enough for further interrogations. Despite previous interrogations and his denials and lack of evidence three charges remained in place. First, conspiring with Beria to make peace with Germany and overthrow the Soviet government. Secondly, he had conducted assassinations of Beria's perceived enemies on Beria's orders, and finally he had supervised the work of the Toxicological Laboratory testing poisons on condemned people, none of these specific cases had appropriate evidence. Sudoplatov also challenged the fact the trial was to be a closed procedure (abolished in April 1956), and he demanded to know why he was not allowed a defence lawyer. He sent 33 appeals to Khrushchev and Rudenko and never had a single reply.

His trial took place in the headquarters of the Supreme Court (Vorovsky Street), and he was not handcuffed. When asked if he had objections to the court, he replied he had none but objected to the closed session and the lack of a defence lawyer. The court was adjourned to check this out and decided that higher authority demanded it continued. He had two witnesses against him, one called Muromtsev, head of the bacteriological research, who surprised the judges that he could not validate statements he had made five years previously, and he could not recall any time when Sudoplatov was involved. Maironovsky, mentioned previously as head of the Toxicology Laboratory, virtually said the same thing naming Khrushchev and Molotov as the two who gave him instructions, implying these murders were sanctioned by those superior to Beria. In any normal court of law with only two witnesses who denied Sudoplatov's involvement he would have been freed. However, they held that the death sentence did not apply but 15 years in jail would be appropriate, of which he had already served five years.

He was transferred to Lefortovo prison where he was able to meet Emma, then transferred to Vladimir prison close to where Emma's sister Cecilia lived, but Sudoplatov was extremely pleased that Emma had not been arrested. Emma turned to work as a seamstress for the high and mighty, which was useful when Khrushchev cut military pensions. Later Emma had discovered that in the purge of Beria, hundreds of officers had suffered, and those who knew too much were shot. She also discovered that Khrushchev had removed over 100 generals for the same reason, expelled from the Party and deprived of their military rank.

Sudoplatov described prison life, kept in solitary confinement for a time with no personal facilities other than a bucket, but sharing with others later. He continued to bombard the necessary authorities with various appeals. In 1960 he met Herman Klimov from the Party Control Committee who for once showed some interest in his case at the trial. It helped Emma's hopes, but according to Sudoplatov it was short lived as 'Procurator Rudenko torpedoed the move to rehabilitate me' (p.413).

Despite interest shown by a few, such as Klimov, in his case and his wife Emma turning every stone she could, nobody dared challenge Sudoplatov's imprisonment. By 1961 Sudoplatov wrote that was the time when illusions of freedom and rehabilitation simply faded. He remained locked in the same prison with the well-known American pilot Gary Powers and Greville Wynne an MI6 agent, though they were both soon released based on exchanges, but Sudoplatov continued to share a cell with his old friend Eitingon. The two of them kept writing appeals to Khrushchev which gained no reply. Using their expertise, they offered some operational suggestions to the KGB in an attempt to show their experience still counted. Their ideas were used, according to Sudoplatov, but all they received were increased food rations.

One appeal for Eitingon was successful, because they had not considered at his sentencing that he had already spent over a year in prison, and this was remedied, and he was released in 1964. As Brezhnev became the key figure it was still apparent that he did not want too many memories of the past, so they relied on the security of past decisions and Sudoplatov stayed locked up. Even when appeals for clemency were presented by the KGB, they were unsuccessful. Sudoplatov's son Anatoli did his utmost best in the appeals but failed, even having his own future career placed in danger. Then suddenly, on 21 August 1968 the day after the Soviet army occupied Czechoslovakia, Sudoplatov was released. He was not a well man, tended to walk with his hands behind his back which was a prison command, and he found sleep difficult when the lights were switched off. Emma had encouraged him to be a translator and, free of restraint, he translated foreign works for publication and authored books himself, which provided a sound income. He was still seeking rehabilitation but in 1988 he was told his case could not be reconsidered. In the same year, his 83-year-old wife Emma who had been so faithful died in the KGB hospital from Parkinson's disease, and her ashes were interred in the wall in the Donskoi Monastery. Sudoplatov remained frail himself as the Gorbachev years started, and his son took up the cudgel once again for his father's rehabilitation. Gorbachev himself was somewhat curious about the past events during Stalin's time. It was noted that Ramon Mercader had been buried as a Hero of the Soviet Union while Sudoplatov was still regarded as a criminal, and he heard Abakumov's case was being reviewed, and finally that his case was also being reviewed, which he assumed was the influence of Gorbachev, but it took months while his reputation as a murderer still persisted. At the end of 1991 both Sudoplatov and Eitingon were rehabilitated. In his closing paragraph of his memoirs he noted that none of his medals had been returned to him. He reflected how he had given his life to the Soviet Union during a period of poverty and under attack until it emerged as a superpower, and 'only when there was no more Soviet Union, no more proud empire, I was reinstated and my name returned to its rightful place' (p.431). He eventually died from presumed natural causes on 24 September 1996.

Sudoplatov, it could be argued, worked for a criminal regime which had no element of mercy and was run by a tyrant who demanded his orders for murdering any possibly critics were carried out instantly and threatening that he should always be fully obeyed. The fall of Beria and then Sudoplatov tells us much about Stalin and his junior bosses in his Mafia style of government.

The total lack of evidence in Sudoplatov's case indicated the corruption of Stalin, and also later men like Khrushchev and Brezhnev who wanted no reminders of the past. It is not a question of liking or disliking a man like Sudoplatov, he was a mere servant for the criminal state but seeing him from the perspective of living under and working for a corrupt system explains the fear which dominated the Soviet world.

Chapter Three

Criminal States

Explores the similarities of Stalin and Hitler's regimes and the inherent dangers arising from tyrannical autocracy.

This is a short chapter of a reflective nature to outline the importance of the concluding chapter. When studying Russian history during the time of Stalin's rule it becomes clear that he was seeing himself as a new Tsar, a totalitarian leader who accomplished his leading role through fear and murder. Communism was more feared in the West than fascism, especially by the rich and powerful who had more to lose should this political system envelop them, having as a stark warning heard the news of the liquidation of the Romanov family and the flight of the Russian wealthy and landowners. Despite this growing fear of communist Russia, the West nevertheless supported the Soviet Union during the Second World War from sheer necessity, even though Stalin had first sided with the Nazis as well as attacking Finland. During these years he became a tyrant like Hitler, becoming known because of the purges to rid himself of any leadership challenge, the Katyń massacres, and his immoral propensity to murder anyone of whom his paranoid mind was slightly suspicious. Any study of an autocracy demonstrates the danger of a state becoming in most eyes criminal and immoral. Stalin managed to achieve this style of single leadership by killing in numerous ways the slightest opposition and using a few trusted henchmen to do his work, then casting them aside if they became too powerful. It was the same with Adolf Hitler who rose through political machinations to rid himself of the Weimar democratic system and surrounded himself with adoring henchmen such as Himmler, Göring, Goebbels to mention just a few. This was happening in the same historical era in places like China, Romania, Italy, and Spain and many other states which had become autocracies.

They achieved their goals through fear. In Germany the Dachau concentration camp was established in March 1933 and the word Gestapo is still used to indicate a sense of terror. In Russia during the time of Stalin the Gulag camps were brutal and life-threatening, with whole families deported to these death traps. In Soviet Russia, the old Tsarist system was taken over and from the Cheka to the NKVD to the KGB instilling the same sense of fear as the German Gestapo. In both countries the ordinary citizen could never feel safe or secure and soldiers knew they had to obey orders even if they had serious moral doubts. In their respective countries both Stalin and Hitler were idolised and became personality cult leaderships, which was alien to democracies and true Marxism. Neither the Nazi nor the Stalin regime hesitated to shift families into prison camps if it suited their purposes, even though such movements were inhumane. Whole populations were moved to distant arid places where death was inevitable both in transition and on arrival.

The similarities of the regimes were always close. Over the concentration camp gate at Auschwitz stood the infamous sign that 'Work Makes you Free' and over most of the Gulag camps were notices that 'Labour is a matter of honour, courage and heroism'. For victims of both regimes these notices indicated their futures were bleak and short once they entered. These regimes grew national youth groups with the Hitler Youth and the Komsomol to fashion the future, designed their own political education, and tried to produce fanatical youngsters for ideological purposes. In Germany protesting students were beheaded by a guillotine, suspected generals were humiliated and hanged by meat hooks, others simply disappeared – known as *Nacht und Nebel* (night and fog). In Russia people also disappeared, but if they had any status they died in fabricated accidents, had sudden fatal medical problems, or it appeared they had committed suicide. In Germany to be a Jew meant death, and in Russia Kulaks were starved to death.

The Germans perpetrated blatant massacres of Jews, Russians, Slavs, Poles, Gypsies, and any possible opposition, and Stalin was no different. Russia had not signed the Geneva Convention although Germany had, which was an international legal obligation, yet the ordinary German soldier was ordered to wipe out Red sub-humanity, leading Poles, and the ethnic cleansing of Jews.

The Second World War occurred because of Hitler's inane wish to dominate Europe, and postwar it was also Stalin's imperial wishes to establish European dominance which alerted the Western powers who had become aware of Soviet demands, especially at Yalta. Churchill saved Greece by old fashion bargaining, but the Soviet Eastern Europe was expansive, and the Cold War started as soon as victory over Nazi Germany had been achieved, leading to establishing the NATO and the Warsaw Pacts. The political fears of the democratic West had been alerted to the immorality and criminality of their one-time ally, even though they had been avoided or glossed over at the Nuremberg Trials, and only a few had any knowledge of Stalin's criminal regime, with many seeing him affectionately as 'Uncle Joe' to Stalin's annoyance. In his diaries the famous Jewish academic Victor Klemperer who survived the Third Reich initially welcomed the Soviet Russians, but a few months later referred to the new form of government as the Fourth Reich.

It is widely understood and accepted by most that the Nazi regime was criminal not just in terms of international law, but the way their population was suppressed through fear, where torture was usual, executions were common on trumped up charges, and an individual had little choice but to conform and obey. The sense of freewill in one's personal and professional life was virtually obliterated because otherwise it meant imprisonment or more likely death. It was no different in the Soviet Union where the ordinary citizen had no choice but to obey and cheer their leader as the greatest person in the world, obliged to treat Stalin as a demi-god, the alternatives were too gross to contemplate. Large pictures of the leaders, whether Stalin or Hitler appeared in their respective cities and towns, a warning to any democratic society where one person has a personal leadership picture on public show in all major public places.

In a genuine voting democracy, it could be argued that the new government is the will of the people, defined by the majority, who place a government in power, and then only for a limited period of time to see if they deserve to stay in control. Unlike Nazi Germany and Soviet Russia, true democracies allow free expression of thought, one can adhere to a religion with its moral demands, live where we choose, vote for whom we choose, often based on taxes and a better standard of living which is often the dominating theme of most elections. The elected leaders are always acutely aware of the voting system and alert to arising issues. When in December 1935 the well-known

Hoare-Laval Pact regarding Italy's invasion of Abyssinia caused public outrage in both Britain and France, and the public won. Churchill was in Washington when news was brought to him about the fall of Tobruk, and he was worried that his leadership would be questioned in the House of Commons. Roosevelt had promised his public they would not be involved in another world war, but as the obvious dangers were emerging his 'fireside chats' became more measured, but it took the attack on Pearl Harbor to generate action from the safety of the American isolationist policy. When Churchill lost the election after the war, Stalin was unbelievably stunned.

In a democratic society, if a person disappears, commits suicide, dies in an accident or even a sudden medical death there is nearly always an autopsy, a police enquiry, a Coroner's Court investigation of known facts, all made public, and if it is somehow linked to a government the free press would have a field-day. If the government proposed euthanasia for people suffering from mental issues (as in Nazi Germany) it is not difficult to predict the public reaction, and it would be the same if a government proposed 'liquidating gypsies' on the grounds that they are a public nuisance and inclined to increase local criminality, the vast majority of the public would be in uproar with disapproval. The treasures of any sound democracy are the exercise of freewill, a free press, free speech, and freedom is the key word, which neither Nazi German nor Stalin's public ever had during this era of war and hatred. When a country kills masses of people, eliminates many of its own citizens, deploys torture, suppresses its own citizens, it is not unreasonable or an exaggeration to call it a criminal State.

However, Nazi Germany was not fought over these issues, but because they were a threat of a military nature, and Stalin was accepted for the same reasons as an Ally. For many people, the value of freedom arose as an issue postwar when the realities of Nazi behaviour became widely known, and it took another decade before the reality of Stalin's rule came to be understood. Nazi Germany and Stalin's Soviet Union are often regarded as immoral, criminal, if not evil. These are powerful words, but it is a human problem. When such people rise to the top and rule, they often succeed because they suppress others, and the question of this almost innate evil has to be pursued. Why, it has often been asked, do some people appear evil? Is it a choice of their free will or are they driven by other factors? The final chapter explores humankind's study of this ongoing human problem.

Chapter Four

Evil Behaviour

Explores how autocratic political authority creates war and oppression by denying its own citizens intellectual and moral freedom and examines the reasons for human conduct and the nature and necessity of Free Will.

Introduction

Sudoplatov was Beria's agent, who served Stalin, and it has been suggested that Stalin led a criminal regime who therefore needed efficient and corrupt servants. In the chapter on Sudoplatov it was noted that this agent befriended a man only to 'liquidate' him with an exploding box of chocolates. It was probably Beria who had suggested the Katyń massacre to Stalin, and enlarged the Gulag camps, and it has been stated that he was 'the most feared man in the Soviet Union during the Second World War'.[1] Under Stalin's orders he arranged the murder of millions of innocent people from behind his desk. Beria followed and encouraged Stalin in many similar barbarous actions. The history of a country raises the question of whether it is a matter of a rotten apple or a rotten barrel and from where such immoral behaviour amounting to evil arises. Naturally, it is a human failure because we can all go wrong with our behaviour, but the issue is raised to a different level when it occurs with leaders like Stalin and Hitler, with correspondingly evil henchmen such as Beria and Himmler with their equally inclined subordinate officers.

Evil has many definitions. but in everyday usage it is generally understood in terms of behaviour which for normal people shocks them to the core. Evil actions often arise from unbalanced behaviour involving revenge, selfishness, the need for dominance, showing no compassion for others. The lives of Stalin, Beria, Sudoplatov, and many others in this text such as Abakumov, appear to exemplify this human problem, but identifying the whys and wherefores needs some unfolding.

Solzhenitsyn proposed evil was a behaviour so barbaric it was irredeemable. However, he wrote later 'the ultimate…is when evil is so utterly condemned that even the criminal is revolted by it', when the actors realise the threshold has been crossed from bad to one of downright evil.[2] This tends to be the case in the story of Sudoplatov, and some have argued that when Beria turned to reform the country it was the same scenario, but it was more likely Beria's ploy of trying to stand out as a potential leader in post-Stalin days, as he was never a reforming person. As for Stalin there was no hope, condemning Russian PoWs on their return, including his own son.

This raises the issue as to how far the role of an historian is to pass any form of judgement on humankind's behaviour, given the immense cluster of moral theories which have and still exist in various global societies. The historian, it has long been argued, has to face the issue of neutrality, not least the better historians avoid nationalistic books proving their country was right in its decisions. The prime duty of a historian is to be factual and tell the truth of what happened. An historian must take into his analysis beliefs, motives, intentions and when looking at the prime figures of the past this must be an important function. This book has been about people and events over the last 100 years mainly set in Europe. From which ever angle we view the history of Europe during this era, it can be agreed by the vast majority of people that events such as the Holocaust, the cruelty of the Gulag camps, massacres of innocent people were wrong. Not in terms of poor decision making, but wrong in the moral sense and legally criminal by most European standards of law. There may be question marks over such areas as nuclear bombs and their indiscriminate killing, as with strategic or carpet bombing, the use of a secret political police force, and killing innocent families after one of their number has been condemned by the State. The murder of the innocent is a very different scenario to the battlefield, and this would disturb the vast majority of people once it comes to light. The question has often been asked how a normal civilised person can be suddenly turned into a mass murderer. Some events were so appallingly immoral that they can only be described as 'evil', and while avoiding passing personal judgment the question ought to be raised as to humankind's understanding of this word.

Religious Insights

For theologians there are two types of evil, namely the moral evil transgressing moral laws, and non-moral evil which includes disasters such as earthquakes, often referred to in legal terms as Acts of God. It is the former definition of evil which should hold our attention as it can be stopped. Soviet machinations had become so degenerate they became as evil as the Nazi Holocaust. The infamous German *Nacht und Nebel* (night and fog) was followed in Russia by people disappearing (even the famous Swedish Wallenberg noted in the text) supplemented by sudden car accidents, so-called suicides, medical explanations, and torture yielding fictional confessions from the victim and others. This amounted to evil machinations, and many academic disciplines have tried to explain the phenomenon of evil, ranging from psychology, criminology, to religion and philosophy. Jurisprudence simply offers a structure, and criminology looks for reasons. Religious perceptions on hovering over the subject of evil offers some insights, but it is in the discipline of philosophy with its study of 'free will' that some valuable thought can be gleaned for the causes for evil, as it is based on a person's individual choice in such matters.

The question is whether people are simply a product of their times, pre-wired in their behaviour, and some by nature appearing almost evil. The question of free will must be explored as well as the influences on a person's character will be pursued. There has been a recent tendency to degrade humanity's free will as if it were fiction. The popular historian Harari has forecast its closure, and gene-research scientists have proposed we are merely copies of our direct ancestors.

However, despite the influences brought to bear on the human mind, freedom of choice remains critical to retain any self-worth of being human. Free will is critical, but it can be argued that free will can be suppressed. The Christian view is that every person is a free agent, by having free will, and is responsible for their actions, albeit that freedom can sometimes be suppressed by other factors. Much of this will relate to Beria and Sudoplatov but will hopefully provoke questions about other major historical figures, and today's universal political instability. Theology and moral philosophy go back nearly 3,000 years and their insights into the subject of evil are pertinent. These two disciplines provide some answers to the question as to why immoral behaviour can descend to evil, leading to serious ramifications.

The religions of the world have identified evil as a major concern, offering explanations for its frequent occurrence. The ancient Persian religion of Zoroastrianism viewed existence as a struggle between the powers of darkness and light with evil being an integral force. Islamic belief explains everything as based upon the doctrine of the 'Will of Allah' with constant reference to the Koran as Christians to the Holy Scriptures, often subjected to various self-serving interpretations. However, Judaism and Christianity have long commented on the issue of evil. The Austrian Jewish philosopher Martin Buber examined the story of Adam and Eve and the forbidden tree of knowledge, and interpreted the fratricidal Cain as 'the story of the first iniquity in the human sense', and 'a deed which is wrong by its very nature'.[3] Buber made it clear that from the earliest of times man was well aware of what was good and evil, placing the responsibility at the feet of man as a free agent.*

The medieval Christian theologian Aquinas argued that because God created 'everything in existence', evil cannot have been created by God as an independent force seen as Satan, which some say blocks the belief that God is all powerful. Some Christians understandably argue that when God made man, he gave them free will making them different from animals. The gift cannot be taken back, so therefore when a man aims a gun at his neighbour, God can not withdraw his gift by blocking the mechanism because free will means that humankind must live by the consequences of their own actions, which is a persuasive argument.

It has long been argued that God created man as a 'free agent', and the nature of free will is implicit in the Christian scriptures and very much alive in the Western legal system, with the necessity of proving *mens rea* (guilty mind, in terms of a wrong intention). St Augustine argued for free will stating that God foreknows all things, but this does not deprive us of freedom of choice, and we are all too conscious of when we go wrong.[4] The message of Jesus Christ was to repent, to change, to look back at previous

---

* Buber renounced his professorship at Frankfurt am Main after Hitler took power in 1933 and left for Jerusalem.

behaviour and become good, and the Koran proposes that strangers must always be treated as welcome guests.

The sense of knowing we have gone wrong, might possibly explain what we call guilt arising from our conscience, which haunts us as a consequence of wrong decisions. Solzhenitsyn wrote that 'Macbeth's self-justifications were feeble – and his conscience devoured him', adding that nearly every person has a conscience of one sort or another.[5] When Sudoplatov killed his so-called enemy with the exploding chocolate box, he claimed that he was happy no bystanders were killed; possibly a late touch of conscience. Nevertheless, conscience and guilt can be variable. A Christian may base his conscience on the Bible, a Muslim on the Koran and a cannibal can feel guilty about letting a potential victim escape. The study of religions indicates that conscience and guilt indicate rules by which we measure our behaviour. In Christian theology and moral philosophy, the argument to explain evil is basically free will, the single factor which produces evil people and situations, making the devil a mere excuse. In other words, the forces of evil emanate from humankind without any prompting of a mythological devil.

Determinism

However, there are contrary arguments, and free will in some philosophical schools is opposed in many ways from a school of thought known as determinism, which claims that free will is meaningless. The question is asked as to how humans can do anything except as a mechanical response arising from their environmental and hereditary inheritance. This viewpoint could be seen to encapsulate the problems raised by human biochemistry, biological instincts, and psychology which will be explored later. Determinists add sociological aspects such as personal history, and many other background factors which is the well-known 'nature and nurture' debate.

When taken to its natural conclusion determinism means no one can be guilty or accused of being evil because a person is merely a bundle of automatic reactions beyond their control. The question of moral or legal blame then becomes questionable. The consequence of this is that prisons should only be used as a means of restraint and not as a means of punishment or correction. Human experience, it is argued, tends to indicate that many of our behavioural and emotional responses are automotive reflexes responding to our psychological, physical make-up, past choices, nurture, and many other factors which could predict the way we react and think. This line of thinking reduces humanity to a status amongst lesser animals, and for many has some truth, but many hollow rings.

Moral Philosophy

Students of philosophy have struggled for generations to define free will, and one of the best exponents in this writer's experience was C.A. Campbell in a series of lectures delivered at the University of St Andrews in the early 1950s and later published under the title *On Selfhood and Godhood*. Campbell was convinced that there is 'a distinctive kind of self-activity involved in moral decision' and our business is to understand this issue.[6] Campbell's style of delivering his argument was intended for students of philosophy and his arguments are too intricate for a brief survey of this nature.* At a base-level his argument suggested that when humans commit themselves to any form of introspection they know that in their inner mental/spiritual self-activity there are decisions of a moral nature that human beings work their way through. To put it another way, when humans are faced by a serious question, usually of a moral nature, they retain the ability to consider the ramifications of their proposed course of action, animals will only consider survival instincts.

However, Campbell notes everyone has 'emotive and conative dispositions which we call his character…and it is in this inner system, this character, which determines what desires will emerge in response to a given situation'.[7] If we know a person well it is possible to predict that person's reactions to a given situation, which was why most people were terrified of Stalin, Beria, Hitler, and Himmler. It is true that a person's character will often formulate the responses they make. The response here is could a person have chosen otherwise? It is this issue which raises the fundamental question of moral responsibility based on free will.

---

* Campbell uses the term 'self', but it could also mean 'mind' or 'Spirit' or 'Soul' and a myriad of other expressions to define that inner part which makes us who we are.

Any normal reflective person can test this idea with what Campbell termed 'introspection', when we are aware that our intentions clash with what we perceive to be the right thing to do. But when a man stands before a judge and states 'he was not himself at the time of the incident', he is often referring to the introspective self which is not a defence in law, because free will does not mean the right decision was made. Campbell noted that 'a man with a passion for power may have resolved to devote all his talents and energies, and to subordinate every other claim, including the claim of morality, to the achievement of this objective', but he remains aware of his choices.[8] The moral verb 'ought' can be used in various ways, from 'I ought to do what is right by what I think is morally correct' to 'I ought to do what I have been instructed to by my superior, be it Hitler or Stalin'.

Men like Himmler, Beria and many other dangerous predecessors and successors could be regarded as accidents of their circumstances or hereditary inclinations, by the view of those who deny free will. In 1945 the notorious Himmler did his best to escape moral judgement by trying to project another side of his nature to the Swedish Count Bernadotte. He claimed the concentration camps were a mere reformatory exercise, the killings were propaganda, and some of his subordinates were out of control. The clever and deceitful Göbbels understood there was no hope of avoiding moral judgement and killed himself, and Göring mendaciously denied any knowledge of the camps and turned his eyes away from the film screens at the Nuremberg Trials, and by removing his earphones when witnesses gave horrendous evidence. Stalin denied any knowledge of the Katyń massacres because he realised that the massacre had been an immoral deed even by his bizarre standards. Solzhenitsyn, an Orthodox Christian and Communist, struggled with the problem of evil which he had experienced during his life, concluding that the source of evil was in man.

Free will and freedom of choice although of paramount importance can be restricted by other factors such as automatic reactions, and an overbearing environment. A person may, as it were, react without thinking, without considering the ramifications, be propelled into action by a myriad of other factors. When a person massacres people and babies, judgment always revolves around freedom of choice which is why the Nuremberg Trial defence of 'obeying criminal orders' was rejected, and the importance of individual choice was judged. Nevertheless, the factors which some argue may affect freedom of choice must be explored in understanding man's behaviour which means turning to psychology.

Psychology

During the Nuremberg Trials the psychiatrist Goldensohn 'shared the belief of the times in the pathology of the leading Nazis…and was especially interested in trying to account for their depravities'.[9] The revelations of mass extermination and massacres were too devastating to be understood by the public who were seeking an explanation. It was felt that such behaviour had to have an explanation which stretched beyond free will and normal behaviour. In an interview with Otto Ohlendorf, not a major war criminal but involved in massacres (for which he was later executed), Goldensohn asked this seemingly 'intellectual man' directly if he were 'some kind of sadist, pervert or lunatic?'[10] For this psychiatrist there had to be some explanation because it appeared impossible that any person could willingly choose whether to follow such commands. Telford Taylor wrote, 'I remember the stunned silence of the audience that followed the SS Officer Otto Ohlendorf's cold, impassive statement that, in southern Russia, his troops had rounded up and killed some 90,000 Jews', adding some form of explanation was needed.[11]

The demand for explanation returned years later during the Adolf Eichmann trial. Primo Levi's reference to the 'banality of evil' was reflected by a reporter named Hannah Arendt, commenting on Eichmann's trial. She pointed out that Eichmann regarded himself as an ordinary law-abiding person. The question Arendt posed was whether Eichmann was simply a bad apple, or was the entire apple-barrel bad.

Christopher Browning made a study of why ordinary people can become immoral. He explored the German Police Battalion 101, which conducted brutal murders of Jews in Poland during the Second World War.[12] These men from Hamburg with non-military backgrounds were the German equivalent of the ubiquitous American John Doe, they were just members of the public who committed massacres. Browning and other historians have clarified that if German soldiers or policemen refused to participate they were not shot, yet the overwhelming majority participated in massacres.

For Browning, the behaviour was explained by the environment of total war changing ordinary people into group murderers. A clash between the historians Goldhagen and Browning is of some interest. Goldhagen in his book *Hitler's Willing Executioners: Ordinary Germans and the Holocaust* treated the perpetrators as 'responsible agents who make choices', whereas Browning based his reasons more on psycho-sociological theories – on 'the assumption of inclinations and propensities common to human nature but not excluding cultural influences'.[13]

The psychologist Stanley Milgram in his experiments with electric shocks tried to demonstrate that ordinary people could inflict powerful electric charges on others, simply because a uniformed authoritative figure informed them it was correct.[14] This was the Nuremberg argument of 'obeying orders', with Milgram testing how far an individual would inflict pain because he was ordered. This appeared to demonstrate that a person can be trained to let personal freedom of choice evaporate when personal responsibility becomes irrelevant. Milgram attempted to demonstrate from this experiment that ordinary people tended to follow orders if they recognised the authority as legally legitimate.[15] Curiously, it was noted that if the person issuing the orders was dressed in laboratory gowns, suggesting a uniform, it was promptly obeyed, but when a civilian took over the role the obedience level dropped by 20 per cent.* It raised the question as to whether people had become accustomed to seeing a uniform as something which must be obeyed.

In another experiment the psychologist Philip Zimbardo gave students role-plays as prisoners and guards.[16] It took a brief time for the guards to become openly sadistic. This research was known as the American Stanford Prison experiment and happened in 1971. It was meant to last a fortnight but was terminated after six days, because its ethical values were questioned because of the procedures. The student prison guards too readily conformed to the social roles they had been given which led to serious brutalisation, and less than 20 per cent came through the experiment as 'good guards.' Later, and most significantly in the above experiment, many of the guards announced

---

* Solzhenitsyn cynically and understandably referred to the secret police officials as 'this branch of the service requires only that they carry out orders exactly and be impervious to suffering – and that is what they do and what they are'. Solzhenitsyn, Aleksandr, *The Gulag Archipelago 1918–56* (London: The Harvill Press, 1985), p.67.

after the experience that they were surprised at their own behaviour. This sense of guilt indicated a sense of morality which for many can be life changing. These psychological experiments explored human reaction but provided no sound answer to the cause of immorality or evil, it was just a certain type of individual's immediate reactions under certain circumstances.

In 2002 Paulus and Williams wrote a paper on *The Dark Triad of Personality; Narcissism, Machiavellianism, and Psychopathy.*[17] They looked at impulsivity, aggression, sexual deviancy, cheating, revenge, and the question of sadism. They asked the old questions whether people are born evil, and they looked at the study of identical and non-identical twins which to them suggested a possible genetic component for narcissism and psychopathy. Psychology has attempted to explain human reactions, but it fails to explain fully the phenomenon of evil in man with its wider connotations. In terms of men like Stalin, Hitler, Beria, Himmler, and their subordinates more is needed.

Psychopathy

Related to psychological research is the study of psychopathy, which is a complex area of study, and of some interest in many academic disciplines. In 1991 the Reed Committee recognised the lack of medical agreement about the diagnosis and treatability of psychopathic disorder.[18] Nevertheless there are ongoing studies from the biological approach looking at faulty biological mechanisms which can be caused by genetic inheritance, biochemistry and neuroanatomy and even viral infection. There is also the behavioural approach as to whether psychopathy results from nature or nurture and this continues to be under investigation.

From the medical investigations it is impossible to make the claim that any of the infamous individuals of history were clinically psychopathic, because their chemistry is not available for scientific study. However, their behaviour indicates that if not total psychopaths they certainly had many of the attributed characteristics. Most experts agree that psychopaths 'lack remorse and empathy and feel emotion only shallowly. In extreme cases, they might not care whether you live or die. These people are called psychopaths. Some of them are violent criminals and murderers. But by no means all'.*

A criminal psychologist Professor Robert Hare claimed that psychopaths see the world in a different way, like colour-blind people, and he established a test of twenty criteria for psychopathic disorders. The features were as follows: 1) Glibness and superficial charm, 2) Grandiose sense of self-worth, 3) Pathological lying, 4) Cunning/manipulative behaviour, 5) Lack of remorse, 6) Emotional shallowness, 7) Callousness and lack of empathy, 8) Unwillingness to accept responsibility for actions, 9) A tendency to boredom,10) A parasitic lifestyle, 11) A lack of long-term realistic goals,12) Impulsivity, 13) Irresponsibility: 14) Lack of behavioural control,15) Behavioural problems in early life, 16) Juvenile delinquency,17) Criminal versatility, 18) A history of conditional release, 19) Multiple Marriages, 20) Promiscuous behaviour.

Psychopaths are good company, but a 'lack of moral scruples and indifference to other people's suffering could be beneficial if you want to get ahead in business'.[19] There are some in the business world who succeed by making impulsive decisions even though it means crushing others to succeed. The defendants at Nuremberg were evaluated for intelligence ratings and with one exception (Rosenberg) they were found to have good to high IQs, and these men were not inhibited by moral concerns and liquidated opponents, thereby demonstrating psychopathic indicators, which would have included Stalin and Beria had they stood trial. In their subservience to their masters Hitler and Stalin, these henchmen had no independence of thought, and 'they held in common a psychopathic unit if such a phenomenon exists'.[20] They simply changed the moral verb 'ought' to the subservience of their masters, discarding moral norms.

Psychopathy is a well-established disorder and has some bearing on a man like Beria, but it offers no explanation for the growth of evil. True psychopathic cases are rare, but some researchers believe it is dependent on nurture rather than nature, though the main question persists as to what the real cause of evil is. Many propose that even psychopaths understand what

---

* Studies done by Torry in 2001 demonstrated that some mental disorders can be related to exposure to virus whilst in the womb.

they are doing is wrong. However, they choose not to agree with the moral norms but follow orders or their own whims. The answer remains evasive but infamous psychopaths have appeared as normal members of society before being revealed, and at a simplistic level it appears they simply have no conscience.

Jurisprudence

Madness brought about by known psychological or medical problems can be regarded in law as a defence. Such mental instability was first recognised under the M'Naghten rules of the 1840s and is a legal defence grounded in sanity being required. More recently Lord Devlin noted with reference to the insanity defence that it is reason which makes a man responsible to the law, reason, and reason alone. It is reason which gives him sovereignty over animate and inanimate things. It is what distinguishes him from animals, which emotional disorder does not, and it is what makes him man and subject to the law. It is, therefore, fitting that nothing other than a defect of reason should give complete absolution.[21] Whether men like Beria and Himmler can be placed in this category is a curious thought, but most unlikely because they were not medically or mentally ill. Therefore, it is worth noting that the Mental Health Act 1983 s.1(2) defined mental disorder as 'mental illness, arrested or incomplete development of mind, psychopathic disorder', which in the case of mass murderers may hold a minor element of interest. It has however been 'amply demonstrated that the relationship between mental abnormality and criminality is an uncertain one'.[22]

Jurisprudence therefore raises the question as to whether law and morality have much in common, a thought often debated by legal scholars. The recognition that an offence is bad in itself is dependent on the law of the land, and on those who made the law. Some countries have laws prohibiting homosexuality while others have laws on political crimes while others have no such laws. The law is simply the applied rules of a society and regarded by others as immoral. A dysfunctional regime has no need of law. There was no law in Germany allowing extermination prisons, nor was there a law in Russia prohibiting brutality in the Gulag camps.

The German philosopher Immanuel Kant noted that 'laws prescribe external conduct whereas morals prescribe internal conduct, that is, morals alone are concerned with subjective factors, such as motive'.[23] It has been argued that an awareness of morality has helped the law develop. In England, a starving man could be hanged for stealing a sheep, but later a jury refused to convict a thief to avoid him suffering the unfair death penalty. Until 1807, Britain allowed its ships to trade in enslaved people, but now it is illegal to abuse ethnic groups. This still does not make the laws of the country necessarily moral, but laws can be regarded as reflecting a sense of morality, while the law of a country reflects a society with no explanation for nationally corrupt laws.

This is a conundrum, because whether a law is moral or immoral is pointless, 'indeed there is no absurdity in conceding that an unjust law forbidding the access of coloured persons to the parks has been "justly" administered, in that only coloured persons genuinely guilty of breaking the law were punished under it and then only after a fair trial'.[24] It is possible for a national law to later be regarded as corrupt, but the law can be regarded as correct if properly administered. In other words, the law as such, is only a servant of the state, moral or immoral. On these grounds the racial laws of the Nazis could be regarded as justly administered according to the law at that time, as well as Stalin's law that Russian soldiers who surrendered were traitors. The Russian Tsarist law of using corporal punishment on peasants, but excluding the upper classes, may be regarded as unjust on the grounds that *prima facie* human beings should be treated alike, and not based on social privilege. The morality of any society may differ greatly. Times and cultures change, but still raises many questions by not explaining the lack of universality in terms of the nature of immorality. David Hume the Scottish philosopher argued that 'human nature cannot by any means subsist without the association of individuals; and that association never could have a place were no regard paid to the laws of equity and justice', outlining the proposal that law and morals should have the same elements.[25]

Different countries at various times in history have enforced corrupt laws, but while many may accept this, there is generally an expectation that a just law ought to have a moral background. Many were incarcerated in Nazi concentration or Gulag camps, or executed for standing by their moral standards, by looking beyond the law for moral justification. The writer Paul Shrimpton studied a group of young students who stood against the Nazi regime and persuaded others to join them in non-violent protests.[26] They were youngsters who demonstrated bravery and became martyrs. They knew the law was immoral and were courageous enough to say so in their homeland, only to be decapitated for their efforts.

The law only reflects any society at a given time, and the legal structure cannot explain why people behave in acts of gross immorality. A corrupt and misled society, such as Nazi Germany and Stalin's Russia will produce evil laws which hypothetically could be administered justly. Nevertheless, a person should not be condemned for being forced by a corrupt State into an act that a person normally would not have done. A bank manager giving the safe keys to robbers because his wife and children were threatened with death, would be regarded as being coerced and not guilty of robbery.

International Law

During the Nuremberg Trials the Chief American Prosecutor Robert Jackson stated that the four victorious nations, by 'staying the hand of vengeance and voluntarily submitting the captive enemies to the judgement of law was one of the most significant tributes that Power has ever paid to reason'. He saw the trial not for making individuals account for their evil behaviour, but as a way of controlling aggression. International law was being elevated to be the controller of moral conduct, by recognising some behaviour as per se evil.

Since the First World War emerged there was a growing recognition that war was the main area in which man's behaviour degenerated to pure evil. War was beginning to be understood as a criminal and immoral act. The importance of individuals both in creating war and their behaviour during the war was becoming identified as a moral question, with which a thinking human being with freedom of choice and action could be identified. There was no question that a courtroom was better than lynching and kangaroo courts which Stalin had once proposed to Churchill. Churchill and Eden, and even the Archbishop of York considered the behaviour of individuals in the Nazi regime so appalling they were prepared to execute them on the spot which was against English law. Eden claimed that 'the guilt of such individuals is so black that they fall outside and go beyond the scope of any judicial process'.[27]

Having an international status, law implied a sense of moral guardianship, but it was flawed in its integrity. The Katyń massacres were ignored, as were Stalin's actions in the invasion of Poland and Finland. In a futile attempt to cover their tracks, the Soviets later executed eight Germans in Leningrad for their alleged role in the Katyń massacre.[28] The Anglo-American strategic bombing was not raised at Nuremberg. It was proposed not to prosecute the Germans for bombing. This was done 'on the advice of the British Foreign Office and this particular charge was quietly withdrawn since it was self-evident that German defence lawyers would have little difficulty in tarring Allied bombing with the same brush.'[29] The U-boat warfare was condemned but Western naval policies were similar, and in Vichy France the Jews had been deported by the French, and both Laval and Darland had pursued a partnership with fascist Germany. There were also many individual Allied commanders and soldiers who went beyond the moral barriers, committing many crimes, as Michael Burleigh's book on *Moral Combat* outlines with many examples.*

There was no question that evil crimes had been committed by the Nazi and Soviet regimes. Some have argued correctly that battlefield crimes were often illegal and immoral and perpetrated by all sides. An American Sergeant West (a cook in civilian life) shot thirty-seven Italian prisoners and later another thirty-six alleging they were snipers, a strange argument since all sides deployed such tactics as snipers. A chaplain and two reporters complained to General Omar Bradley, who spoke to Patton who had turned a blind eye because he had issued the order 'to kill devastatingly'. West was sentenced to life imprisonment but only served a year then reduced to the ranks and returned to duty.[30] Other similar matters came to light when Canadian troops on D-Day took few prisoners, killing most, but 'common sense suggests that one should distinguish between hot-blooded and cold-blooded atrocities', but senior officers were expected to be more detached and exercise better control.[31] However there is a vast difference between individual behaviour

---

* For a classic example involving a senior America general and a sergeant see Burleigh, Michael, *Moral Combat: A History of World War II* (London: Harper Press, 2010), pp.380–1.

on the battlefield compared to immoral and illegal instructions issued from behind the safety of governmental desks, usually based on an evil ideology and its thought processes.

The most important lesson from the Nuremberg Trial was that at this international level, freedom of choice was acknowledged, which was assuming the reality of free will. As the American prosecutor Telford Taylor wrote, 'These outrages were not the work of faceless or anonymous men or agencies', because they were the work of men who freely chose this action.[32]

Biochemistry and Genes

The cause of immorality is considered by a few as a mere question of biochemistry and genes. The question may be raised as to whether some people at birth are lacking the normal bio-chemical make-up in their systems. If true it has been suggested that some people may be born with the seeds for anti-social and immoral actions. Such a possibility removes any reason for moral dimensions and eliminates the need for legal judgment as the fault cannot be helped. Inbuilt into the Western legal system is that a guilty person is guilty because they made the choice themselves to take the action which led them to court proceedings.

Medical science can diagnose some inherent future illnesses, and this may advance in the future. It may be conceivable that the day will come when some basic biochemical fault may explain deviant behaviour. It could be that such behaviour as paedophilia and psychopathy could be the result of breakdowns in molecular mechanisms (alcohol for example) and neural mechanisms such as frontotemporal dementia. There has been considerable interest in comparing identical twins as most books on criminology note, looking for genetic components which may disclose reasons for their conduct.

A good deal of research is being conducted at the genetic level especially in identifying psychopathic genes. However, most serious researchers justifiably remain cautious of using biochemical or genetic data in terms of moral validity or genetic data to diagnose deviance or explain guilt. Most recently Professor Robert Plomin of King's College, London, has published a book called *Blueprint: How DNA Makes us Who We Are*.[33] Basically it means 'that DNA can act as significant predictor, from birth, of a growing multiplicity of traits'.[34] Given this scientist's reputation this writer once communicated with him about the issue and received the following email: 'So I hope it will help a bit if I just say that genes do not determine our choices, even though they influence our choices. Genetic influence on common disorders and complex traits is probabilistic, not deterministic. Genetics nudges us in certain directions, but we certainly have the choice to fight against our tendencies'.[35] This welcome communication from a leading scientist made it clear that although this exploration must look at the various claims made to justify human behaviour, he agrees that free will and the human consciousness still hold validity, namely that we can still from within our inner selves make conscious decisions of our own choice.

Biology

This question of inbuilt or pre-wired behaviour has also attracted the interest of biologists, who see 'aggressiveness as the propensity of an animal to attack another of the same species or of a different species'.[36] Aggression is a natural animal tool deployed when under attack or seeking food or territory. It has been noted that 'each human individual is endowed by heredity with a certain amount of aggressiveness. We know today that this amount can be increased or diminished by chemical substances'.[37] It is always focused on the need for survival and is stronger in some than others. The historian O'Brien argued that when there is a war it is 'essentially one of self-determination by a Darwinian process of armed conflict'.[38] The reference to Darwinism is often used to explain why man behaves in such ways because it is in his makeup, but as man has progressed many religious thinkers and moral philosophers would disagree.

If anything separates man from the animal, it is free will, the freedom of choice. Animals are controlled by their habitat and instincts for survival, but a human-being is capable of breaking free from these restraints out of choice. Animals react instinctively as do humans under trying circumstances, but the history of man is full of examples where individuals stop to think, and they consider their reactions in terms of the future or from a sense of their personal morality.

Biochemistry and biological factors may play a small part in man's reactive behaviour, but it remains minimal and very much in the initial stages of investigation. These sciences give some indicators, but they provide no realistic answer to the nature of humanity's immoral behaviour.

In terms of the causes of major immoral behaviour there are many other factors which have to be considered, but which could take a whole new book. This next section will summarise the various critical components of what makes a governmental regime criminal and immoral. When men like Beria and Goebbels had extra-marital affairs, these sins could almost be described as venial as the sins were less dangerous and potentially forgivable, though not everyone would agree with this thinking. However, when they were participants in the mass murder of innocent people and acting under their own choice, immoral behaviour crosses the boundary to pure evil.

This becomes historically important when criminal behaviour takes control of people through their form of government which can suppress an individual's free will of what they consider to be right or wrong. As Solzhenitsyn wrote, 'Unlimited power in the hands of limited people always leads to cruelty', which is especially valid when they are the accepted leaders.[39]

When human decisions result in war, civil or international, the consequences, history always demonstrates, lead to the grip of criminality and evil. Following a postwar exhibition on Nazi war crimes, one historian noted 'that the exhibition made public what scholars had long known, that there was a direct crucial link between the war and the Holocaust'. Humanity's desire to dominate inevitably leads to evil behaviour.[40] The Holocaust cannot be explained by causal circumstances as some determinists might argue, or as Franco suggested that 'these things happen in war'.* Since the Holocaust the truth of the Stalin Gulag system gradually came to light and post 1945 there have been several genocidal actions which have caught the headlines. These immoral acts originated with leaders and their adherents who knowingly exercised their free will.

---

* 'As the news spread of the extermination camps it filled the world with horror, but Franco simply dismissed it as one of the consequences of wartime problems'. Sangster, Andrew, *Probing the Enigma of Franco* (Newcastle: Cambridge Scholars, 2018), p.184.

Tyrannical Leaders

Edmund Burke wrote that 'the only thing necessary for the triumph of evil is for good men to do nothing' which has its own veracity, but sometimes evil men can convince potentially good men that by following orders, evil acts are justified, which is why understanding history is crucial. It only takes a few people wanting power to provoke a world devastating war which is why the Nuremberg process denounced 'making war' a criminal act. This raises a major issue, which given that we have free will in our decisions, how does a normal individual become so immoral as to be considered evil.

Overly authoritative-type tyrannical leaders can produce behaviours in others which are later realised were morally wrong. This becomes especially true when autocratic figures like Stalin, Hitler, Franco, and an endless list of others turned themselves into worshipped demi-gods. In exploring Beria and others like him, it is therefore important to keep asking the question as to what encouraged them towards their chosen destinies. It could be that they sought power and importance, or feared to disobey as torture and death were a dictator's persuasive tools. Some criminologists suggest 'that criminal and anti-social behaviour results from the interaction between an individual and the environment (which provides criminal opportunities)', and it could be that men like Hitler and Stalin happily provided such opportunities.[41]

This recalls the ongoing debate of nature or nurture. Whether we are by nature 'pre-wired', or as John Locke stated in 1690, that we are *tabula rasa* (blank slate) on which we are formed by our environment. However, there remains the major issue that the vast majority are conscious of having free will. In the early 1960s this writer can still recall a lecture by philosopher H. D. Lewis, who argued that humanity's freedom is contained or hemmed in by three barriers and drew a triangle on a chart. One line represented our born nature, even our genes. The second line was our nurture and environment, and the third represented our past choices. He drew a figure of a person contained within the triangle who was constrained by these three barriers. He then argued that by exercising free will we are able to expand their area of movement, increasing personal freedom. Later, it occurred to the writer the triangle should have been a square, with the fourth line the threat of persuasion and torture. So, for example, a boy born during the First World

War in Germany was obliged to join the Hitler Youth, inundated with anti-Semitic propaganda, indoctrinated in the belief that Germany had been betrayed, and informed he was ethnically superior, which created many resolute SS members. The alternative (the fourth line barrier) was rejection of such influence and being treated as an enemy of the State enforced by prison and torture.

There used to be an old Greek saying that 'a fish rots from the head', giving way to the modern parlance that 'the rot starts at the top'. Shakespeare inferred this when he wrote 'something is rotten in the state of Denmark'. The nature of any tyrant is worth studying if only as a warning because they bring war, oppression, and repress freedom at a national and personal level. Stalin, once an essential ally of the West, was later realised as a dangerous tyrant. Russia under Stalin and Beria was a world where morals and humanism had no point in existing because the idealism of Marxist-Leninism had given way to autocratic behaviour of the worse conceivable type, which was paralleled in Nazi Germany.

There is no escaping the fact that dictators of all shapes and sizes have proved dangerous to men who think they have freedom of will. Mao Zedong killed more of his own citizens than Hitler and Stalin. Mussolini gained power only to be lynched by his own people who turned against him. Franco survived until his death in 1975 but was executing opponents long after the Spanish Civil War finished. Hitler's immoral corruption is probably the most written about, but they were all tyrannous to 'daemonic' proportions. The word daemonic is deployed not just because of the mass murders and torture but the repression of freedom. In both Nazi Germany and Soviet Russia there were known incidents of children betraying their parents, citizens obliged to obey, and the propaganda which tried to instil the government's worth, while threatening them if they disagreed.

All these tyrants managed to surround themselves with powerful henchmen who for their own benefits, sacrificed their own free will for promotion, power, and selfish purposes. Some of them were desktop killers, others enjoyed the torture and the killing as perverse as this may seem. Beria was undoubtedly a clever and intelligent man who had understood that the way to power was simply to 'hitch his wagon' to the man at the top.

Beria, one of the figures in this exploration lived for his personally perceived future and as always working out how best to react to increase his personal status and power. Beria knew that Stalin was ruthless, and he deliberately shaped himself along the same lines. 'Having tea with Beria', mentioned in the text, was the military gossip for being personally beaten and tortured by him, he was known for enjoying being sadistic, personally torturing some individuals, and killing their wives and children. However, he was an intelligent person who deliberately manipulated his way into Stalin's world, having no other motive than making himself important, and this behaviour was his own choice. It was perhaps no surprise that on one well-known occasion Stalin referred to Beria as 'our Himmler'. Two men who were both clever, but who had deliberately cast aside any sense of morality and freedom to gain power like their respective masters, and there were hundreds more who emerged under a tyrant's control.

Repression of Free Will

In all tyrannical States there is the repression of free will. There is a high degree of validity in the claim that sometimes people are 'obliged' to act in what they would normally deem to be immoral. They are given no choice but to respond in a way they would normally have rejected. In this aspect of free reasoning some bearing must be placed on their overall historical background because the influence of a person's historical nurture is significant, with experience indicating it has some impact, but it does not necessarily block an individual from freedom of choice.

The most common example of a non-thinking and automatic response is that of anyone caught up in a battle where survival instincts strongly become the priority, and where personal survival dominates any thinking. There are many causes for the repression of one's personal freedom for decision making which will be commented on later in this discourse, such as the threat of personal reprisal known as putative duress, which creates sheer coercion. Another reason suggested by some apologists for immoral behaviour is 'careerism' which has a less dangerous effect on man's freedom but nevertheless can be significant. Men like Beria, Himmler, Goebbels, fashioned their careers on their plan to be alongside their respective and feared masters, and in the military and even business world many have followed orders which once they would have found repugnant in the hope of promotion.

Putative Duress

One of the major recurring arguments for the suppression of free will is described as putative duress or coercion, summarised by the argument that 'if I do not cooperate then I shall be shot, and my family will suffer', leaving no personal choice. Stalin and Hitler's regimes deployed this threat, warning soldiers and citizens that orders must be obeyed, and if soldiers disobeyed or were taken prisoner, Stalin said they would be regarded as traitors, and their families sent to the camps. This reflected Trotsky who once said that if his soldiers advance, they 'may' be shot, if they retreat, they 'will' be shot.

In his study of a German Police Battalion the historian Christopher Browning noted that a German soldier could refuse to participate in massacres. The commander was called Trappe who stated if the older men did not feel up to the task 'they could step out'.[42] Normally, however, to exercise free will and resist such orders with threats against self and family would take considerable strength of mind. The same putative stress applied in both Nazi Germany and the Soviet Union. From Browning's postwar interviews some appeared to suffer from amnesia, were unclear about details and hid their feelings. Others returned to normal life as if nothing had happened, and many more suffered nightmares at the time, as their consciences returned. However, such putative stress works on most because of the built-in animal instinct for survival, even if it means casting aside free will.

Obeying Orders

In many ways those aggressive autocrats who must be obeyed care nothing for human rights, or humanity in general, and they have as their underlining theme that orders must be obeyed. Obeying orders was frequently raised at Nuremberg where the arguments ranged around the fact that it was universally common for men to obey orders, claiming it had been the law of their country, and that Nuremberg was behaving in a legally retrospective fashion. The infamous Robert Ley stating that, 'I had nothing to do with them [the Jewish people] at all. I was not in charge'.[43]

The main thrust of the argument for obeying an order as noted above was often coercive, and it was argued many had no choice. It has been claimed by one historian that Germans found it psychologically impossible to say no, and he added the further explanations of self-interest and bureaucratic myopia.[44] He could also have added this was not just a German problem, recalling that Solzhenitsyn wrote, 'This is surely the main problem of the twentieth century: is it permissible merely to carry out orders and commit one's conscience to someone else's keeping? Can a man do without ideas of his own about good and evil', pinpointing a major aspect of human life.[45] Nuremberg judicial findings were clear that it was illegal to follow criminal orders, a statement which must hold truth in all sides of a conflict.

Ideological factors

Free Will can be repressed or subverted by the ideological factor in a person's background. During most conflicts and especially in the Second World War many were driven by the prevailing ideology of their own landscape which is perhaps understandable. Ideologies change, in the west democracies were changing, in Germany their society had changed from monarchy to democracy to dictatorship. In Russia, monarchy followed by communism distorted by Stalin into a totalitarian State with him as the leader. An autocratic leader will insist his or her leadership and ideology is the main thrust for their country, often demanding it should be the same in other countries (Comintern). Sudoplatov was driven by his political belief in Stalin's version of communism. By his own descriptions it was clear that for him communism was the main and only ideal in his life. It was the same power of ideology of the extreme Islamic terrorists which preoccupies many today. There is no doubt that an ideology can control a person's thinking to such an extent their personal freedom of choice is subjugated to their political or religious beliefs. Although his academic work concerned anti-Semitism, Goldhagen wrote that 'I maintain that any explanation that fails to acknowledge the actors' capacity to know and to judge, namely to understand and to have views about the significance and the morality of their actions, that fails to hold the actors' beliefs and values as central, that fails to emphasise the autonomous motivating force of Nazi ideology, particularly its central component of anti-Semitism cannot possibly succeed in telling us much about why the perpetrators acted as they did'.[46] An ideology can be so powerful for some people that it provides them with motivation and often means sacrificing the follower's own freedom of thought, but this is no excuse or reason for illegal and immoral actions which is more likely to happen when free will is cast aside as unnecessary.

As this is being written there is a raging debate about loss of freedom for human minds with AI (Artificial intelligence). This is a point made by Yuval Noah Harari in his book *21 Lessons for the 21st Century* in which he suggested that the normal influences of religion and nation are minimalised, and humanity will soon live in a kind of matrix with our free will (if it exists) diminishing. He claimed that 'the twin revolutions of infotech and biotech could reconstruct not just economics and societies but our very bodies and minds'.[47] This all amounts, whether emanating from autocrats like Stalin and Hitler, to AI hacking the human mind, and amounts to a downgrading of humankind.

Reactions of Individuals

Where autocratic tyranny reigns, free will is repressed, the citizen suffers from oppression, and war is nearly always likely. One of the factors which must be considered is the influence of personal background. Those who obey a tyrant ruler and his henchmen have lost their freedom of will. They may have lost it through fear, because of propaganda, a misled belief for a better future, fallen to what we today we call 'celebrity status', and they had taken the last step to the adoration of their demi-god. For some people this was a total renunciation of their own free will, for others a degree of unawareness as they assumed others knew better.

An individual's personal involvement, in what is generally regarded as criminalised immoral acts, is a complex problem. The historian Burleigh asked the question bluntly when he wrote that 'the notion of moral crimes is superficially tautological. It becomes clearer if one recalls postwar prosecutors asking these men whether, if ordered, they would also have shot their own children, to which the response was indignantly negative. Since that suggests they retained a sense of crime and wrongdoing, how did they reconcile this with their own heinous actions?'[48]

A sense of conscience, as noted earlier, prompts a feeling of guilt, which implies they knew or were aware they had made a wrong decision, which underlines the knowledge they had freedom of choice. Men like Beria, Stalin, Himmler, and Hitler appeared to be free of the restraints of conscience, yet when Göring refused to watch the films and hear the witnesses of the Holocaust at Nuremberg this raises doubts. They had used their freedom of choice to opt for power and dominance over others, knowing that what they were doing was morally unacceptable. The historian Christopher Browning's book *Ordinary Men*, an account of the massacres in Poland, pointed out that Trappe, a commander of these events, was upset at his orders stating that 'if this Jewish business is ever avenged on earth, then have mercy on us Germans'.[49]

When Goldhagen, author of *Hitler's Willing Executioners* posed the question that 'it must be shown how people can be brought to commit acts to which they would not inwardly assent, acts which they would not agree are necessary or just', the reasons are sadly many, but the main thrust must be the tyrannical authority of a lead figurehead.[50] Battlefield combat must have its own context because this 'often leads to an automaton-like state in which much of the conscious mind closed itself down and instinct took over', but even so 'only about two per cent of combat soldiers are reckoned to have positively revelled in lethal violence'.[51]

Power-seeking autocratic leaders who take a grip over their citizens both in mind and body become all-powerful, and they restrict the freedom of their people by controlling their minds. Both Huxley and Orwell in their dystopian novels noted these insights. The Nuremberg Trials were correct in making aggressive war a criminal act because it dehumanises the individuals by changing them from being free agents into automatons. When aggressive war becomes total war the sense of normal morality is often inverted at a national and personal level, and only a few manage to retain norms of morality and their free will. It provokes a sense of revenge; sometimes so powerful the moral norms of the day are cast aside. The director of the International Peace campaign, Philip Noel-Baker approved of bombing claiming it was 'almost civilised compared to the concentration camps and to the Himmler terror'.[52] The Church of England tended to condone the policy, and when a petition was raised against such bombing the Dean of St Pauls refused to sign. There was a campaign against night-bombing because it was perceived as too inaccurate, signed by Bishop Bell of Chichester, George Bernard Shaw, Gilbert Murray, Vera Brittain, and many others who tried to hold a moral balance. War has an escalating effect, each side responding to what they consider the other side's violations, and as Solzhenitsyn noted, the horrors of war behaviour spilled over into everyday life on both sides of the divide. Propaganda made it clear that the Germans had 'sowed the wind and would reap the whirlwind'. It becomes a matter of the old Biblical *Lex talionis* (an eye for an eye and a tooth for a tooth) and it was no surprise as Overy points out, that the RAF reflected this in their operational names of *Gomorrah*, *Millennium*, and *Chastise*.[53]

However, it must be noted in this section, which even for this writer seems full of gloom and doom, there were some who retained a sense of personal free will, a sense of the traditional teaching of right and wrong, and a desire to act in a humane way and avoid criminal and immoral orders. It should be recalled that the Gulag was noted for human suffering because some had dared to oppose Stalin, and in Germany Dachau was always full. In Nazi Germany it must not be forgotten there was resistance against the Nazi regime. It ranged from rebellious Hitler Youth to university students, to diplomats and many in the military. There are many examples where people under serious stress retained a sense of morality and free will under the most extreme circumstances. There is the well-known account of Maximilian Kolbe, a Polish priest who in 1941 offered himself to be executed in a German concentration camp to spare the life of a married man. His sense of humanity and conscience defied the Nazi State's effort to mould him to their shape, and he rose above the animal instinct of survival. The historian Burleigh offered various accounts of German soldiers who risked their lives to save Jewish people, again clearly indicating that some people managed to retain their human sense of freedom. Reinhold Lofy refused to shoot an elderly Jew when ordered, and when he was promoted to Lieutenant refused to send his men out on a suicide mission, and made detrimental comments on Nazi policy, even though this moral attitude had him sentenced to six years in a penal battalion. Corporal Anton Schmidt was a middle-aged soldier, he was no intellectual, never read a book, ran a truck repair garage when at home as a civilian, but he forged false papers 'to spirit 300 Jews out of Vilna, depositing them in the smaller towns of Lithuania where they seemed safer', for which action he was executed.[54] In 1939 Major Helmuth Stieff, a German staff officer, wrote to his wife that he felt guilty on seeing the ruins of Warsaw, and that 'it shamed me to be a German'.[55] General Blaskowitz wrote and complained about the atrocities. Not every German co-operated or agreed with the barbaric orders, and many understood that it was morally reprehensible. There were businessmen like Oskar Schindler, Friedrich Graebe and Franz Fritzsch who decided not to cooperate with immoral deeds, and they did not allow themselves to be moulded by the political controls of the mind. There were many such people generally overlooked, indicating that the power of a tyrant's influence does not necessarily dictate a person's behaviour or attitudes, and free will could still be activated.

The problem is almost like a mathematical formula with precise patterns of outcome. An autocratic leader adds his ideology to his propaganda, which leads to persuasion, influence, and results in subservience. This is followed by total control of citizens who are compelled to abandon their right of freedom of choice. Those who are strong enough to retain any sense of freedom are in prison or eliminated, those unsure are given no choice if they wish to survive. This system demands the support of henchmen also seeking power and position, and as a consequence there is repression and nearly always war, which inevitably is fought under criminal and immoral orders resulting in evil conditions.

Himmler once had reason to discipline an officer called Globocnik for immoral behaviour, but he promptly promoted him, and he became the driving force for the Final Solution in Poland. Beria was a man who gratified his appetites both sexually and in power politics. As Solzhenitsyn noted men 'were possessed and directed by the two strongest instincts of the lower sphere, other than hunger and sex: greed for power and greed for gain. Particularly for power. In recent decades it has turned out to be more important than money'.[56]

Men like Beria, Himmler, Stalin, and Hitler made animals appear decent and normal. They, unlike animals, created evil because they had freedom of choice by removing the free will of their own citizens. Without freedom of thought and expression, without free will and conscience with its sense of guilt, the appalling aspects of evil will control humanity and the problem still exists. It is a matter of recognising such people and not allowing them to rise to authority over others.

Appendix

Solzhenitsyn and the Gulag

In his book on the *12 Rules for Life* Jordan Peterson made the point that to avoid despair which can be endemic to humanity, people should treat the world personally, but if treated too objectively there remains a distance.[1] The message is that if we are asked to think about a prisoner's life in the third person, the result is not so animating when it is done in the first person, namely it is better to understand the situation as if *I am the prisoner*. As such, Solzhenitsyn in his work on *The Gulag Archipelago* takes us inside the mind and daily conditions of the Gulag prisoner at a personal level. The book is not a novel but a serious historical reconstruction. Solzhenitsyn wrote that 'For a few decades the word *Holocaust* has served us well as a shorthand term for modern man's inhumanity to man. In recent years, a second such shorthand has entered our working vocabulary, *Gulag*'.[2] Solzhenitsyn was such a prisoner describing in his work the camps in painful detail, bringing home the appalling reality of what Stalin and Beria imposed upon ordinary and all too frequently innocent people.

Solzhenitsyn described the fear of arrest because of the well-known consequences, and the sense of isolation as one's world disintegrates. A prisoner's home was searched looking for incriminating evidence. Solzhenitsyn related the account of a railway engineer called Inoshin, in whose rooms was a coffin with the body of his recently dead child. The body was tipped out of the coffin and searched before being tossed on the floor.[3] Those members of the family who were not arrested were told there was no right of correspondence with the prisoner, which often indicated the prisoner was to be executed.

The officials were given quotas for the necessary slave labour and would eliminate anyone who dared criticise the State. Solzhenitsyn described throughout his work the assorted reasons given for an arrest. He described how some young girls collected a few grains of wheat and received twenty years for being 'an organised gang'. He wrote of a shepherd swearing at his 'collectivised' cow, children in a playground who knocked down a government notice, a fourteen-year-old child, Lida, picking lost grain up from the path, and another young girl called Iruna Tuchinskaya who was arrested leaving church on the purported grounds that she had been praying for Stalin's death.[4]

Later Russian soldiers and civilians who had been captured by the Germans were often arrested as traitors, but the real reason was that they had seen too much of Western life, and they might be in danger of talking about what they had witnessed. In the years that Solzhenitsyn experienced, he listed other reasons for arrests, they ranged from spying to praising American technology, democracy, or 'Toadyism' towards the West. It had been established in Article 12 of the Criminal Code of 1926 that children from the age of twelve could be arrested, but when families were arrested even younger ones left for the camps. Solzhenitsyn was naturally cynical about the whole *raison d'être*, pointing out the old Russian proverb that a 'stone is not a human being, and even stones get crushed'. He reflected on Tsarist days, noting the differences, recalling out that Lenin's brother had been executed for attempting to kill Tsar Alexander III, but Lenin had still been allowed to study law at university, adding that 'no Genghis Khan ever destroyed so many peasants as our glorious *Organs*, [his term for Soviet secret police] under the leadership of the Party'.[5]

Solzhenitsyn wrote about the interrogations, mentioning their methods, including torture. Few people would have possibly predicted 'that prisoners would have their skulls squeezed within iron rings, that a human being would be lowered into an acid bath; that they would be trussed up naked to be bitten by ants and bedbugs; that a ramrod heated over a primus stove would be thrust up their anal canal; that a man's genitals would be slowly crushed beneath the toe of a jackboot'.[6] Only Peter the Great may possibly have used this type of torture against only ten or twenty people. Solzhenitsyn lists thirty detailed means ranging from the psychological to outright torture to encourage victims to confess to crimes they or others had never committed. Solzhenitsyn reminds his readers that it was impossible to imagine this hell on earth unless one had experienced the process. He wrote that it was comparable to trying to explain to a medieval peasant the speed of a jet plane.

The transportation to the remote camps often resulted in deaths and killings on the way. The camps were remote, and any escape was unlikely given the wide-spread freezing regions where these camps were placed. There were some specialised camps for scientists and technicians, and what were called TONs intended for Special Purpose Prisons for long-term prisoners, designed to isolate rebels. They were all labour camps with much in common, namely death which was administered by brutal work, long hours, appalling rations, and a cold climate. The camp inmates described three weeks at logging as 'dry execution', and even when the weather improved life remained tenuous.[7] Random killing frequently happened and Solzhenitsyn described the time a guard decided that someone was about to break rank, so he 'opened fire and killed five prisoners, he was put in detention for fifteen days (in a warm guardhouse, of course)'.[8]

Solzhenitsyn noted that 'at the end of the workday there were corpses left on the work site. The snow powdered their faces. One of them was hunched over beneath an overturned wheelbarrow, he had hidden his hands in his sleeves and frozen to death in that position'.[9] 'Those who lagged behind were beaten with clubs and torn by dogs. Working in 50 degrees below zero Fahrenheit, they were forbidden to build fires and warm themselves'.[10] Solzhenitsyn described in detail the effects of hunger and how it was always central to one's thinking, and the effects on women at the mercy of the *trustees*. Solzhenitsyn persistently pointed out that his account sounded unbelievable unless a person had the experience, but his book managed to convey the ruthless barbarity from which the prisoners suffered which was imposed by Stalin and his men. According to Solzhenitsyn the camps lived off constant fear, servitude, secrecy and mistrust, universal ignorance, and squealing. Betrayal was a form of existence, corruption, and lies were all a means of staying alive, as was cruelty and slave psychology.

The West generally remained ignorant of this absolute wicked cruelty until Solzhenitsyn's work was published. Stalin, Beria, and their men ensured that the outside world received only their version of the reformative nature of hard labour. Marx himself had noted that hard labour was good for the criminal, but as Solzhenitsyn noted, Marx had never picked up an axe or pick in his lifetime. The Nazi concentration and labour camps have had a considerable wealth of literature and history written about them, but the

Soviet system remains somewhat hidden to this day. Solzhenitsyn was always astounded at the ignorance of the West and even more so at their ignorance of what happened to prisoners of war who were dutifully returned to Stalin, the West not understanding the ramifications even as late as 1973.[11]

When in 1929 Gorky had visited the camps, they were suddenly organised to look healthy, and the prisoners forced to appear grateful. Solzhenitsyn related how one brave boy told him all the facts and was shot when Gorky left, and Gorky's article claimed that 'it was nonsense to frighten people with Solovki, and that prisoners lived remarkably well there and were being well reformed'.*

In 1934 the State Publishing House produced a book called *The White Sea-Baltic Stalin Canal* which was an extension of the Gorky project *Histories of Factories and Plants*. 'The collective authors do not simply keep silent about the deaths on the Belomor Canal during the construction…they write directly that *no one* died during construction', they wrote that criminals (who are being reformed) are the result of the repulsive conditions of former times.[12] In *Life* magazine it was reported that a Supreme Court Judge in New York had paid a similar 'organised' visit, writing that 'in serving out his term of punishment the prisoner retains a feeling of dignity', to which Solzhenitsyn replied 'how much you have harmed us in your vain passions to shine with understanding in areas where you did not grasp a lousy thing!'**

It remains difficult even now (as Solzhenitsyn constantly warned his readers) to understand the gross inhumanity and evil of these camps, but his work conveyed some of the impact that men like Stalin and Beria had imposed on their own citizens and peoples of other nations. It is not difficult to use the words 'pure evil' when describing the Holocaust and the gas-chambers, but the Gulag system although different in some ways, was an evil which Solzhenitsyn brought to the world's attention.

---

* The Solovki camp was set up in 1923, an island in the White Sea. It was remote and inaccessible and was used as a place of detention for political opponents. At first these prisoners had a special status, but under Stalin they became labour (death) camps. The camps system policy evolved from the Solovki camp.

** Solzhenitsyn, Aleksandr, *The Gulag Archipelago 1918–56* (London: The Harvill Press, 1985), p.215.

Abbreviations

Cheka	1917–1922 The All-Russian Extraordinary Commission, (VChK) Secret Police.
Comintern	Communist International, ECCI.
FSB	Federal Security of the Russian Federation.
FSK	Federal Counter-Intelligence Services.
GPU	State Political Directorate, Secret Police.
GRU	1934–1941 Red Army Intelligence Unit.
GUGB	1934–1941 Main Directorate of State Security within NKVD
Gulag	Main Administration of Camps
INO	Inostrannyi Otdel, Foreign Intelligence of OGPU, targeting émigrés.
KGB	1954–1991 Committee for State Security.
MB	1991–93 Ministry of Security
MOR	Monarchist Association of Central Russia.
MGB	1946–1953 Ministry of State Security
MVD	1953–1954 Ministry of Internal Affairs
NKGB	1941–43 People's Commissariat for State Security.
NKVD	1934–1941 The Peoples' Commissariat for Internal Affairs.
OGPU	See GPU, Secret Police.
Okhrana	Department for Protecting the Public Security and Order: The Tsar's Secret Police.
SMERSH	Cover name for three counter-intelligence services in Red Army (late 1942).
Sovnarkom	Council of Peoples' Commissars.
SPO	Secret Political Department.
SVR	Foreign Intelligence Service.
TASS	Soviet News Agency
VeCheka	See Cheka.

Notes

Introduction

1. Michel, Henri, *The Second World War* (London: Deutsch, 1975), p.241.
2. Ibid., p.8.
3. Ferris, John (Ed.), *The Cambridge History of the Second World War, Volume I: Fighting the War* (Cambridge: CUP, 2015), p.639.
4. Roberts, Andrew, *The Storm of War* (London: Allen Lane, 2009), p.492.
5. Ibid., p.643.
6. *The Guardian*, 18 July 2020.
7. See Arendt, Hannah, *The Origins of Totalitarianism* (London: André Deutsch, 1951), pp.434–5.
8. Suny, Ronald Grigor, *The Structure of Soviet History: Essays and Documents* (Oxford: OUP, 2014), p.xiii.
9. O'Brien, W.V. (Freedman, Lawrence, Ed.), *War* (Oxford: OUP, 1994), p.180.
10. See the opening pages of Lockhart, R.H. Bruce, *Memoirs of a British Agent* (London: The Folio Society, 2003)
11. Seton-Watson, Hugh, *The Russian Empire 1801–1971* (Oxford: OUP, 1967), p.587.
12. Service, Robert, *The Penguin History of Modern Russia: From Tsarism to the Twenty-first Century* (London: Penguin, 2015), p.19.
13. Lockhart, R.H. Bruce, *Memoirs of a British Agent* (London: The Folio Society, 2003), p.43.
14. Crawford, Donald in Smith, Douglas (Brenton, Tony (Ed.)), *Historically Inevitable? Turning Points of the Russian Revolution* (London: Profile Books, 2016), p.66.
15. Hellbeck, Jochen in Suny, Ronald Grigor, *The Structure of Soviet History: Essays and Documents* (Oxford: OUP, 2014), p.198.
16. Andrew, Christopher & Gordievsky, Oleg, *KGB: The Inside Story* (London: Hodder & Stoughton, 1990), p.19.
17. Antonov-Ovseyenko, Anton, *The Time of Stalin: Portrait of a Tyranny* (London: Harper & Row, 1981), p.123.
18. Andrew, Christopher, *The Secret World: A History of Intelligence* (London: Penguin Books, 2019), p.556.
19. Andrew, Christopher & Gordievsky, Oleg, *KGB: The Inside Story*, p.43.
20. Churchill, Winston, *Great Contemporaries* (Delaware: ISI Books, 2012, original publication 1937), p.133.
21. Antonov-Ovseyenko, Anton, *The Time of Stalin: Portrait of a Tyranny*, p.45.
22. Quoted from *Iz istorii VchK* (History of the Cheka), Moscow 1958 and quoted in Antonov-Ovseyenko, Anton, *The Time of Stalin: Portrait of a Tyranny*, p.151.
23. Montefiore, Simon Sebag, *Stalin: The Court of the Red Tsar* (London: Weidenfeld & Nicolson, 2003), p.158.
24. Deutscher, Isaac, *Stalin: A Political Biography* (New York: OUP, 1967), p.228.
25. Figes, Orlando, *A People's Tragedy: The Russian Revolution 1891–1924* (London: The Bodley Head, 2014), p.794.

26. Alliluyeva, Svetlana, *Only One Year* (London: Hutchinson, 1969), p.147.
27. Andrew, Christopher & Gordievsky, Oleg, *KGB: The Inside Story*, p.81.
28. See Montefiore, Simon Sebag, *Stalin: The Court of the Red Tsar* (London: Weidenfeld & Nicolson, 2003), p.85.
29. See Gellately, Robert, *Stalin's Curse: Battling for Communism in War and Cold War* (Oxford: OUP, 2013).
30. Montefiore, Simon Sebag, *Stalin: The Court of the Red Tsar*, p.218.
31. Antonov-Ovseyenko, Anton, *The Time of Stalin: Portrait of a Tyranny*, p.124.
32. Kotkin, Stephen, *Stalin, Vol II: Waiting for Hitler, 1928–1941* (London: Allen Lane, 2017), p.501.
33. See Bullard, Julian and Margaret (Eds), *Inside Stalin's Russia: The Diaries of Reader Bullard 1930–1934* (Oxfordshire: Day Books, 2000), pp.202–203.
34. Antonov-Ovseyenko, Anton, *The Time of Stalin: Portrait of a Tyranny*, p.117.
35. Montefiore, Simon Sebag, *Stalin: The Court of the Red Tsar*, p.154.
36. See Alliluyeva, Svetlana, *Twenty Letters to a Friend* (New York: Harper & Row, 1967), p.83.
37. Ibid.
38. Koestler, Arthur, *Darkness at Noon* (London: Penguin Books, 1947).
39. See Antonov-Ovseyenko, Anton, *The Time of Stalin: Portrait of a Tyranny*, pp.91–3.
40. Knight Amy, *Beria Stalin's First Lieutenant* (Princetown: University Press, 1993), pp.67–8.
41. See Andrew, Christopher, *The Secret World: A History of Intelligence*, pp.594–5.
42. Lewin, Moshe, *The Soviet Century* (London: Verso, 2016), p.92.
43. Kotkin, Stephen, *Stalin, Vol II: Waiting for Hitler*, p.589.
44. Antonov-Ovseyenko, Anton, *The Time of Stalin: Portrait of a Tyranny*, p.183.
45. Ferris, John (Ed.), *The Cambridge History of the Second World War, Volume I: Fighting the War*, p.648.
46. Rees, Laurence, *World War II Behind Closed Doors: Stalin, The Nazis and the West* (London: BBC Books, 2008), p.223.
47. Suny, Ronald Grigor, *The Structure of Soviet History: Essays and Documents* (Oxford: OUP, 2014), p.168.

Chapter 1

1. See Montefiore, Simon Sebag, *Stalin: The Court of the Red Tsar, Stalin*, p.67.
2. See Kotkin, Stephen, *Stalin, Vol II: Waiting for Hitler, 1928–1941*, p.139.
3. Wittlin, Thaddeus, *Commissar: The Life and Death of Lavrenty Pavlovich Beria* (New York: Macmillan, 1972), p.xix.
4. Knight, Amy, *Beria: Stalin's First Lieutenant*, p.16.
5. See Montefiore, Simon Sebag, *Stalin: The Court of the Red Tsar*, p.447.
6. See Kotkin, Stephen, *Stalin, Vol II: Waiting for Hitler, 1928–1941*, p.139, and Montefiore, Simon Sebag, *Stalin: The Court of the Red Tsar*, p.67.
7. See Kotkin, Stephen, *Stalin, Vol II: Waiting for Hitler, 1928–1941*, p.541.
8. Knight, Amy, *Beria: Stalin's First Lieutenant*, p.21.
9. Kotkin, Stephen, *Stalin, Vol II: Waiting for Hitler, 1928–1941*, p.139.
10. Ibid., p.140.
11. Alliluyeva, Svetlana, *Only One Year*, p.387.
12. Montefiore, Simon Sebag, *Stalin: The Court of the Red Tsar*, p.67.
13. Ings, Simon, *Stalin and the Scientists: A History of Triumph and Tragedy 1905–1953* (London; Faber & Faber, 2017), p.300.
14. Quoted in Montefiore, Simon Sebag, *Stalin: The Court of the Red Tsar*, p.40.
15. Montefiore, Simon Sebag, *Stalin: The Court of the Red Tsar*, p.42.

16. Kotkin, Stephen, *Stalin, Vol II: Waiting for Hitler, 1928–1941*, p.549.
17. Knight, Amy, *Beria: Stalin's First Lieutenant*, pp.32–3.
18. Antonov-Ovseyenko, Anton, *The Time of Stalin: Portrait of a Tyranny*, p.71.
19. See Knight, Amy, *Beria: Stalin's First Lieutenant*, pp.35–6.
20. Kotkin, Stephen, *Stalin, Vol II: Waiting for Hitler, 1928–1941*, p.515.
21. See Montefiore, Simon Sebag, *Stalin: The Court of the Red Tsar*, p.112.
22. This letter can be found in Knight, Amy, *Beria: Stalin's First Lieutenant*, p.40.
23. See Kotkin, Stephen, *Stalin, Vol II: Waiting for Hitler, 1928–1941*, p.140.
24. See Montefiore, Simon Sebag, *Stalin: The Court of the Red Tsar*, p.103.
25. Ibid., p.79.
26. Kotkin, Stephen, *Stalin, Vol II: Waiting for Hitler, 1928–1941*, p.140.
27. Antonov-Ovseyenko, Anton, *The Time of Stalin: Portrait of a Tyranny*, p.148.
28. See Knight, Amy, *Beria: Stalin's First Lieutenant*, p.53.
29. Montefiore, Simon Sebag, *Stalin: The Court of the Red Tsar*, p.115.
30. Ibid., p.161.
31. See Knight, Amy, *Beria: Stalin's First Lieutenant*, p.58.
32. Kotkin, Stephen, *Stalin, Vol II: Waiting for Hitler, 1928–1941*, p.260.
33. Knight, Amy, *Beria: Stalin's First Lieutenant*, p.62.
34. Service, Robert, *Stalin: A Biography*, p.360.
35. Kotkin, Stephen, *Stalin, Vol II: Waiting for Hitler, 1928–1941*, p.301.
36. Antonov-Ovseyenko, Anton, *The Time of Stalin: Portrait of a Tyranny*, p.125.
37. Kotkin, Stephen, *Stalin, Vol II: Waiting for Hitler, 1928–1941*, p.502.
38. Ibid., p.503.
39. Ibid., p.505.
40. Montefiore, Simon Sebag, *Stalin: The Court of the Red Tsar*, p.179.
41. Ibid., p.222.
42. Kotkin, Stephen, *Stalin, Vol II: Waiting for Hitler, 1928–1941*, p.506.
43. Ibid., p.507.
44. Antonov-Ovseyenko, Anton, *The Time of Stalin: Portrait of a Tyranny*, p.125.
45. Kotkin, Stephen, *Stalin, Vol II: Waiting for Hitler, 1928–1941*, p.549.
46. Quoted in Kotkin Stephen, *Stalin, Vol II*, p.626.
47. Rubenstein, Joshua, *The Last Days of Stalin* (London: Yale University Press, 2016), p.195.
48. See Knight, Amy, *Beria: Stalin's First Lieutenant*, pp.82–3.
49. See Kotkin, Stephen, *Stalin, Vol II: Waiting for Hitler, 1928–1941*, p.517.
50. Ibid., p.518.
51. Kotkin, Stephen, *Stalin, Vol II: Waiting for Hitler, 1928–1941*, p.520.
52. Gellately, Robert, *Stalin's Curse: Battling for Communism in War and Cold War*, p.37.
53. Siegelbaum, Lewis and Sokolov, Andrei, *Stalinism as a Way of Life: A Narrative in Documents* (London: Yale University Press, 2000), pp.241–2.
54. Kotkin, Stephen, *Stalin, Vol II: Waiting for Hitler, 1928–1941*, p.511.
55. Alliluyeva, Svetlana, *Twenty Letters to a Friend* (New York: Harper & Row, 1967).
56. See Antonov-Ovseyenko, Anton, *The Time of Stalin: Portrait of a Tyranny*, p.124.
57. Service, Robert, *Stalin: A Biography*, p.368.
58. Solzhenitsyn, Aleksandr, *The Gulag Archipelago 1918–56* (London: The Harvill Press, 1985), pp.30 and 44.
59. See Knight, Amy, *Beria: Stalin's First Lieutenant*, p.88.
60. Kotkin, Stephen, *Stalin, Vol II: Waiting for Hitler, 1928–1941*, p.542.
61. Ibid., p.512.
62. Ibid., p.501.

63. Khlevniuk, Oleg V., *Stalin: New Biography of a Dictator* (London: Yale UP, 2015), p.332fn.
64. Figes, Orlando, *The Whisperers: Private Life in Stalin's Russia* (London: Penguin Books, 2008), p.279.
65. Service, Robert, *Stalin: A Biography*, p.368.
66. Christopher, Andrew & Oleg, Gordievsky, *KGB: The Inside Story of its Foreign Operations from Lenin to Gorbachev* (London: Hodder & Stoughton, 1990), p.130.
67. Montefiore, Simon Sebag, *Stalin: The Court of the Red Tsar*, p.244.
68. Kotkin, Stephen, *Stalin, Vol II: Waiting for Hitler, 1928–1941*, p.605.
69. Quoted in Montefiore, Simon Sebag, *Stalin: The Court of the Red Tsar*, pp.216–17.
70. Alliluyeva, Svetlana, *Twenty Letters to a Friend*, p.19.
71. Montefiore, Simon Sebag, *Stalin: The Court of the Red Tsar*, p.255.
72. Burleigh, Michael, *Moral Combat: A History of World War II* (London: Harper Press, 2010), p.89.
73. See Knight, Amy, *Beria: Stalin's First Lieutenant*, p.92.
74. Figes, Orlando, *The Whisperers: Private Life in Stalin's Russia*, p.280.
75. Montefiore, Simon Sebag, *Stalin: The Court of the Red Tsar*, p.261.
76. Sudoplatov, Pavel and Anatoli, *Special Tasks: The Memoirs of an Unwanted Witness – A Soviet Spymaster* (London: Little, Brown and Company, 1994), p.41.
77. Conquest, Robert, *The Great Terror: A Reassessment* (New York: OUP, 1990), p.627.
78. Service, Robert, *Stalin: A Biography*, p.369.
79. Lewin, Moshe, *The Soviet Century* (London: Verso, 2016), p.107.
80. Ibid., p.111.
81. Figes, Orlando, *The Whisperers: Private Life in Stalin's Russia*, p.537.
82. Lewin, Moshe, *The Soviet Century* (London: Verso, 2016), p.113.
83. Burleigh, Michael, *Moral Combat: A History of World War II*, p.87.
84. See Ings, Simon, *Stalin and the Scientists: A History of Triumph and Tragedy 1905–1953* (London; Faber & Faber, 2017), pp.431–2.
85. See Service, Robert, *Stalin: A Biography*, p.374.
86. Lewin, Moshe, *The Soviet Century* (London: Verso, 2016), p.118.
87. Montefiore, Simon Sebag, *Stalin: The Court of the Red Tsar*, p.267.
88. Gellately, Robert, *Stalin's Curse: Battling for Communism in War and Cold War*, p.49.
89. Siegelbaum, Lewis and Sokolov, Andrei, *Stalinism as a Way of Life*, p.263.
90. See Kotkin, Stephen, *Stalin, Vol II: Waiting for Hitler, 1928–1941*, p.745.
91. A copy of this letter can be found in Sudoplatov, Pavel and Anatoli, *Special Tasks: The Memoirs of an Unwanted Witness – A Soviet Spymaster* (London: Little, Brown and Company, 1994), pp.476–8. See also Appendix Two.
92. Moore, Bob, in *The Cambridge History of the Second World War, Vol 1* (Cambridge: CUP, 2015), p.666.
93. See Knight, Amy, *Beria: Stalin's First Lieutenant*, p.105.
94. See Ings, Simon, *Stalin and the Scientists: A History of Triumph and Tragedy 1905–1953* (London; Faber & Faber, 2017), pp.312–13.
95. Christopher, Andrew and Oleg, Gordievsky, *KGB: The Inside Story*, p.195.
96. Hastings, Max, *The Secret War: Spies, Codes and Guerrillas 1939–1945* (London: William Collins, 2015), p.129.
97. Knight, Amy, *Beria: Stalin's First Lieutenant*, p.109.
98. Sudoplatov, Pavel and Anatoli, *Special Tasks: The Memoirs of an Unwanted Witness – A Soviet Spymaster*, p.117 & p.122.
99. See Ibid., p.121.

100. Clark, Alan, *Barbarossa: The Russian-German Conflict 1941–1945* (London: Phoenix Press, 1965), p.49.
101. Sangster, Andrew, *Field-Marshal Kesselring: Great Commander or War Criminal?* (Newcastle: Cambridge Scholars, 2015), p.65.
102. Knight, Amy, *Beria: Stalin's First Lieutenant*, pp.110–11.
103. Quoted in Kotkin, Stephen, *Stalin, Vol II: Waiting for Hitler, 1928–1941*, p.880.
104. Service, Robert, *Stalin: A Biography*, p.410.
105. Gellately, Robert, *Stalin's Curse: Battling for Communism in War and Cold War*, p.59.
106. Montefiore, Simon Sebag, *Stalin: The Court of the Red Tsar*, p.333f.
107. Service, Robert, *Stalin: A Biography*, p.415.
108. Quoted in Montefiore, Simon Sebag, *Stalin: The Court of the Red Tsar*, p.330.
109. Christopher, Andrew and Oleg, Gordievsky, *KGB: The Inside Story*, p.220.
110. See Montefiore, Simon Sebag, *Stalin: The Court of the Red Tsar*, p.336.
111. Khlevniuk, Oleg V., *Stalin: New Biography of a Dictator*, p.203.
112. Sudoplatov, Pavel and Anatoli, *Special Tasks: The Memoirs of an Unwanted Witness – A Soviet Spymaster*, p.127.
113. Knight, Amy, *Beria: Stalin's First Lieutenant*, p.113.
114. Hastings, Max, *The Secret War: Spies, Codes and Guerrillas 1939–1945*, p.175.
115. Burleigh, Michael, *Moral Combat: A History of World War II*, p.154.
116. Montefiore, Simon Sebag, *Stalin: The Court of the Red Tsar*, p.360.
117. Ibid., p.338.
118. See Christopher, Andrew and Oleg, Gordievsky, *KGB: The Inside Story*, pp.220–1.
119. Sudoplatov, Pavel and Anatoli, *Special Tasks: The Memoirs of an Unwanted Witness – A Soviet Spymaster*, p.135.
120. Ibid., p.136.
121. Burleigh, Michael, *Moral Combat: A History of World War II*, p.348.
122. Ibid., p.225.
123. Gellately, Robert, *Stalin's Curse: Battling for Communism in War and Cold War*, p.194.
124. See Sudoplatov, Pavel and Anatoli, *Special Tasks: The Memoirs of an Unwanted Witness – A Soviet Spymaster*, p.163.
125. Montefiore, Simon Sebag, *Stalin: The Court of the Red Tsar*, p.390.
126. Sudoplatov, Pavel and Anatoli, *Special Tasks: The Memoirs of an Unwanted Witness – A Soviet Spymaster*, p.129.
127. Montefiore, Simon Sebag, *Stalin: The Court of the Red Tsar*, p.349.
128. See Hastings, Max, *The Secret War: Spies, Codes and Guerrillas 1939–1945*, pp.178–9.
129. Sudoplatov, Pavel and Anatoli, *Special Tasks: The Memoirs of an Unwanted Witness – A Soviet Spymaster*, p.148.
130. Montefiore, Simon Sebag, *Stalin: The Court of the Red Tsar*, p.376.
131. Quoted in Knight, Amy, *Beria: Stalin's First Lieutenant*, p.123.
132. Montefiore, Simon Sebag, *Stalin: The Court of the Red Tsar*, p.400.
133. Gellately, Robert, *Stalin's Curse: Battling for Communism in War and Cold War*, p.180.
134. Ibid., p.182.
135. Ibid.
136. Ibid., p.186.
137. Ibid., p.199.
138. Ibid., p.202.
139. Knight, Amy, *Beria: Stalin's First Lieutenant*, p.127.
140. Montefiore, Simon Sebag, *Stalin: The Court of the Red Tsar*, p.419.
141. Knight, Amy, *Beria: Stalin's First Lieutenant*, p.130.

142. See Montefiore, Simon Sebag, *Stalin: The Court of the Red Tsar*, p.410.

143. Gellately, Robert, *Stalin's Curse: Battling for Communism in War and Cold War*, p.80.

144. Ibid., p.158.

145. Montefiore, Simon Sebag, *Stalin: The Court of the Red Tsar*, p.494fn.

146. Service, Robert, *Stalin: A Biography*, p.508.

147. Gellately, Robert, *Stalin's Curse: Battling for Communism in War and Cold War*, p.142.

148. Sudoplatov, Pavel and Anatoli, *Special Tasks: The Memoirs of an Unwanted Witness – A Soviet Spymaster*, p.173.

149. Volodarsky, Boris, *Stalin's Agent: The Life and Death of Alexander Orlov* (Oxford: OUP, 2015), p.484.

150. Sudoplatov, Pavel and Anatoli, *Special Tasks: The Memoirs of an Unwanted Witness – A Soviet Spymaster*, p.xiv.

151. Gellately, Robert, *Stalin's Curse: Battling for Communism in War and Cold War*, p.163.

152. Hastings, Max, *The Secret War: Spies, Codes and Guerrillas 1939–1945*, p.123.

153. Sudoplatov, Pavel and Anatoli, *Special Tasks: The Memoirs of an Unwanted Witness – A Soviet Spymaster*, p.187.

154. Hastings, Max, *The Secret War: Spies, Codes and Guerrillas 1939–1945*, p.526.

155. Knight, Amy, *Beria: Stalin's First Lieutenant*, p.134.

156. Quoted in Christopher, Andrew and Oleg, Gordievsky, *KGB: The Inside Story*, p.310.

157. Ibid., p.312.

158. Gellately, Robert, *Stalin's Curse: Battling for Communism in War and Cold War*, p.343.

159. See Sudoplatov, Pavel and Anatoli, *Special Tasks: The Memoirs of an Unwanted Witness – A Soviet Spymaster*, p.221.

160. Ibid., p.222

161. Ibid., p.231

162. Christopher, Andrew and Oleg Gordievsky, *KGB: The Inside Story*, p.279.

163. See Knight, Amy, *Beria: Stalin's First Lieutenant*, p.141.

164. Brent, Jonathan and Naumov, Vladimir P., *Stalin's Last Crime: The Plot Against the Jewish Doctors, 1948–1953* (New York, Harper Collins, 2003), p.153.

165. Christopher, Andrew and Oleg, Gordievsky, *KGB: The Inside Story*, p.314.

166. Ibid., p.315.

167. See Knight, Amy, *Beria: Stalin's First Lieutenant*, p.142.

168. Montefiore, Simon Sebag, *Stalin: The Court of the Red Tsar*, p.460.

169. Alliluyeva, Svetlana, *Twenty Letters to a Friend*, p.187.

170. Service, Robert, *Stalin: A Biography*, p.577.

171. Christopher, Andrew and Oleg, Gordievsky, *KGB: The Inside Story*, p.316.

172. Ibid., p.336.

173. Montefiore, Simon Sebag, *Stalin: The Court of the Red Tsar*, p.448.

174. Alliluyeva, Svetlana, *Twenty Letters to a Friend*, pp.22–3.

175. Alliluyeva, Svetlana, *Only One Year*, p.363.

176. Antonov-Ovseyenko, Anton, *The Time of Stalin: Portrait of a Tyranny*, p.294.

177. Service, Robert, *Stalin: A Biography*, p.523.

178. Quoted in Montefiore, Simon Sebag, *Stalin: The Court of the Red Tsar*, p.462.

179. Ibid., p.460.

180. Alliluyeva, Svetlana, *Only One Year*, p.352.

181. Ibid., p.395.

182. Ibid., p.396.

183. Knight, Amy, *Beria: Stalin's First Lieutenant*, p.153.

184. Alliluyeva, Svetlana, *Only One Year*, p.353.

185. Alliluyeva, Svetlana, *Twenty Letters,* p.193.
186. Montefiore, Simon Sebag, *Stalin: The Court of the Red Tsar,* p.456.
187. Ibid., p.549.
188. Knight, Amy, *Beria: Stalin's First Lieutenant,* p.157.
189. Montefiore, Simon Sebag, *Stalin: The Court of the Red Tsar,* p.541.
190. Sudoplatov, Pavel and Anatoli, *Special Tasks: The Memoirs of an Unwanted Witness – A Soviet Spymaster,* p.299.
191. See Montefiore, Simon Sebag, *Stalin: The Court of the Red Tsar,* p.476.
192. See Williams, Alan, *The Beria Papers* (Frogmore: Panther Books, 1974).
193. See Montefiore, Simon Sebag, *Stalin: The Court of the Red Tsar,* p.548.
194. Khlevniuk, Oleg V., *Stalin: New Biography of a Dictator,* p.305.
195. Sudoplatov, Pavel and Anatoli, *Special Tasks: The Memoirs of an Unwanted Witness – A Soviet Spymaster,* p.313.
196. Montefiore, Simon Sebag, *Stalin: The Court of the Red Tsar,* p.561.
197. See Knight, Amy, *Beria: Stalin's First Lieutenant,* p.165.
198. See Montefiore, Simon Sebag, *Stalin: The Court of the Red Tsar,* p.270.
199. See Sudoplatov, Pavel and Anatoli, *Special Tasks: The Memoirs of an Unwanted Witness – A Soviet Spymaster,* p.285.
200. Ibid., p.309.
201. See Knight, Amy, *Beria: Stalin's First Lieutenant,* p.169.
202. Brent, Jonathan and Naumov, Vladimir P., *Stalin's Last Crime: The Plot Against the Jewish Doctors, 1948–1953,* p.179.
203. Ibid., p.67.
204. Ibid., p.184.
205. Ibid., p.131.
206. See Conquest, Robert, *Power and Policy in the USSR* (New York: Harper & Row, 1967), p.171.
207. Brent, Jonathan and Naumov, Vladimir P., *Stalin's Last Crime: The Plot Against the Jewish Doctors, 1948–1953,* pp.66–7.
208. Gorlizki, Y. & Khlevniuk, Oleg in Suny, Ronald Grigor, *The Structure of Soviet History: Essays and Documents* (Oxford: OUP, 2014), p.321.
209. Montefiore, Simon Sebag, *Stalin: The Court of the Red Tsar,* p.559.
210. Christopher, Andrew and Oleg, Gordievsky, *KGB: The Inside Story,* p.347.
211. See Hingley, Ronald, *The Russian Secret Police: Muscovite, Imperial Russian and Soviet Political Security Operations* (New York: Simon and Schuster, 1970).
212. Montefiore, Simon Sebag, *Stalin: The Court of the Red Tsar,* p.545.
213. Gorlizki, Y. & Khlevniuk, Oleg in Suny, Ronald Grigor, *The Structure of Soviet History: Essays and Documents,* p.322.
214. Alliluyeva, Svetlana, *Twenty Letters to a Friend,* pp.6–7.
215. See Montefiore, Simon Sebag, *Stalin: The Court of the Red Tsar,* p.570.
216. Gellately, Robert, *Stalin's Curse: Battling for Communism in War and Cold War,* p.378.
217. Knight, Amy, *Beria: Stalin's First Lieutenant,* p.179.
218. Alliluyeva, Svetlana, *Twenty Letters to a Friend,* p.7.
219. Ibid., p.11.
220. Quoted in Rubenstein, Joshua, *The Last Days of Stalin* (London: Yale University Press, 2016), p.9.
221. Ibid., p.14.
222. Brent, Jonathan and Naumov, Vladimir P., *Stalin's Last Crime: The Plot Against the Jewish Doctors, 1948–1953,* p.320.

223. Service, Robert, *Stalin: A Biography*, p.592.

224. Ibid., p.587.

225. Christopher, Andrew and Oleg, Gordievsky, *KGB: The Inside Story*, p.349.

226. Sudoplatov, Pavel and Anatoli, *Special Tasks: The Memoirs of an Unwanted Witness – A Soviet Spymaster*, p.354.

227. Rubenstein, Joshua, *The Last Days of Stalin*, p.101.

228. Knight, Amy, *Beria: Stalin's First Lieutenant*, p.182.

229. See Service, Robert, *Stalin: A Biography*, p.495.

230. See Sudoplatov, Pavel and Anatoli, *Special Tasks: The Memoirs of an Unwanted Witness – A Soviet Spymaster*, p.xvii.

231. Ibid., p.358.

232. Ibid., p.339.

233. Ibid., p.108.

234. Khrushchev, N., *Khrushchev Remembers* (Boston: Little, Brown & Co, 1970), p.330.

235. Ibid., pp.327–8.

236. See Sudoplatov, Pavel and Anatoli, *Special Tasks: The Memoirs of an Unwanted Witness – A Soviet Spymaster*, p.363–4.

237. Gellately, Robert, *Stalin's Curse: Battling for Communism in War and Cold War*, p.385.

238. Christopher, Andrew and Oleg, Gordievsky, *KGB: The Inside Story*, p.350.

239. Rubenstein, Joshua, *The Last Days of Stalin*, p.206.

240. See Knight, Amy, *Beria: Stalin's First Lieutenant* and Rubenstein, Joshua, *The Last Days of Stalin*.

241. Sudoplatov, Pavel and Anatoli, *Special Tasks: The Memoirs of an Unwanted Witness – A Soviet Spymaster*, pp.372–3.

242. Quoted in Christopher, Andrew and Oleg, Gordievsky, *KGB: The Inside Story*, p.350.

243. Knight, Amy, *Beria: Stalin's First Lieutenant*, p.198.

244. Alliluyeva, Svetlana, *Only One Year*, p.354.

245. Knight, Amy, *Beria: Stalin's First Lieutenant*, p.199.

246. See Sudoplatov, Pavel and Anatoli, *Special Tasks: The Memoirs of an Unwanted Witness – A Soviet Spymaster*, p.363.

247. Knight, Amy, *Beria: Stalin's First Lieutenant*, p.204.

248. *Izvestiia*, TsK KPSS, No. 1 (1991): pp.141–7 and quoted in Knight, Amy, *Beria: Stalin's First Lieutenant*, p.205.

249. See Sudoplatov, Pavel and Anatoli, *Special Tasks: The Memoirs of an Unwanted Witness – A Soviet Spymaster*, pp.146–7.

250. Quoted in Knight, Amy, *Beria: Stalin's First Lieutenant*, p.216.

251. Quoted in Rubenstein, Joshua, *The Last Days of Stalin*, p.226.

252. Knight, Amy, *Beria: Stalin's First Lieutenant*, p.3.

253. See Service, Robert, *Stalin: A Biography*, p.573

254. See Hastings, Max, *The Secret War: Spies, Codes and Guerrillas 1939–1945*, p.355.

255. Sudoplatov, Pavel and Anatoli, *Special Tasks: The Memoirs of an Unwanted Witness – A Soviet Spymaster*, p.60.

256. On this subject see Knight, Amy, *Beria: Stalin's First Lieutenant*, p.97.

257. See Figes, Orlando, *The Whisperers: Private Life in Stalin's Russia*, p.402.

258. See Rubenstein, Joshua, *The Last Days of Stalin*, p.10.

259. Montefiore, Simon Sebag, *Stalin: The Court of the Red Tsar*, p.448.

260. Ibid., p.450fn.

261. Conquest, Robert, *The Great Terror: A Reassessment*, p.432.

262. See Alliluyeva, Svetlana, *Only One Year*, p.413.

263. See Montefiore, Simon Sebag, *Stalin: The Court of the Red Tsar*, p.108.

264. Kotkin, Stephen, *Stalin, Vol II: Waiting for Hitler, 1928–1941*, p.502.

265. Solzhenitsyn Aleksandr, *The Gulag*, p.12.

266. Kotkin, Stephen, *Stalin, Vol II: Waiting for Hitler, 1928–1941*, p.626.

267. Christopher, Andrew and Oleg, Gordievsky, *KGB: The Inside Story*, p.196.

268. Quoted in Ibid., p.216.

269. Montefiore, Simon Sebag, *Stalin: The Court of the Red Tsar*, p.426.

270. Ibid., p.579.

271. Solzhenitsyn, Aleksandr, *The Gulag Archipelago 1918–56*, p.126.

Chapter 2

1. Hastings, Max, *The Secret War: Spies, Codes and Guerrillas 1939–1945*, pp.18–21.

2. Sudoplatov, Pavel and Anatoli, *Special Tasks: The Memoirs of an Unwanted Witness – A Soviet Spymaster* (London: Little, Brown and Company, 1994).

3. Christopher, Andrew and Oleg, Gordievsky, *KGB: The Inside Story*, p.133.

Chapter 4

1. Service Robert, *The Oxford Companion to the Second World War* (Oxford: OUP, 1995), pp.123–4.

2. Solzhenitsyn, Aleksandr, *The Gulag Archipelago 1918–56*, p.80.

3. Buber, Martin, *Images of Good and Evil* (London: Routledge and Kegan Paul, 1952), pp.19, 26–7.

4. Augustine, *De libero arbitrio*.

5. Solzhenitsyn, Aleksandr, *The Gulag Archipelago 1918–56*, p.77.

6. Campbell, C.A., *On Selfhood and Godhood* (London: George Allen and Unwin, 1957), p.148.

7. Ibid., p.150.

8. Ibid., p.190.

9. Gellately, Robert, *The Nuremberg Interviews* (London: Pimlico, 2007), p.xxi.

10. Ibid., p.xxvii.

11. Telford, Taylor, *The Anatomy of the Nuremberg Trials* (New York: Alfred A Knopf, 1992), p.5.

12. See Browning, Christopher, *Ordinary Men* (London: Penguin Books, 2001).

13. Ibid., p.221.

14. Milgram, Stanley, *Obedience to Authority* (New York: Harper and Row, 1974)

15. See Milgram, Stanley, 'Behavioural Study of Obedience' in *Journal of Abnormal and Social Psychology*, (67, 371–378) 1963.

16. Zimbardo, Philip, *The Lucifer Effect: Understanding How Good People Turn Evil* (London: Rider, 2007).

17. *Journal of Research in Personality*, 36(6): 556–563, December 2002.

18. See Peay, Jill in Maguire, Morgan, Reiner (Eds), *The Oxford Handbook of Criminology* (Oxford: Clarendon Press, 1995), p.1146.

19. Chivers, *Daily Telegraph*, 19 August 2017.

20. Sangster, Andrew, *Göbbels, Himmler and Göring: The Unholy Trinity* (Newcastle; Cambridge Scholars, 2018), p.435.

21. Quoted in Peay, Jill in Maguire, Morgan, Reiner (Eds), *The Oxford Handbook of Criminology* (Oxford: Clarendon Press, 1995), p.1122.

22. Ibid., p.1144.

23. Freeman, Michael D.A., *Lloyd's Introduction to Jurisprudence* (6th Edition) (London: Sweet & Maxwell, 1994), p.57.

24. Hart, H.L.A., *The Concept of Law* (Second Edition) (Oxford: Clarendon Press, 1994), p.161.
25. Hume, David, *A Treatise of Human Nature*, III. ii, 'Of Justice and Injustice.'
26. See Shrimpton, Paul, *Conscience Before Conformity: Hans and Sophie Scholl and the White Rose Resistance in Nazi Germany* (Leominster: Gracewing Publishing, 2018).
27. Overy, Richard, *Interrogations: Inside the Mind of the Nazi Elite* (London: Penguin Books, 2002), p.7.
28. See Burleigh, Michael, *Moral Combat: A History of World War II*, p.549.
29. Overy, Richard, *The Bombing War: Europe, 1939–1945* (London: Allen Lane, 2013), p.630.
30. See Burleigh, Michael, *Moral Combat: A History of World War II*, pp.380–1.
31. Ibid., p.381.
32. Telford, Taylor, *The Anatomy of the Nuremberg Trials*, p.24.
33. Plomin, Robert, *Blueprint: How DNA Makes Us Who We Are* (London: Penguin, 2018).
34. Saturday *Times Magazine*, 29 September 2018, p.39.
35. Email to this writer on 15 October 2018 from Professor Robert Plomin, MRC Research Professor, Social, Genetic and Developmental Psychiatry Centre, Institute of Psychiatry, Psychology and Neuroscience, King's College London.
36. Aron, Raymond (Freedman, Lawrence, Ed.), *War* (Oxford: OUP, 1994), p.77.
37. Ibid., p.78
38. O'Brien, W.V. (Freedman, Lawrence, Ed.), *War*, p.181.
39. Solzhenitsyn, Aleksandr, *The Gulag Archipelago 1918–56*, p.285.
40. Bartov, Omer, Grossmann, Atina and Nolan, Mary (Eds), *Crimes of War: Guilt and Denial in the Twentieth Century* (New York: The New Press, 2002), pp.xiv–xiv.
41. Farrington, D. in Maguire, Mike, Morgan, Rod and Reiner, Robert (Eds), *The Oxford Handbook of Criminology* (Oxford: Clarendon Press, 1995), p.555.
42. See Browning, Christopher, *Ordinary Men*, p.2.
43. Overy, Richard, *Interrogations, Inside the Mind of the Nazi Elite* (London: Penguin Books, 2002) p.165.
44. Goldhagen, Daniel, *Hitler's Willing Executioners: Ordinary Germans and the Holocaust* (London: Abacus, 1997), pp.11–12.
45. Solzhenitsyn Aleksandr, *The Gulag*, p.385.
46. Goldhagen, Daniel, *Hitler's Willing Executioners: Ordinary Germans and the Holocaust*, p.13.
47. Harari, Yuval Noah, *21 Lessons for the 21st Century* (London: Jonathan Cape, 2018), p.7.
48. Burleigh, Michael, *Moral Combat: A History of World War II*, p.405.
49. Browning, Christopher, *Ordinary Men*, p.58.
50. Goldhagen, Daniel, *Hitler's Willing Executioners: Ordinary Germans and the Holocaust* (London: Abacus, 1997), p.13.
51. Burleigh, Michael, *Moral Combat: A History of World War II*, pp.363 and 366.
52. Overy, Richard, *The Bombing War: Europe, 1939–1945*, p.250.
53. Ibid., p.631.
54. Burleigh, Michael, *Moral Combat: A History of World War II*, pp.464–5.
55. Telford, Taylor, *The Anatomy of the Nuremberg Trials*, p.23.
56. Solzhenitsyn, Aleksandr, *The Gulag Archipelago 1918–56*, pp.68–9.

Appendix
1. Peterson, Jordan, *12 Rules for Life: An Antidote to Chaos* (London: Allen Lane, Reprint Ed, 2018).
2. Solzhenitsyn Aleksandr, *The Gulag*, p.xi.
3. Ibid., p.5.
4. Ibid., p.26, p.240–1.

5. Ibid., p.430.
6. Ibid., p.39.
7. Ibid., p.221.
8. Ibid., p.385.
9. Ibid., p.205.
10. Ibid., p.211.
11. Ibid., p.34.
12. Ibid., p.200.

Bibliography

Published Books

Alliluyeva, Svetlana, *Only One Year* (London: Hutchinson, 1969)

——, *Twenty Letters to a Friend* (New York: Harper & Row, 1967)

Andrew, Christopher, *The Secret World: A History of Intelligence* (London: Penguin Books, 2019)

Andrew, Christopher and Gordievsky, Oleg, *KGB: The Inside Story* (London: Hodder & Stoughton, 1990)

Antonov-Ovseyenko, Anton, *The Time of Stalin: Portrait of a Tyranny* (London: Harper & Row, 1981)

Arendt, Hannah, *The Origins of Totalitarianism* (London: André Deutsch, 1951)

Aron, Raymond (Freedman, Lawrence, Ed.), *War* (Oxford: OUP, 1994)

Augustine, *De libero arbitrio*

Bartov, Omer, Grossmann, Atina and Nolan, Mary (Eds), *Crimes of War: Guilt and Denial in the Twentieth Century* (New York: The New Press, 2002)

Brent, Jonathan and Naumov, Vladimir P., *Stalin's Last Crime: The Plot Against the Jewish Doctors, 1948–1953* (New York: Harper Collins, 2003)

Browning, Christopher, *Ordinary Men: Reserve Police Battalion 101 and the Final Solution in Poland* (London: Penguin Books, 2001)

Buber, Martin, *Images of Good and Evil* (London: Routledge and Kegan Paul, 1952)

Bullard, Julian and Margaret (Eds), *Inside Stalin's Russia: The Diaries of Reader Bullard 1930–1934* (Oxfordshire: Day Books, 2000)

Burleigh, Michael, *Moral Combat: A History of World War II* (London: Harper Press, 2010)

Campbell, C.A., *On Selfhood and Godhood* (London: George Allen and Unwin, 1957)

Christopher, Andrew and Oleg, Gordievsky, *KGB: The Inside Story of its Foreign Operations from Lenin to Gorbachev* (London: Hodder & Stoughton, 1990)

Churchill, Winston, *Great Contemporaries* (Delaware: ISI Books, 2012, original publication 1937)

Clark, Alan, *Barbarossa: The Russian-German Conflict 1941–1945* (London: Phoenix Press, 1965)

Conquest, Robert, *The Great Terror: A Reassessment* (New York: OUP, 1990)

——, *Power and Policy in the USSR* (New York: Harper & Row, 1967)

Crawford, Donald in Smith, Douglas (Brenton, Tony (Ed.)), *Historically Inevitable? Turning Points of the Russian Revolution* (London: Profile Books, 2016)

Deutscher, Isaac, *Stalin: A Political Biography* (New York: OUP, 1967)

Farrington, D. in Maguire, Mike, Morgan, Rod and Reiner, Robert (Eds), *The Oxford Handbook of Criminology* (Oxford: Clarendon Press, 1995)

Ferris, John (Ed.), *The Cambridge History of the Second World War, Volume I: Fighting the War* (Cambridge: CUP, 2015)

Figes, Orlando, *A People's Tragedy: The Russian Revolution 1891–1924* (London: The Bodley Head, 2014)

———, *The Whisperers: Private Life in Stalin's Russia* (London: Penguin Books, 2008)

Freeman, Michael D.A., *Lloyd's Introduction to Jurisprudence* (6th Edition) (London: Sweet & Maxwell, 1994)

Gellately, Robert, *Stalin's Curse: Battling for Communism in War and Cold War* (Oxford: OUP, 2013)

———, *The Nuremberg Interviews: An American Psychiatrist's Conversations with the Defendants and Witnesses* (London: Pimlico, 2007)

Goldhagen, Daniel, *Hitler's Willing Executioners: Ordinary Germans and the Holocaust* (London: Abacus, 1997)

Gorlizki, Y. & Khlevniuk, Oleg in Suny, Ronald Grigor, *The Structure of Soviet History: Essays and Documents* (Oxford: OUP, 2014)

Harari, Yuval Noah, *21 Lessons for the 21st Century* (London: Jonathan Cape, 2018)

Hart, H.L.A., *The Concept of Law* (Second Edition) (Oxford: Clarendon Press, 1994)

Hastings, Max, *The Secret War: Spies, Codes and Guerrillas 1939–1945* (London: William Collins, 2015)

Hellbeck, Jochen in Suny, Ronald Grigor, *The Structure of Soviet History: Essays and Documents* (Oxford: OUP, 2014)

Hingley, Ronald, *The Russian Secret Police: Muscovite, Imperial Russian and Soviet Political Security Operations* (New York: Simon and Schuster, 1970)

Hume, David, *A Treatise of Human Nature*, III. ii, 'Of Justice and Injustice.'

Ings, Simon, *Stalin and the Scientists: A History of Triumph and Tragedy 1905–1953* (London; Faber & Faber, 2017)

Iz istorii VchK (History of the Cheka), Moscow 1958

Izvestiia, TsK KPSS, No. 1 (1991): pp.141–7

Khlevniuk, Oleg V., *Stalin: New Biography of a Dictator* (London: Yale UP, 2015)

Khrushchev, N., *Khrushchev Remembers* (Boston: Little, Brown & Co, 1970)

Knight, Amy, *Beria: Stalin's First Lieutenant* (Princeton: Princeton University Press, 1993)

Koestler, Arthur, *Darkness at Noon* (London: Penguin Books, 1947)

Kotkin, Stephen, *Stalin, Vol II: Waiting for Hitler, 1928–1941* (London: Allen Lane, 2017)

Lewin, Moshe, *The Soviet Century* (London: Verso, 2016)

Lockhart, R.H. Bruce, *Memoirs of a British Agent* (London: The Folio Society, 2003)

Macintyre, Ben, *Operation Mincemeat: The True Spy Story That Changed the Course of World War II* (London: Bloomsbury, 2010)

Michel, Henri, *The Second World War* (London: Deutsch, 1975)

Milgram, Stanley, *Obedience to Authority* (New York: Harper and Row, 1974)

———, 'Behavioural Study of Obedience' in *Journal of Abnormal and Social Psychology*, (67, 371–378) 1963

Montagu, Ewen, *The Man Who Never Was* (London: Naval Institute Press, 2001)

Montefiore, Simon Sebag, *Stalin: The Court of the Red Tsar* (London: Weidenfeld & Nicolson, 2003)

Moore, Bob, in *The Cambridge History of the Second World War, Vol 1* (Cambridge: CUP, 2015)

O'Brien, W.V., (Freedman, Lawrence, Ed.), *War* (Oxford: OUP, 1994)

Overy, Richard, *Interrogations: Inside the Mind of the Nazi Elite* (London: Penguin Books, 2002)

———, *The Bombing War: Europe 1939–1945* (London: Allen Lane, 2013)

Peay, Jill in Maguire, Mike, Morgan, Rod & Reiner, Robert (Eds), *The Oxford Handbook of Criminology* (Oxford: Clarendon Press, 1995)

Peterson, Jordan, *12 Rules for Life: An Antidote to Chaos* (London: Allen Lane, Reprint Ed, 2018)

Plomin, Robert, *Blueprint: How DNA Makes Us Who We Are* (London: Penguin, 2018)

Rees, Laurence, *World War II Behind Closed Doors: Stalin, The Nazis and the West* (London: BBC Books, 2008)

Roberts, Andrew, *The Storm of War* (London: Allen Lane, 2009)

Rubenstein, Joshua, *The Last Days of Stalin* (London: Yale University Press, 2016)

Sangster, Andrew, *Field-Marshal Kesselring: Great Commander or War Criminal?* (Newcastle: Cambridge Scholars, 2015)

——, *Göbbels, Himmler and Göring: The Unholy Trinity* (Newcastle: Cambridge Scholars, 2018)

Service, Robert, *The Oxford Companion to the Second World War* (Oxford: OUP, 1995)

——, *Stalin: A Biography* (London: Pan Books, 2010)

——, *The Penguin History of Modern Russia: Frin Tsarism to the Twenty-first Century* (London: Penguin, 2015)

Seton-Watson, Hugh, *The Russian Empire 1801–1971* (Oxford: OUP, 1967)

Shrimpton, Paul, *Conscience Before Conformity: Hans and Sophie Scholl and the White Rose Resistance in Nazi Germany* (Leominster: Gracewing Publishing, 2018)

Siegelbaum, Lewis and Sokolov, Andrei, *Stalinism as a Way of Life: A Narrative in Documents* (London: Yale University Press, 2000)

Solzhenitsyn, Aleksandr, *The Gulag Archipelago 1918–56* (London: The Harvill Press, 1985)

Sudoplatov, Pavel and Anatoli, *Special Tasks: The Memoirs of an Unwanted Witness – A Soviet Spymaster* (London: Little, Brown and Company, 1994)

Suny, Ronald Grigor, *The Structure of Soviet History: Essays and Documents* (Oxford: OUP, 2014)

Telford, Taylor, *The Anatomy of the Nuremberg Trials* (New York: Alfred A Knopf, 1992)

Volodarsky, Boris, *Stalin's Agent: The Life and Death of Alexander Orlov* (Oxford: OUP, 2015)

Williams, Alan, *The Beria Papers* (Frogmore: Panther Books, 1974)

Wittlin, Thaddeus, *Commissar: The Life and Death of Lavrenty Pavlovich Beria* (New York: Macmillan, 1972)

Zimbardo, Philip, *The Lucifer Effect: Understanding How Good People Turn Evil* (London: Rider, 2007)

Newspapers and Journals

Daily Telegraph, Chavers 19 August 2017

Izvestiia, TsK KPSS, No. 1 (1991): pp.141–7

Journal of Research in Personality, 36(6):556–563, December 2002

Saturday Times Magazine, 29 September 2018

The Guardian, 18 July 2020

Index

Abakumov, Viktor, 43, 47, 58–9, 61–2, 67,
    71, 117, 118, 126–7, 129, 131–4, 136,
    138, 140, 146
Anti-Semitism, 55, 70, 72, 121,
    130–1, 168–9
Autocratic issues, 142–5

Bagirov, Mircafar, 7, 18, 20, 25, 66, 88
Beria, Lavrenty, x, xviii, xxv, xxvii, xxix–
    xxx, xxxii–xxxiii, 1–98, 101, 103–105,
    108–10, 112–13, 115, 117, 119–20, 123,
    125, 129–40, 146–8, 151–2, 155–7,
    163–6, 170, 172–4, 176–7
    ambition, 4, 7, 13, 15–16, 19, 40, 47, 56,
        60, 65, 78–9, 84, 93
    background, 1–2, 4–5, 9
    fall of, 85–8, 90, 134
    fear of, 32, 46, 81, 85–6, 136, 166
    personality, 20, 29, 45, 47, 96
    ruthless, 8, 10, 12, 21, 25–6, 31, 34–5, 41,
        48–9, 91
    sadism, 12, 23–4, 30, 41, 94
    sex addiction, 68, 92–3
    with Stalin, xxvii, xxx, 13, 19, 26, 28, 51,
        59, 63, 66, 91, 93–4
Bohr, Niels, 118–20, 122–3
Brezhnev, Leonid, 33, 50, 67, 73, 77, 130,
    139, 141
Bukharin, Nikolai, xxiv, xxvi, 10, 22, 77
Bulganin, Nikolai, 59, 64, 69, 76–7, 85, 88,
    91, 133, 135
Burgess, Guy, 101

Cairncross, John, 115, 117
Chuikov, General, 43
Churchill, Winston, xxii, xxvii, xxxii,
    51–2, 57, 93, 96, 111, 122, 124–5, 144,
    145, 159

Cold War era, x, xiv, 1, 50, 53, 57, 97,
    123–7, 131, 136, 144
Comintern, xxii, xxix, xxxii, 125, 168

Dekanozov, Vladimir, xxxi, 7, 36, 90, 95
Doctors' Plot, xxv, 43, 61, 63, 67, 70–3, 79,
    131–3, 135–6
Dzerzhinsky, Feliks, xxiii, xxiv, xxvi, 45

Eitingon, Leonid, 70, 100–101, 104–106,
    112, 126, 130–1, 133–4, 137, 139–40
Enigma, 115, 124, 163

Fermi, Enrico, 118–23
Fuchs, Klaus, 11, 55, 121, 123

Gofman, Grigory, 26
Golikov, Filipp, xxxii, 36
Gorbachev, Mikhail, 79, 89, 129, 140
Göring, Hermann, 8, 90, 110, 142,
    152, 170
Great Terror, xxx, 28, 31
Gulag prison camps, x, xxvi, 32–3, 35, 48,
    50, 56, 79, 89, 91, 143, 146, 154, 157–8,
    163, 171, 174, 177

Harriman, Averell, 70, 125, 131
Himmler, Heinrich, xvii, 8, 14, 23, 32–4,
    41, 46, 96, 114, 142, 146, 151–2, 155,
    157, 166, 170–3
Hitler, Adolf, xvi, xix, xxxi, xxxiii, 6, 13,
    19, 22, 28, 36–8, 40, 42, 54, 57, 72, 95,
    110–11, 113, 125, 131, 133, 142–4,
    146, 149, 151–2, 154–6, 164–5, 167,
    169–71, 173

Ilyin, Viktor, 117–18
Intelligence work, xiii–xv, xx, xxviii

Kaganovich, Lazar, xxvii, 17, 27, 39, 69, 71, 74, 77, 88
Kamenev, Lev, xxiv, xxviii, 70–1
Kapitsa, Petri, 54, 56
Katyń massacres, xiv, xxxii, 1, 35, 129–30, 142, 146, 152, 160
Kedrov, Mikhail, 8
Kerensky, Alexander, xix
Kesselring, Field Marshal, xvi, 38
Khandzhian, Aghasi, 20–1
Kheifetz, Gregory, 119
Khrushchev, Nikita, xxv, xxxii–xxxiii, 5, 15, 25–7, 30–1, 33, 49–51, 58–9, 61, 64, 66–70, 72–82, 84–91, 109–10, 127, 133, 135, 137–9, 141
    seeks power, 80, 82–5
Kirov, Sergei, xxviii, xxix, xxx, 5–6, 20, 102
Kobulov, Bogdan, 23, 35, 90
Konovalets, Yevhen, 99–100
Kruglov, Sergei, 58
Kurchatov, Igor, 54–5
Kuznetsov, NKVD Special Agent, 63, 113
Kvantaliani, Nika, 10–13, 24

Lakoba, Nestor, 13, 17, 21, 24
Leningrad Case, 62, 134
Lenin, Vladimir, xix, xxi, xxiii, xxv–xxvi, xxviii–xxix, 3, 5, 9, 18, 20, 22, 24, 65, 77, 86, 89, 175
Litvinov, Maxim, 23, 71, 94–5

Maclean, Donald, 53, 58, 92, 108, 118–19, 126
Maironovsky, Professor, 129–30, 138
Malenkov, Georgy, xxvii, 17, 27, 29, 41, 59–63, 65–7, 69, 74, 76–8, 82, 84–91, 132–3, 135
Manhattan Project, 54, 119–20
Marshall Plan, 58, 125
Max, Special Soviet Spy, 116–18
Mein Kampf, 37, 111
Menzhinsky, Vyacheslav, xxiii–xxiv, xxvi
Mercader, Caridad, 105
Mercader, Ramon, 100, 104–106, 140
Merkulov, Vsevolod, 11, 19, 27, 30–1, 41, 54, 58, 87, 90, 115–16, 126
Mikhoels, Solomon, 55, 61, 79–80, 132

Miklashevsky, Boris, 110
Mikoyan, Anastas, 35, 39, 63–4, 69, 74, 76, 85, 93
Molotov, Vyacheslav, xxvii, xxxi–xxxii, 27, 32–6, 39, 54–5, 57, 59, 61–2, 65–6, 69, 76, 78, 83–4, 88, 93, 95, 109, 120, 125–7, 132, 138
Moskalenko, General, 85, 87
Musavat Government, 4–6, 26, 88, 90

Nacht und Nebel (Night and Fog), 8, 143, 148
Neledov, Count, 114
Nina, Beria's wife, 9–10, 16, 67–8, 86, 93

Okhrana, xvii–xix
Operation Barbarossa, xxxii, 39, 54, 111–13
Operation Monastery, 45, 116, 118
Oppenheimer, Robert, 55, 107, 118–19, 121–3
Orakhelashvili, Mamia, 17–18, 24
Ordzhonikidze, Sergo, xxix, 6, 9–10, 12, 14, 16–18, 22
Orlov, Nikolsky, 101, 104, 126–7

Pavlov, General, 43
Pervukhin, Mikhail, 73, 77, 135
Philby, Kim, 111, 117
Poskrebyshev, Mikhail, 63, 73
Potsdam Conference, 52–3, 57

Redens, Stanislav, 15–16
Red Orchestra, 114–15
Ribbentrop, Joachim von, xxxi, 34, 39, 108–109
Roosevelt, President, 52, 57, 96, 119–20, 125, 145
Rosenberg, husband and wife spy team, 121, 156
Rudenko, Roman, 87, 90, 138–9

Saburov, Maksim, 73, 77, 135
Savinkov, Boris, xxii–xxiii
Secret Police work, xvi–xvii, xx–xxi, xxv
Sergo, Beria's son, 12, 52, 66, 77, 84, 90, 93
Shtemenko, Marshal, 70
Siqueiros, David Alfaro, 105

Skorzeny, Otto, 51, 113
Solzhenitsyn, Aleksandr, 27, 34, 48, 89,
    94, 96, 147, 150, 152, 154, 163, 168,
    171–2, 174–7
Sorge, Richard, xxxi–xxxii, 36
Spanish Civil War, 98, 100, 104–105, 165
Special Tasks (Yasha Groups), 44, 51, 92,
    97–8, 103, 112, 182–7
Stalin, Joseph, xx, 164
    background, xx, xxiv
    cruelty, xxix, 30, 43, 49, 117
    death of, 73, 75–6
    personality, xxvi, xxvii, xxxi, 6, 10, 37,
        38, 42
    suspicious nature, xxiii–xxiv, 12, 48, 51,
        58, 64, 66, 69, 113, 132–3
    the tyrant, x, xxi, xxx, 15, 22, 36, 133, 142
Stalin's daughter, xxv, xxviii, 9–10, 27, 29,
    61, 63, 65, 75–6, 86, 93, 133
    see also Svetlana, Stalin's daughter
Sudoplatov, Emma, 92, 99, 103, 109,
    132, 138–40
Sudoplatov, Pavel, xxxiii, 37, 40, 42, 45–6,
    53, 57, 63, 69, 79, 81, 83
    and the purges, 107
    atomic secrets, 118–19, 122–4
    background, 97–8
    in prison, 137, 139
    office friction, 103, 109, 117, 126
    rehabilitated, 140
    ruthless, 100
    the obedient servant, 98, 104, 106, 114
    views on Stalin, 102, 107–108, 111, 113,
        125, 130
    with Beria, 101, 112, 115, 120
    with Stalin, 100, 117, 134
Svetlana, Stalin's daughter, 10, 93, 133
Szilard, Leo, 118

Tehran Conference, 51, 113
Timoshenko, Marshal, 38–40, 95
Tito, Josip, 62, 76, 80–1, 97, 134, 136
Troika system, xvii, xxi, 8, 24
Trotsky, Leon, xix, xxiii–xxiv, xxix, 53, 70–1,
    91, 97, 100, 102–107, 133, 167
    his assassination, 104

Truman, President, 54, 57, 80, 124
Trump, President, xv, 112
Tsarist rule, xviii–xix, 145
Tukhachevsky, General, xxx, 107–108

Ulbricht, Walter, 82–3, 89

Views on the nature of evil, 148
    biochemistry and genes, 161–2
    biology, 162
    determinism, 150–1
    ideological factors, 168
    international law, 159, 161
    Jurisprudence, 157–8
    moral philosophy, 151–2
    obeying orders, 167
    psychology, 153–5
    psychopathy, 155–6
    putative duress, 167
    reactions of individuals, 169–72
    religious insights, 149–50
    repression of free will, 166
    the result of tyranny, 164–6
Vlasik, General, 67, 72–3, 86
Voroshilov, Kliment, 39, 50, 74, 77, 85,
    93, 108
Voznesensky, Nikolai, 39, 62–3
Vyshinsky, Andrey, xxvii, 27, 61–2

Wallenberg, Raoul Gustaf, 128–9, 148

Yagoda, Genrikh, xxiv, xxvi, xxix, 22, 71, 89
Yalta Conference, 51, 57, 96, 109, 125, 144
Yegorov, General, xxx, 31
Yenukidze, Avel, xxviii
Yezhov, Nikolai, xxvi–xxviii, 5, 22, 26–32,
    89, 93–4, 100, 104, 129
Yezhovshchina, 29, 31

Zarubin, husband and wife spies in
    USA, 121–2
Zhdanov, Andrei, 60–3, 65, 71
Zhukov, Marshal, 38–40, 42, 44, 50, 66, 85,
    116, 133
Zinoviev, Grigory, xxiv, xxviii, xxix, 70–1